a time for truth

Sarah is an award-winning bereaved children and victims' rights campaigner and one of the youngest authors in Irish history. Born in Ireland, her mother died tragically when she was twelve weeks old and, when Sarah was four, her family moved to the US when her father remarried.

Sarah and her older brother Jack were left orphaned when their father, Jason Corbett, was killed by their stepmother, Molly Martens, and her father, Tom Martens, in August 2015. Sarah and Jack then returned to Ireland to be raised by Jason's sister, Tracey, and her husband, Dave.

This tragic loss instilled in Sarah a burning desire to campaign for other bereaved children and for victims' rights and to help others impacted by violent crime, which she has actively done in the US and Ireland in the years since.

At just thirteen years old, Sarah wrote an illustrated book, *Noodle Loses Dad*, to help children cope with bereavement and loss. Her book was later adopted by children's rights groups, professionals, counselling services, and schools as a valuable teaching aid. For her work, Sarah received a special National Garda Síochána award and a Limerick Young Person tribute.

A native of Limerick, now living in County Clare, Sarah is also an accomplished singer, actor, and dancer. A qualified swim teacher and lifeguard, she loves to snorkel, surf and sea swim, and she has just qualified as a commercial diver with An Bord Iascaigh Mhara.

a time for truth

my father Jason and my search for justice and healing

SARAH CORBETT LYNCH

HACHETTE
BOOKS
IRELAND

Copyright © 2025 Sarah Corbett Lynch

The right of Sarah Corbett Lynch to be identified as the author of the work has been asserted by her in accordance with the Copyright, Designs and Patents Act 1988.

First published in Ireland in 2025 by
HACHETTE BOOKS IRELAND

6

All rights reserved. No part of this publication may be reproduced, stored in a retrieval system, or transmitted, in any form or by any means without the prior written permission of the publisher, nor be otherwise circulated in any form of binding or cover other than that in which it is published and without a similar condition being imposed on the subsequent purchaser.

Some dialogue within this text has been reconstructed.

'Summer Days' by Sarah Corbett Lynch is produced by Pierce O'Rahilly. Lyrics reproduced with kind permission of author.

Cataloguing in Publication Data is available from the British Library

ISBN 9781399740937

Typeset in Times New Roman by Bookends Publishing Services, Dublin
Printed and bound in Great Britain by Clays Ltd, Elcograf S.p.A.

Hachette Books Ireland policy is to use papers that are natural, renewable and recyclable products and made from wood grown in sustainable forests. The logging and manufacturing processes are expected to conform to the environmental regulations of the country of origin.

Hachette Books Ireland
8 Castlecourt Centre
Castleknock
Dublin 15, Ireland

A division of Hachette UK Ltd
Carmelite House, 50 Victoria Embankment, London EC4Y 0DZ

www.hachettebooksireland.ie

*For those who have been denied
the chance to share their story*

*Special thanks to Kathryn Rogers
for her help in writing this book*

Contents

Prologue   *1*
Chapter 1 – The Healing Room   *6*
Chapter 2 – A Sky Full of Goodbyes   *18*
Chapter 3 – Strong Enough   *31*
Chapter 4 – In Her Shadow   *45*
Chapter 5 – Victims   *53*
Chapter 6 – The Nightmare   *68*
Chapter 7 – The Swim Coach   *72*
Chapter 8 – Dragonfly   *88*
Chapter 9 – Big Little Lies   *97*
Chapter 10 – Family   *103*
Chapter 11 – The Spy Among Us   *115*
Chapter 12 – The Bonds That Bind   *131*
Chapter 13 – Truth on Trial   *138*
Chapter 14 – Spanish Point   *147*
Chapter 15 – Ladies' Day   *153*
Chapter 16 – Secrets   *165*
Chapter 17 – Molly Said   *172*

Chapter 18 – The Holiday   *182*

Chapter 19 – Resolve   *188*

Chapter 20 – Writing to Recovery   *198*

Chapter 21 – The Scheme   *206*

Chapter 22 – A Badge and a Bat   *215*

Chapter 23 – Endgame   *222*

Chapter 24 – Rehearsals   *234*

Chapter 25 – Bad Habits   *242*

Chapter 26 – A Hollow Victory   *246*

Chapter 27 – After the Storm   *264*

Chapter 28 – Disbelief   *268*

Chapter 29 – When Crime Pays   *274*

Chapter 30 – Release   *282*

Chapter 31 – Aftermath   *290*

Chapter 32 – A New World   *302*

Acknowledgements   *309*

PROLOGUE

Kilkee, County Clare
October 2023

I stare at a document on my screen, empty apart from the blinking cursor. My fingers are on the keys, willing the right words to come, but I'm struggling. How can I sum up my father's life and the chasm left by his absence in a few paragraphs? How do I capture the essence of Dad – his warmth, huge booming laugh and kindness – through a keyboard?

I type the title 'Victim Impact Statement' and focus on that middle word: 'impact'. Just six letters. Such a small word for an unending ache.

It feels impossible to convey the impact of Dad's killing eight years ago. The sense of loss is endless: birthdays, holidays, Christmases and many milestones in my life have already passed without my father's presence. Future moments are also forever stolen: twenty-firsts, graduations, weddings, births, christenings, the grandchildren he'll never hold. The ripples expand endlessly.

People tell me to write about how Dad's death has affected my life. They make it sound simple, but how do you express the inexpressible? While friends are having fun, I am in therapy, trying to unload an invisible but crushing weight. I've spent endless hours crying, trying to process my grief, trauma, loss and regret. I can't count the number of sleepless nights or the nightmares where I wake screaming. Nor can I calculate the days I've spent with officials, my voice raw with grief as I repeat what I experienced, desperately hoping for a response greater than sympathetic nods and scribbled notes.

How do I explain that I view the world through a permanently altered lens? 'Victim Impact Statement' seems like an emotionless term for someone who has seen her father's bloody handprint trailing down his bedroom door, a silent testament to his desperate attempt to escape. But the law is black and white, and heartless.

In 2017, Molly Martens and her father Tom Martens were convicted of the second-degree murder of my father, Jason Corbett, who they killed on 2 August 2015. However, their convictions were quashed on appeal in 2020, with the appeal upheld by the North Carolina Supreme Court in 2021, after they had served three-and-a-half years of their twenty-to-twenty-five-year sentences.

The North Carolina Supreme Court upheld the decision for a new trial in 2021. The court found that evidence that could have supported the Martens' claims of self-defence had been improperly excluded during the original trial. A retrial was ordered and their prison sentences ended in April 2021.

They have now been free for two years, back to living their normal family lives in Tennessee as they wait for the next step in the legal process. Meanwhile, my father's remains lie under a marble stone in Castlemungret Cemetery, near our former home in Limerick. My only consolation is that in death, Dad has been reunited with my birth mother Mags, his first wife, and the love of his life.

However, we received news weeks ago that the Martens' retrial will not happen. They have struck a plea deal with the prosecutors and will plead guilty to voluntary manslaughter. Instead of a retrial, they will have a sentencing hearing. I will never now have the chance to take the stand in court.

Throughout the twisting legal process since my father's killing, I've begged the prosecution to let me take the stand in court. I have lost count of how many times I've written, emailed and called since the Martens began lodging their appeals after their sentencing in 2017. I have implored the District Attorney himself. I've asked everyone to give me a chance to confront my father's killers and present what I know to a jury and judge.

They kept telling me I was too young and that giving evidence in court would be too traumatic. But I've imagined being in the courtroom a hundred times, standing on the witness stand and telling my truth. The assurances from the District Attorney's office that I would get my chance in a retrial have proven hollow. The only bone thrown by the District Attorney's office is the offer of making a Victim Impact Statement – a few minutes standing in the courtroom to summarise a lifetime of loss.

I don't even know if I can make a statement. No one can tell us how many of our family may address the court. If we're only allowed one statement, my brother Jack is older than me, so maybe he'll be the one to speak.

I have two parents in heaven, but I also have two living ones. Dad, in his wisdom, legally appointed his sister Tracey and her husband David Lynch as our guardians. He loved and trusted them, and they have repaid his trust many times over. They have been to hell and back saving Jack and me from Molly Martens' grip, all while relentlessly pursuing justice for Dad. They have spent eight years fighting the Martens through America's legal system. This courtroom date at the end of this month will be their twenty-fifth journey to the United States as Dad's representatives.

Tracey and David's entire lives and that of their sons, Adam and Dean, have been upended since our father's killing. Their voices deserve to be heard too.

One statement, two or three – it feels like a mockery of everything we've done. We're being offered a few footnotes in the margins of a long battle for justice for my father. After the trauma of losing Dad, a statement is a poor substitute for the closure I had hoped for.

The Word document on my screen still remains empty apart from its bureaucratic title. I gaze out at the street through the rain-streaked bedroom window of our home in Kilkee instead. As I do, memories of Dad run through my mind. I recall the feel and warmth of my small hand in his on the beach at Spanish Point in Clare. I remember him sitting in the rocking chair in my room in North Carolina, reading another bedtime story. Every memory is like reopening an old wound, painful but strangely comforting. Each reminds me of a more innocent time before the heartache began.

Tears are welling, but a tiny spark of determination flickers. If this statement is all I get, I'll make every single word count. I'll tell the world what a decent and caring person my father was. I will take what little control I have to set the record straight. Every anecdote I tell and each character trait I outline will be part of his enduring legacy. My words about Dad will be captured for posterity in the transcripts, his permanent case file and the public record. If I can capture a true picture of Dad, my statement will help preserve his memory.

I am determined that the judge knows that the life Tom and Molly Martens extinguished was much loved and valued.

My words will also be an act of defiance. The Martens brutally silenced my father, but they can't silence me any longer. I will do my best to inform the court what happened in our home at 160 Panther Creek Court in North Carolina on that August night in 2015.

I know I will write and rewrite this statement a hundred times over the coming weeks, but I make a start. The judge must understand that my father is more than another crime statistic or a file in the Davidson County Sheriff's Office. He is more than his assigned number – forty-two – of the seventy-eight victims of domestic violence listed in 2015 by the North Carolina Coalition Against Domestic Violence. And he's a lot more than the bloodied corpse the judge will see in crime-scene photographs.

Your Honour
You know my dad as the deceased, but he had a name. It was Jason. I am proud to be the daughter of such a kind and gentle man. I am proud to be Jason Corbett's daughter.

CHAPTER 1

THE HEALING ROOM

Your Honour

Please do not think I haven't or do not try to heal – I do. I have been in talk therapy for eight years. While my friends are out having fun and going to parties, I am seventeen years old and in therapy.

Kilkee, County Clare
September–October 2023

I hadn't felt the need to see my psychologist for ages. But as Tom and Molly Martens' sentencing hearing loomed, my fingers hovered again over her familiar number.

Stepping into the familiarity of Dr Mary Hayes' office and seeing her face spread into a smile has always been reassuring. Her office in Castletroy, Limerick, has only changed slightly since I first went there in 2016 aged nine. The room always seems to be bathed in natural light, highlighting the sparse furnishings: a light wood desk and two comfortable black-leather chairs. Blue curtains frame one side of the window, looking over nearby brick buildings, and a clock hangs on the yellow walls. I have spent many hours gazing at those curtains and that clockface, looking anywhere to avoid meeting Mary's eyes.

As we settled in our facing chairs, Mary assumed her usual position, balancing her notepad and pen on her knee. My throat felt tight, but I was relieved to be in this room again. Mary would be an anchor in the storm about to come.

'I thought I was doing okay,' I began.

Her presence was as steadying as it had been when I was a child. 'And now?'

Like a dam breaking, the tears and words tumbled out. I told Mary what had happened. 'They made a plea deal,' I cried, sharing my fears that I might never get the closure I hoped for.

In September 2023, I was on a sleepover with my friend Alva at her Limerick home when I saw an email arrive from District Attorney (DA) Garry Frank – the man in charge of my father's case in North Carolina. Alva and I were on a call with a friend, so I swiped away the email until we finished. I was about to open it minutes later when Tracey rang.

'Don't open the email, love,' she said. She explained that my brother Adam, who is six years older than me, was in Limerick that evening and would drive me halfway home to Kilkee, and they would collect me and bring me the rest of the way. 'Pack your things, and we'll talk when we see you.'

My heart sank. Tracey and David had become my guardians after my father's death. I soon grew to regard them as my parents, implicitly loving and trusting them. So I didn't ask what was happening that night, but I knew it wasn't good. All I knew was our schoolgirl sleepover was over.

Sometimes, when I was with my friends, I could almost forget about my double life and be like any other teenager. Then, a single email or a newspaper report could thrust me back into adult concerns of legal arguments, appeals, evidence and court cases. Tracey and David have always been protective, trying to shield my brother Jack and me from the slow grind of the American legal system. But I have felt caught between two worlds since I was eight – sometimes a carefree child; other times weighed down by my dad's loss and the fight for justice.

Adam collected me but had no idea why Tracey and David wanted to talk to me so urgently. The sun was setting when he pulled in at a service station in Darragh. The village was a halfway point between my school in Limerick and our new family home in Kilkee, more than an hour away. Tracey and David were waiting and, as I changed cars, Tracey talked with Adam for a few minutes.

It had been a beautiful September day. The sky looked on fire in a blaze of red and orange as we left Darragh and drove towards home. But I couldn't enjoy the glorious scene, as Tracey and David's troubled silence made me anxious.

'What's going on?' I finally asked.

Tracey turned to me, reaching back from the front passenger seat to grab my hand. That's when I learned that District Attorney Garry Frank had dropped the murder charges against the Martens. The prosecutors felt that their chances of getting a successful murder conviction at retrial were small. Instead, Tracey explained, the Martens had been offered a plea deal and were being charged with the voluntary manslaughter of my father.

I felt winded.

I couldn't breathe.

My mind raced with the implications of this news.

'Sarah, love, please talk to me,' Tracey urged but, for the next twenty minutes, I couldn't form any words.

Garry Frank and his legal team had successfully prosecuted Molly and Tom Martens for second-degree murder in 2017. Since then, they had lodged appeals using several arguments, including alleging jury misconduct in an appeal that they had been denied in December 2017.

They had begun a broader process in 2018. We had been gutted when, in 2020, the North Carolina Court of Appeals agreed that the Martens were entitled to a new trial. However, the prosecution immediately appealed to North Carolina's Supreme Court, and we were hopeful that the Court of Appeals decision would be overturned.

In March 2021, we had been told that the Court of Appeals decision was being upheld by the state's Supreme Court. A retrial was announced and the Martens were to be freed soon after. The date for a retrial was uncertain.

Two years after the courts had freed the Martens, the threat of a plea deal had disappeared – the retrial had been postponed because of the Covid-19 pandemic. However, we finally had a date for October 2023, and we focused our energies on this last battle. I thought I would finally be given a chance to tell my side of the story and get justice for Dad. It was a massive blow to hear a retrial would never happen.

We only had the bare details of the plea deal that had been accepted, but those details ran around my head. Tom Martens would plead guilty to voluntary manslaughter and Molly Martens would plead no contest to voluntary manslaughter.

Instead of a retrial, my father's killers would only face a

sentencing hearing, which would decide what additional jail time they would serve, if any.

Before being released, they had only spent three-and-a-half years in jail – out of the twenty-to-twenty-five-year sentences imposed on them when they had been convicted of second-degree murder in 2017. With time served, the pair could walk free or return to prison for years.

The notion of the Martens being convicted of 'voluntary manslaughter' angered me because there was nothing voluntary about Dad's death. He didn't choose to leave my brother Jack and me. The people who were meant to love all three of us tore him from us.

David pulled in near the cliff walk at Diamond Rocks in Kilkee. None of us wanted to go straight home. Darkness surrounded us now, but Tracey stepped into the buffeting Atlantic wind to have a moment alone. I got out of the car and went my own way, pulling my school jacket close and feeling my long wool skirt whipping off my legs. Gazing into the black ocean void, I felt like shrieking in sheer frustration. I wanted the world to swallow me whole.

Without a trial, I would never be a witness in court. Jack and I could never reveal what we'd seen and experienced. We could never explain the lies we had told to social workers about our father in the days following his killing, or why we had told them. I'd lost the only opportunity to speak up for my father in a court of law. In one swoop, they had disempowered me.

I felt outraged by the Martens' plea deal and betrayed by the legal system. The Martens had thrown money at expensive lawyers, launching one appeal after another, and their strategy had succeeded. The legal narrative had also changed. Like snakes shedding their skin, they would shake off the title 'murderers'. Once convicted of voluntary manslaughter, the Martens could only be called 'killers'. A plea deal didn't feel like justice – it felt like the Martens were getting away with murder.

As the wind chill intensified, Tracey and I returned to the car and went home.

The District Attorney's decision was irrevocable, so I knew we couldn't fight it. I cried all that night instead.

Now, back in Mary's office, I related the latest twist in the legal process, along with many other issues that whirled around my head. Over many appointments with Mary before the sentencing hearing started, I tried to articulate all my concerns about our return to America. I needed to build resilience for the weeks ahead.

The prospect of seeing Molly Martens again was one of several issues I raised. I'd seen my former stepmother for the first time in seven years at a pre-trial hearing in March 2022, eighteen months before the prosecutors agreed to a plea deal. It was also the first time I had attended a court proceeding about Dad's case. I was fifteen.

For that week, Tracey had found accommodation near the Davidson County Courthouse so we could walk to the hearing each day. On the opening day, as we approached the courthouse, I got my first experience of the media circus that would surround the case as photographers and TV reporters surrounded us.

I could see Tom Martens and his wife Sharon ahead, but was relieved to see no sign of Molly. I didn't want any contact with her outside of the formal situation of the courthouse. Molly was unpredictable and I was nervous about how she might react to seeing me for the first time since 2015.

Tracey had warned us that nothing would prepare us for the daily media gauntlet. But she also urged us to hold our heads high, reminding us that the only ones who should hang their heads going into court were the Martens. Feeling protected with my family around me, I looked straight ahead as the flurry of cameras clicked and big lenses surrounded us.

We took the lift to the courtroom floor and, when we emerged, everyone stopped, glancing around, unsure of which direction to take. As we hesitated, I felt my anxiety rise. *Molly will come out of that lift any minute now*, I thought. On cue, I heard a soft ping. The lift door slid open, and out stumbled Molly with two women friends, their heads thrown back and laughing hysterically.

I was right in front of Molly and our eyes locked. Her laughter trailed off, replaced by a look of stunned recognition. I saw what I could only describe as a shadow pass over her face. She regained her composure in an instant, turned back to her cheery friends and walked right past me.

I didn't expect it, but that brief encounter stirred up a world of memories, emotions and anxieties.

As Molly strode off, flanked by her protective pals, I felt my heart race and my chest heave for breath. Then I broke down in gasping sobs – my composure crumbling in that courthouse corridor.

Even while I was crying, I realised my tears had little to do with Molly. Of course, her laughter and her carefree demeanour caught me off-guard – it had been unsettling to see the person who had killed my father look jovial before her case – but it was more about my anxiety facing a courtroom for the first time. Tracey and David had sheltered Jack and me from the courtroom dramas up to this point. I had insisted I be there this time – but, suddenly, the process had all become real, and I felt overwhelmed.

Tracey wrapped her arms around me as I cried. 'It's okay, love,' she said. 'You're not going in there. We're going back to the hotel.'

As soon as I heard those words, I took a deep breath, wiped my tears and steadied myself. 'I'm okay. I'm going in,' I said determinedly.

A year later, in the safety of Mary's office, I unburdened every worry I had so that I wouldn't experience that visceral response again when I returned to the courtroom. Even though the Martens had agreed a plea deal, their jail time still had to be decided by a judge in a sentencing hearing. The prosecution would produce a body of evidence to ensure that their sentences would be as long as possible. The Martens' defence team would use everything in their power to see their clients walk free with time already served.

Tracey and David had warned us we'd need resilience to get through some evidence. 'We won't lie and say it will be fine,' Tracey said. 'You'll hear and experience things you'll wish you hadn't. As bad as you think the courtroom will be, it will probably be worse.'

I felt terrible apprehension about being exposed to crime-scene photographs. I had a beautiful picture of Dad in my head, and I didn't want that replaced by any horror images of his death. Tracey, David and other family and friends had already been through that trauma. They can never unsee the viciousness, rage and horror inflicted on my dad.

My memories of Dad were of him smiling and I wanted to keep it like that. Mary agreed I should not be exposed to those photographs, and I would leave the court during the testimony from the crime-scene experts. It helped ease some of my concerns about the hearing.

Though I had lost any chance to testify as a witness, I still hoped to deliver my Victim Impact Statement. However, I needed to build up my emotional strength first. I wanted to stand in court and make my statement without breaking down. These are the challenges I worked through with Mary before going to America.

The plea deal was difficult to swallow and made harder because we couldn't discuss it in public. Judge David Hall had imposed a gag order, preventing us from speaking about any aspect of the case. DA Garry Frank had warned we could subject ourselves and the prosecution to 'serious negative consequences' if we made any public statement before the sentencing hearing concluded.

However, I could talk about anything in the privacy of that quiet room with Mary. I could also think and breathe. As each session wound down, I felt that usual mix of exhaustion and greater clarity.

I feel fortunate that Tracey and David had sought psychological support for Jack and me soon after they had brought us home to Ireland. As guardians, they provided us with the most supportive and caring family environment that we could have asked for. As qualified foster parents, they also had the insight to know my bright smile was only a veneer and that, behind it all, I was suffering from profound loss and grief.

They had found Mary, the most caring clinical psychologist I could have hoped for. She offered the experience and objectivity that only experts can provide.

Mary knows me better than I know myself, and her office has become another safe and confidential place to explore my feelings, a place where the tangled, most complex parts of myself can unravel safely. I've been with her for years grappling with a world bereft of safety, where loved ones could disappear overnight. I still carry the dread that those I cherish may vanish from my life. But the losses of my maternal grandad to cancer and paternal grandmother to Covid-19 in the intervening years have taught me that even natural death brings pain that cuts deeply.

Between Tracey and Mary, I have received all the emotional and psychological support I needed. Few are lucky to have the backing of a formidable team like mine. But therapy wasn't an easy process for any of us. In the beginning, I had refused to share anything about the past. At the start of every session, Mary had laid out colouring materials – vibrant crayons, soft-coloured pencils and vivid markers alongside colouring books or white sheets of paper. And, week after week, I had bounded into Mary's office, ponytails swinging, and settled down to colour, and tell her nothing. Drawing had enabled me to avoid eye contact and made it easier to talk, and I spoke for Ireland about nothing of any consequence.

'I went horse riding yesterday and rode Millie and today in art class, I drew a big rainbow. I'll do another rainbow now ...'

As I'd strive to fill the air with forced cheer, I regaled her with tales of parties, school, new hobbies and clothes. I was all sunshine and rainbows, a smile frozen on my face. I was so used to maintaining that chirpy facade of a happy, obedient child that I hadn't even been aware that I was wearing a mask. Problem? What problem?

Mary and I had sat on the same side of her desk through every session, and through the non-threatening medium of art, she had helped me to express my thoughts and feelings. In the beginning, I had seen Mary regularly. She'd listened, validated my feelings and ensured that I felt heard. It took time and patience, but I'd begun to open locked doors in my head. As I coloured, I'd started disclosing concerning memories, often without even realising.

As the years went on, my appointments with Mary became less frequent. After each session, Tracey or David were waiting with a hug as I walked out, often with eyes swollen red from crying. They never asked what I discussed with Mary, and Tracey always assured me that everything between Mary and me was confidential. However, I told Tracey everything anyway. In recent years, I only made appointments with Mary when I needed them.

Despite my trust in Mary and Tracey, I didn't disclose a few distressing flashbacks until a year or two ago. Some were painful memories that were always deep within me, but others were troubling recollections that had resurfaced as I got older. If I'd articulated those thoughts, I knew I'd have to accept that they were real, and I wasn't always prepared to do that.

I couldn't always talk it out, and I often sought refuge in my music and writing during times when I felt silenced by the courts and unheard in my struggles. It was a challenging experience, so, in an attempt to express the toxic feelings I was carrying, I wrote a song called 'Summer Days' when I was just 13. With the help of a friend, we brought the music to life and recorded it. In 2022, I shared it on my Instagram and Twitter pages, and though no one knew the depth of my experiences, creating that song provided me with a sense of control amidst the chaos. It felt as though I was suffocating by the injustice of it all and having my words weaponised against me by the Martens in public. Each small action I took served as a release valve. Little by little, those creative outlets helped me find a way to cope and accept my circumstances, allowing me to navigate my journey with a bit more peace. The lyrics represented my way of gaining control and feeling a sense of empowerment.

'Poolside, best life, that's what everyone thought. But I was lost inside, I had nowhere to hide, you locked me up and made me blind. Summer days smiling, no one ever saw the mind games, I never had a voice, and I was only five. Summer days smiling, it's all going to be ok, that's what you told me when you said get over it, but I miss him every day and someday they will know who you are and what's inside your mind ... Those summer days ... your mind games ... your lies to confuse us ... those summer days.'

I guarded a particularly troubling memory for years, carrying it around like a rock in the darkest reaches of a deep pocket. But one day, something shifted, and the incident ballooned in my head.

Mary has always assured me she's always available, but I was in two minds. The rational part of my brain told me I could make an appointment with her as usual, but my growing panic screamed otherwise. The pressure built until I couldn't stop myself. I rang Mary's private number and, like a lifeline, she answered on the first ring. I just needed to hear her reassuring voice say everything would be okay. Mary has always shown that she's there for me when I need her.

I've exposed every traumatic recollection in therapy now, but Mary has warned me that some more may surface when I'm older. Some disclosures will be kept between Tracey, Mary and me. I can't say that I always felt better when I talked about ordeals from my past. They've already happened, and I can do nothing to change them.

I also struggle because guilt compounds my grief. But I keep talking in the hope that it will help me heal or at least soften the sharpest edges of the pain. And Mary's office will always be a healing room, a place to gather strength during a long journey of grief, loss and betrayal.

CHAPTER 2

A SKY FULL OF GOODBYES

Your Honour
Just like that, I had to leave house, home, community and country.
I will never come to terms with that ...

Lexington, North Carolina
Sunday, 29 October 2023
Tracey, David, Jack and I had landed at Washington's Dulles International Airport just days before the sentencing hearing and made the six-hour drive to Winston-Salem in North Carolina.

Dad's twin brother Wayne, his sister Marilyn and her partner Sharon followed the next day with Dad's best friend and my godfather, Paul Dillon. My brothers, Dean and Adam, flew out days later. All ten of us stayed in an old, rambling house in downtown Winston-Salem that Tracey had found on Airbnb. The sentencing hearing was expected to take two weeks.

Jack and I invited Dad's friends, former colleagues and family to gather in his name outside his former Lexington workplace on Sunday afternoon, the day before the hearing started. We held the event beside a memorial plaque to Dad that had been placed by his colleagues.

Dad started a tradition with Jack and me of releasing balloons on the anniversary of our mother's passing. I loved to watch those balloons sail into the winter sky where Daddy said Mommy was always watching over us.

The day before the Martens' sentencing hearing began, we released balloons again. But, this time, there was a poignant echo because this time they were in memory of our father rather than our mother.

Jack and I never got to know our mother, Margaret 'Mags' Corbett. She'd died from an asthma attack in 2006 when Jack was two and I was twelve weeks old. But Jack and I know we were born into love, and to a couple who had adored each other.

Dad never let Mom's anniversary – 21 November – pass unnoticed. He liked to show us videos of her. They were grainy and out of focus sometimes, but they offered us a tantalising glimpse of what our lives were and what they might have been if she hadn't died.

One clip shows Dad returning home after a work trip, and I see my brother toddling towards him and Dad swooping him up. Mom is pregnant with me as she films, and it's lovely to see how they were together, to hear the melodic lilt of her laughter around

Dad. I love these videos, but they're all too short, offering only fragments of what I desperately long to know more about.

I have a brief clip of Mom in the hospital hours after giving birth to me. The quality is not great because the light is poor, but she's in bed, showing Jack her bare tummy. He's poking it, saying 'baby', and Mom points to me in the bassinet to show him I have arrived. Dad's voice is behind the camera, filming Jack as he goes to peer into the transparent hospital cot. I can see a blurred outline of myself, a sleeping swaddled bundle. I can hear Dad lovingly praise my mom in the background. 'You were brilliant, absolutely brilliant …'

I have another video of Mom weeks later, on Jack's second birthday. She could never have imagined that it would be her last birthday with her little boy or that she would never live to see my first birthday. I can hear the background chatter of many people gathered in the kitchen, but Dad focuses the camera on Mom and Jack. Mom is watchful, holding on to the back of Jack's sweater while the candles flicker on the cake before he and everyone sings 'Happy Birthday'. Jack stands on his chair, delighted to be the centre of attention, as he blows out the two candles. Mom and Jack clap with pure joy, and everyone around them applauds and cheers. The house is full of laughter. Watching some of these videos feels like I'm trying to peer through a window, my face pressed against the glass. But there's a sadness knowing that I'm forever separated from the life inside.

One of my favourite clips is Mom getting ready on her wedding day. It's a professional wedding video, and it's lovely to witness her on one of the happiest days of her life. Her bridesmaids are tightening the laces of her off-the-shoulder white wedding dress.

She is slight in figure. Her hair is short and feathered, topped with a delicate tiara with small sprays of seed pearls. The camera zooms in as one bridesmaid fastens a gold crucifix around her slender neck. Everything about her that day is simplicity and elegance.

The videographer placed a soundtrack over the video – 'The Voyage', a sentimental Christy Moore song. But I can hear Mom say in the background, 'I'm fine! Honestly, I'm fine!' She's trying to reassure everyone as they fuss about her in the room. And she *is* fine. She has natural warmth and grace, and her smile is sweet, reaching her hazel eyes. She looks so beautiful and radiant, a fleeting dream from the past. The world must have seemed so full of promise for her that day.

We watched those videos many times over. It was important to Dad to impart something of our mother's spirit and help us build a connection to the woman he had loved and who had given us life.

The date of the balloon release coincided with Domestic Violence Awareness Month (DVAM) in America.

By then, we knew the Martens' defence team were planning to paint Dad as an aggressor and abuser at the sentencing hearing. By arranging the event and hundreds of biodegradable purple balloons – the official colour of DVAM – I'd hoped to correct the narrative and highlight that our father was a victim of domestic abuse, not the perpetrator. With the balloon event, I also hoped to show other children who were victims of abuse they were not alone.

It was comforting to be in the warm embrace of a community that knew and loved Dad the day before facing his killers in

Davidson County Courthouse. It was also wonderful to reconnect with many of Dad's friends and neighbours – many of whom I hadn't seen since my father had died. So many familiar faces turned up and reintroduced themselves, and seeing all these people from our past brought memories of our years in America rushing back.

I have never forgotten Dad showing us our new home in North Carolina for the first time, even though I was only four when we moved to America. He drove us through the manicured Meadowlands Golf estate in Wallburg, northeast Davidson County, about ten miles from the city of Winston-Salem. The leafy estate was filled with grand family homes among spreading trees. He turned onto a curved driveway and pulled up before an imposing two-storey brick building.

As I craned forward in the car, the house looked vast, dwarfing the homes I'd known in Limerick. The red-brick property's roofline had multiple pointed gables and dormer windows, and the rounded tower at one side reminded me of a fairytale turret.

When Dad unlocked the white front door, it swung open into a cavernous interior. I twirled slowly, mouth agape, in the dramatic two-storey high foyer and living space. Sunlight streamed in from the tall windows as I ran through the house, my footsteps echoing on gleaming hardwood floors. I flung open doors to vast, unfurnished spaces, wide-eyed with amazement and curiosity. I remember asking where my bedroom was.

Dad pointed up the open staircase in the hall, and I dashed up, squealing, 'Show me! Show me!'

Dad laughed as I ran in circles around the space that was my bedroom. 'Just wait until we get your toys and furniture in here,' he said.

'Will I have a new bed?'

'Of course. Can't have my princess sleeping on the floor.' He always called me his princess. 'We'll put your big princess bed over there,' he said, tracing an imaginary outline near one wall.

'A real princess bed?'

'Yep, and right here, we'll set up your princess dressing table.'

I whooped excitedly as Jack and I continued our helter-skelter house tour. Molly and Dad wandered hand in hand through each room, discussing new furniture and where everything would go. We were all in high spirits, looking forward to this fresh start in beautiful surroundings.

Our vast home had six bedrooms with a traditional-style kitchen with cherrywood cabinets in the heart of it. Jack and I darted out onto a first-floor deck floating on stilts over the garden. We ran down the wooden steps, raced through half an acre of gardens and explored the forest of trees around the perimeter.

Overnight, the Corbett family from Limerick became part of a gated community with a network of walking and biking trails and a golf course for my father. Dad and Molly quickly met other couples with young children around the estate's swimming pool. Our new home was also a quick drive from all the amenities of Winston-Salem, a city consistently ranked among America's top places to live.

The defining feature of our first summer was the nightly chorus of crickets. Those noisy little insects were a constant reminder that I was living in a strange new land. They burst into song as the intense heat faded and the sky mellowed into a dark honey glow.

My abiding memory of those summer evenings in North Carolina is the sound of the crickets outside my bedroom window while Dad read me stories.

Molly Martens instigated our family's move to North Carolina. She had arrived in Limerick from Tennessee in her mid-twenties to work for my widowed father as a nanny for Jack and me. My brother was three and I was seventeen months old when Molly moved in with us and, very quickly, she and Dad became a couple. They announced their engagement three years later and, by then, Molly said she was homesick for America.

Initially, Dad had hesitated at the prospect of uprooting Jack and me from our extended family in Limerick. However, he also wanted his fiancée to be happy, especially as she was the woman who Jack and I considered our mother. He didn't want to risk us losing another mother figure. Dad had little option but to transfer from his company, Multi Packaging Solutions (MPS) in Limerick, to the firm's North Carolina operations, where he secured a position as the plant manager. Dad had a thirty-minute commute from our house in Meadowlands estate to his office at the plant off Lexington Parkway.

With his usual optimism, Dad embraced his new life in America and the opportunities offered by this unexpected relocation. Heartbroken after losing the love of his life, Mags, he believed he was creating a new start for us all. He had found a place where Molly could be happy and a sanctuary where he could create cherished childhood memories for Jack and me. It must have seemed like a slice of the American dream for Dad. He could never have known this relocation would end so tragically only four years later.

I hadn't expected the turnout we got at our balloon-releasing event for Dad. My heart swelled with pride to know he had lived on in the memories of many of the people he had worked with in Lexington and lived among in Meadowlands eight years after his death. Jury members who had convicted Tom and Molly of murder were also among the gathering that day. Understandably, they were particularly upset by the Martens' plea-deal arrangement.

That afternoon brought another face from my past in North Carolina when I turned to see a man approach me from the crowd. He was strikingly tall, and something about him tugged at my memory. He was like a half-remembered dream, a towering man with a shaven head, but I couldn't place him.

'I don't know if you remember me,' he said, his warm Southern accent tinged with uncertainty. Tracey recognised him straightaway as a witness from the Martens' 2017 trial.

She reintroduced me. 'This is the man who carried you down the stairs that night.'

Everything around me went silent for an instant, and I saw myself, a small and frightened child jolted from my sleep by a shadowy figure. My heart pounded as I made out a stranger, towering and bald, by my bed. I was confused at first. I looked again and believed Grandpa Tom (Martens) had gone bald. When I scrambled upright, the police badge on the man's shirt came into focus.

Corporal Clayton Stewart Dagenhardt of the Davidson County Sheriff's Office was the first officer to reach the scene of my father's killing at approximately 3.15 a.m. on Sunday, 2 August 2015.

Using his mobile phone, he had captured the first photographs of the scene with my father's naked, blood-stained body lying on his bedroom floor. I had never seen those photographs, but I knew they documented blood on the walls, floor, bed and hallway.

After emergency services removed Dad's body and his killers from the crime scene, Corporal Dagenhardt made his way upstairs with another policeman to wake Jack and me. Speaking kindly and softly, he inspired enough trust that I agreed to leave my bedroom with him. He asked me to promise to walk backwards and keep my eyes shut before he led me downstairs.

Then, he walked me out of my cosy bedroom for the last time. I never saw it again. As we emerged onto the landing, I saw Jack being walked backwards by another police officer. But as we reached the stairs, I hesitated. Earlier that night, I'd felt dizzy and sick and suffered hallucinations. I still felt unsteady, so I nodded when the officer asked if I wanted to be carried. I tried to look back at Jack, but the officer held my head against his white shirt and the nape of his neck and covered the side of my face with his large hand.

At the top of the stairs, I heard the clamour of frantic activity – strangers' voices and the sounds of multiple boots on the wooden floors. It sounded like there were many people downstairs, but the pressure of the officer's hand meant I saw nothing. As we neared the bottom of the stairs, everything went quiet. There was a hush as if everyone downstairs had disappeared. All I heard were Officer Dagenhardt's boots and those of the other officer who was guiding Jack.

I've never forgotten the sense of safety I felt in that officer's arms with his whispered reassurances that everything would be all right. Much later, I learned that he had shielded me from a nightmarish river of blood, trailing from Dad's bedroom on the ground floor to the hall door – the result of my father's body being removed from the house on a gurney.

The officer's hand over my eyes also ensured I remained blissfully ignorant of the scene of butchery inside and around Dad and Molly's bedroom. I realised we had reached the basement door when I heard the creak of its stiff hinges as he pulled it open. Almost as soon as his foot hit the tread of the stairs to descend, the frenzied activity and voices I'd heard earlier started again.

The cold basement air hit me before the officer removed his hand and lowered me to the ground. The police brought us to the large bedroom we called the 'blue room' where Molly's parents, Tom and Sharon Martens, had stayed that night when they visited us in Meadowlands.

When he opened the door, Sharon was sitting in bed, reading her book, with our dog Rory and her dogs, Homer and Guthrie, around her.

'You guys just stay here for a while,' said Officer Dagenhardt.

But Jack wanted to know what was going on. 'Where's Mom and Dad?' he asked.

The officer said nothing as he left, and Jack looked at Sharon.

'I don't know,' Sharon said. 'Just wait like the officer said.'

I took my cue from Sharon. She seemed calm and composed. She read her book under a clip-on light as the three dogs settled back to sleep. The room became quiet, save for the soft rustle of paper as Sharon turned the pages of her book. Sharon Martens was included in a wrongful death claim along with Tom and Molly, however she has never been criminally charged with my dad's killing.

That night, I remember moving to the window. The trees and garden looked dark and eery, painted with shifting red-and-blue lights pulsing through the trees. I couldn't see the emergency vehicles. I don't know how long I sat by the window, leaning on the sill, dozing and jerking awake. Every time I opened my eyes, those lights were still flashing their warning in the darkness.

Seeing Clayton Dagenhardt again brought memories of that night flooding back. My tears flowed as I reached to hug my guardian angel. 'I never got to thank you,' I said.

Clayton was still in the police force and was now a lieutenant. I learned he shouldn't have been working that night, but he had stayed late and received the emergency call that sent him to our house at Panther Creek Court.

He introduced me to his wife, whom he had woken that night when he got home. He'd wanted to talk about the little girl who he'd had to shield from the slaughtered remains of her father. The officer's wife explained the case affected him more than many because he had a baby daughter at home, also called Sarah.

Clayton's wife had followed me on social media ever since and related my progress to him. He explained he had wanted to reach out to me, but the cases and appeals had dragged on, and he had to keep a professional distance.

My rescuer also confirmed everything I remembered of that night. I believe therapy has retrieved many memories that might otherwise have remained buried. It explains why I remember so much about the past, and Jack remembers less. I've engaged in many therapies, but Jack has a different way of coping. He is more reserved about expressing his feelings, and there's nothing wrong with that. But he recalls nothing about the police officer who brought him from his room, whereas I remember everything.

The night of 2 August will always hold traumatic memories, but it could have been much worse without Clayton Dagenhardt's humanity and compassion. I was glad to have had the privilege of thanking him at the balloon release for Dad.

I addressed the crowd at one point, telling them how the day was inspired by Dad's tradition of giving Jack and me balloons on the anniversary of our birth mother's passing. I explained that just as Dad wanted to preserve Mom's presence in our lives, Jack and I were similarly trying to preserve his spirit and carry memories of him forward in our lives. That day began a new tradition built upon the strong foundation Dad had given us.

I didn't tell the people assembled that I was still young and naive enough to wish for things that I could never have. Or that I bartered with God that day. *If I can't have Dad back, let me tell him I'm sorry I lied. If I can't have that, please give me a sign that he knows I'm sorry.* The longing to explain to Dad my statements to the social workers became so intense some days that it was almost unbearable. The balloon release in North Carolina was one of those days.

When the formalities had concluded, we turned our heads skywards as we freed our balloons in unison. Purple and lilac orbs rose in ones and twos and then in a rush, until the sky was covered. My eyes brimmed with tears as I watched our balloons ascend into the sky, drifting away on the breeze like unbreakable vows to always remember him.

Unfortunately, Dad's former workplace in Lexington, which was renamed Westrock, announced its imminent closure three months after our balloon release. I felt a deep sadness hearing this, not just for losing this connection to my father, but for all the 153 workers – Dad's colleagues and friends – who had lost their livelihoods as part of Westrock's merger with the Irish company Smurfit Kappa.

Before the plant closed forever, his American colleagues shipped Dad's memorial plaque back to Ireland, where it will be installed at the Smurfit Westrock plant in Raheen, Limerick. This means that Dad's memorial stone has come full circle and is back where he had started his career as a young general operative thirty years earlier. Dad would have been sorry to see the closure of his North Carolina plant, but he'd smile seeing a lasting memorial to him in a place he associated with many of the happiest years of his life.

CHAPTER 3

STRONG ENOUGH

Your Honour

I was hoping there would be a retrial so my truth and my brother's truth could both be heard. Instead, all we have is this, a Victim Impact Statement.

Courtroom 6, Davidson County Courthouse
Day 1: Monday, 30 October 2023
Music has always been therapeutic, lifting and energising me when I feel at my lowest. I've always been drawn to singing because my dad sang. Jack's a naturally gifted singer like Dad, but I had to train my voice. When I was ten, Tracey encouraged me to go to lessons in the Voice Box in Limerick. She recognised singing was a vital release for me but also saw my frustration when I couldn't reach some notes. I can only sing the way I do because I worked at it, training for hours until I got my voice to sound how it should.

'Jar of Hearts' by Christina Perri is my go-to song when I'm feeling low. It's a difficult song, a powerful ballad that builds with an emotional intensity that pushes my voice to its heights. Inside, it feels like I'm screaming when I sing it, releasing something raw and visceral. I am letting grief, anger and pain pour out in a torrent of song. When I sing, it's not about applause or perfection. Singing gives me a sense of release. It enables me to exorcise demons.

Ryan Tubridy had been taken aback on his RTÉ radio show when I said 'Jar of Hearts' was my 'scream' song. The interview took place in 2019 when I was promoting a children's book I had written entitled *Noodle Loses Dad*.

'That sounds quite sad, Sarah,' he'd said.

But it isn't. When I pour all my voice into an emotional song, something shifts, and every note becomes empowering. If I ignore my emotions, they build like steam in a pressure cooker. Singing helps release this build-up of toxic stress before it becomes harmful. I have to be vigilant about this, like managing a chronic condition.

The Martens' actions have left me with this lasting burden – one I need to be mindful of to maintain my well being. Singing is a release valve, sometimes giving me the strength to move through what I'm feeling. When I scream-sing, it's also a declaration of survival and resilience.

The morning after our balloon release, two carloads of us set off for Davidson County Superior Court for the first day of the sentencing hearing. Tracey cranked up the music for the twenty-minute journey. She'd come armed with a soundtrack to steel us for the fight ahead.

We sang along to Whitney Houston's upbeat 'Step by Step'. The lyrics, about never giving up and moving on, resonated that morning. Cher's 'Strong Enough' pulsed through the speakers afterwards. 'Strong Enough' has always been Tracey's and my go-to anthem; its girl-power lyrics bolstered our resolve that morning.

My shoulders straightened a little as we sang and my chin rose a bit higher. Within minutes, my spirits lifted and my anxiety reduced.

Our songs became like an extra layer of armour as we hurtled towards each tension-filled and often disturbing day in court. I drew strength from having a little order, predictability and motivational music before the turmoil of the courtroom day.

Davidson County Courthouse was a vast and newly renovated, three storey building with towering modern glass windows punctuating its brown-and-cream brick walls. As we pulled into its car park, we conducted a quick recce. On that first morning, we prepared like soldiers going into battle.

David wanted to avoid any unnecessary confrontation with any members of the Martens family. The day was stressful enough without bumping into them. He reminded us of the security protocols – phones and bags had to be locked in the car, save for Tracey's bag, which contained her inhaler.

'Let's do this!' we said, using the American-flavoured catchphrase I'd used as a child and which had always amused my family.

Then everyone moved as one, falling into formation as we walked towards the courthouse entrance – David and Dean led from the front, Tracey and I were in the middle, Jack and Adam were at the back, and everyone else milled around us too. Heads held high, we made our way through the media gauntlet.

The intense media scrutiny outside the courthouse didn't faze me initially, even though some in our group found the attention unnerving. Amid the chaos, I watched an RTÉ cameraman, his equipment balanced effortlessly on his shoulder, reversing at speed as he captured us striding towards the courthouse. I was in awe of his dedication, risking life and limb for a brief news clip.

Inside, we navigated the armed-police security and metal detectors. Tracey and David, courthouse veterans, exchanged greetings with the staff they knew. Then, passing a large window, we faced a wall of cameras pressed against the glass, hoping for one last shot.

Before we'd left the house that morning, David had already prepped everyone on what was going to happen. We knew that first we had to take the lift to the District Attorney's office at the top of the courthouse. We met our assigned liaison officer and Assistant District Attorney Alan Martin, who had been appointed by the DA Garry Frank as the lead counsel for the prosecution. Alan was a familiar face to Tracey and David as he had been a key part of the original team that had successfully prosecuted the Martens for murder years earlier. We also met his fellow Assistant DAs, Marissa Parker and Kaitlyn Jones. We exchanged pleasantries and took the stairs to Courtroom 6 on the first floor.

Our legal battleground was a spacious, modern room with harsh fluorescent panels overhead, grey walls and grey-hued industrial carpet. The judge's bench, attorneys' desks and jury box were made of light oak and stood out in the sea of grey.

A central aisle ran through the courtroom like no-man's land, separating the defence and prosecution sides.

Jack and I sat behind Alan Martin on the right. David positioned himself on our outside like a human shield to protect us from Tom and Molly Martens, who were sitting ten feet away on the left side of the aisle. That's where David ensured he sat every day to protect us in the only way he could in that courtroom. All I had to do was lean back and the Martens disappeared from my view.

That morning, Tom's wife Sharon and two of their three sons, Bobby and Connor, sat behind Tom, Molly and their defence teams. Sharon's brother, Michael Earnest, and his wife, Mona, were also part of their support team. Members of the media crowded into their rows behind the Martens.

The bailiff's voice rang out at 10 a.m. sharp, 'All rise! The Honourable Judge David Hall presiding.'

Judge Hall, a man in his mid-fifties, ascended to his raised bench draped in traditional black robes. His bald pate reflected the lights above him and he wore spectacles that lent him an air of gravitas. After motioning to everyone to sit, he folded his arms on the bench before him, and his first words were to warn the people in the courtroom against any reactions or interruptions. He added that he had the power to remove anyone 'who even grimaces' for the duration of the proceedings. He scanned the courtroom as he said this, adjusting his glasses and taking in the attorneys, defendants, media and spectators with a sweeping glance. He made it clear that he planned to keep a vice-like grip of control over proceedings.

I knew I had to exercise restraint in the courtroom, no matter how difficult it became. And I vowed not to let my emotions get the better of me. I was there to represent Dad and I couldn't let myself be provoked, no matter what the defence did or said. If we showed any volatility, it would play into the defence's hands. They would use an emotional response to imply that we were a reflection of my father, who they wanted to portray as violent and abusive. Still, I knew it would be hard to remain mute when every interested party had a voice in this sentencing hearing except the victim's family.

Alan Martin then rose to address the judge. A middle-aged man with a shock of nearly black hair and heavy, black-rimmed glasses, Alan had a calm and composed air about him. Nothing ruffled him.

He confirmed the news we had received weeks earlier – that the DA in Davidson County would not be proceeding with a retrial of the second-degree murder charges. Alan told the court that the plea agreement had taken months to negotiate and had only recently been fully resolved. These months of negotiation were news to us. The deal, he stated, was in 'the best interest of justice'.

Justice for whom? I couldn't see any justice for my dad. After our long fight, a plea deal was not the conclusion we had expected or wanted.

DA Garry Frank had seriously considered charging the Martens with first-degree murder. He had achieved the longest sentence possible for second-degree murder for people with no previous convictions – twenty to twenty-five years. And now we were discussing voluntary manslaughter? It was a steep decline from first-degree murder, and it just didn't feel right or justifiable.

However, in the days after the sentencing hearing, the DA Garry Frank insisted that, from 'day one', his office had considered voluntary manslaughter in the case against the Martens. He said his office had backed off the manslaughter charge when the case went forward on the basis of second-degree murder, as it could not pursue both at the time.

He had explained to us earlier that the grounds for the Martens' appeal meant a successful outcome in a retrial would be more difficult.

The Martens had claimed there was an improper exclusion of testimony. Tom Martens' statement that he had heard Molly yell 'Don't hurt my dad' during the altercation that killed my father was excluded as hearsay. The defence successfully argued that this was erroneous, as it was relevant to Tom Martens' state of mind at the time.

If we had gone to retrial, our statements to social workers, in particular, would have been brought into evidence. Garry Frank had said in a newspaper interview that the rule changes regarding evidence would make it 'more likely that the defence's theory about this being domestic violence, and the dad [Tom Martens] being a hero for coming in and protecting his daughter [Molly]'. He added that this could be 'possibly believed by at least one juror, and that's all it would have taken to derail conviction'.

Jack and I were devastated to know statements that the Martens coached us to make could be used to defend them, our dad's killers.

Garry Frank also discussed problems with my birth mom's post-mortem in Ireland. The medical experts commissioned by his office disagreed with the conclusions of the Irish medical team. He said the report had 'left some things open' that could have been pursued by the defence.

In the 2017 trial, prosecutors had described Dad's killing as 'heinous, atrocious and cruel'. These were not the words being used in this sentencing hearing.

The Martens' lengthy prison sentences also did not apply. The prosecution told us that their new sentences could range from thirty-eight to fifty-eight months (three to five years) to eighty to 108 months (six to nine years). The state would argue for the latter, but the defence would argue for probation, meaning the Martens could walk free with time served. Even the thought of the Martens being released felt agonising.

Typically, a sentencing hearing for a guilty plea to voluntary manslaughter in North Carolina lasts thirty minutes. Perhaps because the case had attracted widespread and international media coverage, the hearing for the Martens was scheduled to last two weeks. We knew the defence would use those two weeks to establish mitigating circumstances and thereby persuade the judge that Molly and Tom had killed my father in self-defence. They would do everything in their power to reduce their sentences and destroy our father's reputation as they did so.

My expression remained impassive as Molly was called on to enter her plea. This wasn't difficult because I felt little seeing her apart from disdain. I knew I would have to remind myself to stay strong in the coming days. She and her defence team would say things that were not the truth, and I couldn't let my emotions get the better of me. My focus was on my father, not Tom or Molly Martens.

That morning, Molly, wearing shades of baby blue, stood with her left hand on the Bible and, affecting her sweetest tones, entered her guilty plea. Tom then stood and entered his guilty plea. In all the previous court cases, he had presented himself in a sharp dark suit, white shirt and black tie, as if he'd just stepped out of his office. However, at this hearing, he presented a softer, more 'grandfatherly' appearance. He had exchanged his slick FBI-style suit for a casual grey sports jacket and a blue open-neck shirt.

Judge Hall explained to the court that Molly's no-contest plea to voluntary manslaughter was still considered a guilty plea and meant she would remain a convicted felon. We learned that a no-contest plea meant that she did not admit guilt but also did not dispute the charges. Molly essentially accepted a conviction without admitting to the criminal act. This plea could be beneficial to her if we took civil proceedings, as it could not be used as evidence of liability in civil court. By pleading guilty, Tom Martens would also have a Felony D criminal conviction.

The judge explained that the Martens could face maximum sentences of up to 204 months (seventeen years) but quickly added that this upper limit would not apply as they had no prior criminal record.

He said that he could impose a sentence at the lower end of the scale or even decide that there were 'exceptional mitigating circumstances' that would enable the defendants to walk free on probation. My worst fear was that Tom and Molly, all smiles and hugs for their family, would stroll out of the courtroom.

When Molly and Tom confirmed that they understood the implications of accepting a guilty plea, Judge Hall said he would ratify the deal.

The state asked the court to consider the fact that children (Jack and me) were in the house at the time of Dad's killing as 'an aggravating factor'. This meant the judge was asked to regard our presence in the house when the Martens carried out our dad's killing as grounds for a harsher sentence. They wrapped up the plea deal in forty-five minutes.

As a family, all we could do now was to ensure that the Martens' sentencing reflected the severity of their offence and defend our father's name in whatever way we could. Our attendance signalled our support for the prosecution's case and would hopefully strengthen their argument for a more severe sentence.

The sentencing hearing started with opening statements from the prosecution and defence, outlining some of the evidence that lay ahead. Assistant DA Kaitlyn Jones rose to give an overview of the events of the night of 2 August 2015. She said Dad had been killed in the primary bedroom on the ground floor of our home in Panther Creek Court. She explained that Molly and her father were claiming self-defence, saying Dad had attacked them and threatened their lives.

Tom Martens' version of events was that he had discovered Dad choking his daughter and rushed to her rescue, hammering my father repeatedly with an aluminium baseball bat. During the struggle, Molly had come to her father's aid by smashing Dad's head with a concrete paver stone that had been sitting on her nightstand.

The courtroom heard the recording of Tom's 911 call placed at 3.02 a.m., which revealed they only started CPR when instructed to by the operator. The operator had said to 'make sure his mouth and nose are clear'.

We heard Tom reply. 'It's a mess.'

The operator had explained the procedure for chest compressions, and Tom had said, 'I'm somewhat familiar with this.' His voice had been composed throughout the call. His breathing was normal, and there was no sense of panic. He could have been talking about the weather when he said, 'I think I may have killed him.'

Kaitlyn moved on to describe the stomach-churning injuries Dad had suffered. She said he had been struck so many times that the pathologist Dr Craig Nelson wasn't sure how many impacts there had been. He could only say that Dad had been hit *at least* twelve times.

During the 2017 trial, he'd said that the skull fractures were the types of injury that were normally seen in falls from great heights or in car crashes. In Nelson's evidence, he had also said that any individual blow could have rendered my father unconscious and ensured he was no longer a threat. But that they had continued their savage attack, literally beating a man's brains out. A juror had vomited when a photograph of Dad's head was shown.

During the trial, a Davidson County Emergency Medical Services paramedic testified that while attempting to lift Dad's chin to prepare him for intubation, his fingers 'went inside the skull'. The prosecution showed pictures of Dad's autopsy, where his head had been bashed in with such violence that pieces of his skull from the back of his head had fallen out on the gurney.

One of the foremost US experts in blood-spatter evidence also told the 2017 trial that he believed the first blow to Dad's head had happened when he was lying in bed. The expert, Dr Stuart James, had testified that some blows had been made as Dad fell to the ground, and another was struck when his head was on or near the floor. He said blood spatters on the inside lower hem of Tom Martens' shorts indicated that the blood had come from below to where he was standing.

However, the prosecution presented little of the damning evidence heard in the trial during this sentencing hearing. The new plea deal also specified that prosecutors could not introduce 'any theory that includes premeditation or malice as an element of the offence'. I was in disbelief and couldn't grasp how the defence could cherry pick the evidence to be produced in the sentencing hearing. Yet, that was how it was.

Assistant DA Jones noted that, despite Dad's colossal injuries, Tom and Molly Martens were unmarked at the scene. The pair claimed they had fought for their lives that night, but none of the first responders on the scene observed injuries to either killer.

The excessive force used in killing Dad was an Achilles' heel for counsel defending Tom and Molly Martens. Even the plea agreement conceded that the level of force used was excessive. The defence needed to explain and excuse Tom and Molly's savagery to reduce their sentence.

In his opening statement, Jay Vannoy, counsel for Tom, stood to tell the court that he would show 'an extraordinary amount of mitigating factors' in this sentencing case. Clean-shaven, with short, neat, salt-and-pepper hair, Vannoy said his client was 'accepting responsibility that his actions were excessive'.

'We don't deny that he hit multiple times,' he said. 'The question at sentencing is why?'

Vannoy said that Tom had been so distraught at seeing Dad assault Molly that it had impaired his perception and cognition.

Vannoy also reminded the judge that Tom had lived 'an exemplary life'. He was a qualified lawyer and had served with the FBI for thirty years, climbing the bureau ladder until he received top-secret clearances.

Vannoy noted that Molly and Tom had already spent forty-four months in prison. He said that if someone searched Tom Martens' name, all they would read about him is that he is a 'murderer, a cold, calculated murderer'.

I shook my head. He seemed to imply that Tom was an innocent victim of public perception; that this portrayal of him as a cold killer was unjustified and unfair. He seemed to forget that Tom had been convicted of second-degree murder by a jury of twelve of his peers.

Then Molly's defence counsel, Douglas Kingsbery, rose and began pacing the courtroom with intent, outlining what he would present to the judge over the coming days. He didn't waste any time portraying Dad as an abusive wife-beater. Molly 'confided in multiple witnesses' that Dad had killed his first wife and that she feared she was next.

Kingsbery also announced defence and prosecution experts agreed that my birth mom did not die of an asthma attack, adding, 'Homicide by manual strangulation is a possibility.'

So is an alien landing, I thought, gazing at Kingsbery in astonishment.

It was clear that the defence were hell-bent on portraying my birth mom as a murder victim. To defend Molly, they would stop at nothing to cast my father as a cold-blooded killer.

No one would have given Kingsbery a second glance in a crowded room. His appearance was bland and unimpressive.

He looked deflated with an oversized suit that drooped at the shoulders and pooled at his ankles. However, appearances are deceptive because Kingsbery was ruthless. He was the courtroom's showman and the defence's Rottweiler from the first day.

He moved on to talk about the statements Jack and I made to social workers in the immediate aftermath of Dad's killing. He said our statements had supported Molly's claims of a history of domestic violence in the house. *Of course they did because that is what she told us to say.* He didn't mention that we recanted those statements soon after.

The defence had already successfully used the words of two scared children to help quash the Martens' murder convictions during their appeals. Now, they were about to use those statements again during their sentencing hearing to keep our father's killers from returning to jail.

I took a deep breath at the end of that first day. It was only day one, and I already knew this would be the longest two weeks of my life.

CHAPTER 4

IN HER SHADOW

Your Honour
I treasured a framed photograph that my dad got for me of him and my birth mom, Mags, on their wedding day. Molly threw it down the stairs ... Molly Martens began her mind games when I was five years old. What kind of mother tells a five-year-old girl that her father killed her birth mom?

Winston-Salem, North Carolina
October 2023

In the evenings, I wrote and revised my Victim Impact Statement. I had so much to say about Molly's impact on my life.

Without being expressly told, I grew up knowing not to mention my birth mother in front of Molly. She bristled at any reminder of her, so Jack and I knew our birth mother was she-who-must-not-be-named.

Within a year of moving to Ireland and starting a relationship with my dad, Molly insisted that he sell the home he'd built with our mom. Our stone-clad home near the village of Ballyneety in Limerick had to go because Molly claimed she could no longer live 'in the shadow' of my birth mother.

My birth mother had compiled a scrapbook detailing the construction of the cottage in Ballyneety. It contained a picture of her and Dad standing by the sold sign at the site outside the village. I love that photo. Dad's arms are wrapped around Mom, and both are beaming at the camera, standing on their new property – essentially a muddy field. Mom recorded every detail of the construction and added handwritten notes and quotations for the build. I have that scrapbook now and treasure it. The Ballyneety cottage represented some of the happiest times in my parents' lives.

Dad always encouraged us to talk about Mom. He gave me a photograph of her and him on their wedding day, which was one of my most precious possessions. Dad placed the image in a pink 'princess' frame and always reminded me that Mom had chosen the name Sarah, which means princess in Hebrew. He always referred to me as his 'little princess'.

As a child, that wedding photograph fascinated me. I gazed at my mom's features, musing about whether or not I looked like her and wondering about the life I might have had if she had lived. People in our family say I have her mannerisms. I wrinkle my nose in a certain way like she did and I have her laugh, including the snort. People say you can't miss what you never had, but that's not true. I miss not knowing her as a mother. She has the most soulful eyes, and I treasure every connection to her.

After I'd looked at it, I always tucked the photograph away at the back of my bedside drawer. I knew it would injure Molly's feelings to see it, and I never wanted to hurt her. My behaviour and every thought was dictated by Molly. I always had a push-button smile, eager to do whatever she wanted. But I was alert, watching for every shift in her expression that might reveal her state of mind. Her moods swung in an instant, so I was hyper-vigilant, always living with a certain sense of dread.

I'd take my birth mom's photo out when I was alone in my room but, one day, when I was seven years old, I was careless and forgot to hide it. My heart sank when Molly spotted it the minute she entered my bedroom. Snatching the photo, she turned on me, her face contorted with rage.

'This woman is dead!' she screamed into my face, furiously jabbing the photo. 'She is dead! Do you hear me? I am your mother! That woman is dead!'

I shrank, terrified, but she came even closer to shriek at me. 'I. AM. YOUR. MOTHER!'

Still clutching the frame, she stormed onto the landing and flung the frame with force down the stairs, and I heard the crash of it shattering. The sound broke my heart. But she sauntered down the stairs barefoot, walking over the splintered picture frame and through shards of glass as if nothing had happened.

I was cleaning the mess up when Dad arrived home.

'What happened here?' he asked.

Of course, I never told him. I wouldn't dare tell on Molly. I gave him some excuses about dropping the photo on the stairs. Dad helped me clean up the shattered glass and, using super glue, he reassembled the frame, which had snapped in two with the force of Molly's fury. I'm still reminded of that event when I see the cracks on the frame today. I never left the photo anywhere

Molly might see it again. But, today, that picture sits on top of my bedside table.

The Martens' fiction about Dad murdering my birth mom was a focus of the sentencing trial, and I could already imagine the headlines the next day. But it was old news to me. As a child, the only time Molly ever lifted the ban on mentioning my birth mother was to tell me how Dad had killed her. She had been accusing Dad of smothering my birth mom for years behind his back.

'You know how your birth mom died, don't you?' she'd say, lowering her voice as if she was telling me in confidence. 'Your dad suffocated her with a pillow.'

I don't know why she repeatedly told me this because it wasn't something that I could easily forget. I learned much later that this was obviously nothing near the truth of what happened.

She started telling me the story of how Dad had killed Mom from the time I was around five years old. Even though her words shocked me, I never dared repeat her accusation to Dad. I knew her words would deeply wound my father. I would never dare break Molly's confidence anyway. She always fostered a sense of her and me as a secret team – 'us versus Dad'. But I remember feeling conflicted and confused. *Why was she saying this to me?* I knew Daddy never did what she said. He was a gentle and kind man, who only spoke lovingly about my birth mother, so it made little sense.

On our last Father's Day with Dad – Sunday, 21 June 2015 – Molly raised the topic of my 'murdered' birth mom again. Dad, Jack and I had gone to a pet superstore to buy an aquarium and fish that day. However, the fish died while we were out at the cinema that evening, and Molly shrieked at Dad, blaming him for the dead fish and for upsetting me.

As Molly, Jack and I buried the fish in the garden that night, she looked back towards the house, glaring at Dad. He was standing in the kitchen's light, still trying to figure out what had gone wrong with the air pump or filter.

'HIM!' Molly said, with unconcealed disgust. 'Killing things again!' Without mentioning my mother's name, it was clear what she was implying.

Instinct never allowed me to believe what she said about Dad, but I longed to erase the niggling doubt that Molly had tried to instil. I was desperate to know the details of how my birth mother had died.

A few days later, I seized my chance to quiz Dad as he collected the post from the mail lady. Molly exerted a lot of control in the house, and I was rarely able to talk to Dad out of her earshot.

Approaching him was a spur-of-the-moment thing, so I had no preamble. 'Dad, what happened to my mom?'

He had been flicking through the mail, but he stopped. 'You know what happened, Sarah. She died of an asthma attack. We've spoken about it.'

'Yes, but what *really* happened?' I insisted.

He had no idea what lay behind my urgent questioning, so he shook his head, smiling ruefully. 'I promise I'll tell you in more detail when you're older, Sarah, okay?'

And that was it. I followed Dad back to the house, deflated and worried. *Why won't he tell me what happened?*

Now that I am older, I can understand why Dad didn't discuss it with me in detail at that time. I was too young, and it would have been painful to revisit that night and explain it to me.

Molly's constant accusations about my father made me anxious. I felt burdened with this terrible secret, which I longed to unload, but I suspected there might be terrible consequences if I did. I didn't know what to believe but, in my heart, I knew Dad couldn't have done what Molly had accused him of. Still, questions rolled round and round in my head.

Several nights before he died, I woke to hear Molly and Dad arguing. I crept onto the landing, sat against the bookshelves and listened at the open staircase. Whenever they rowed, that was my spot. I heard Molly shrieking, her voice sharp and furious. Then, suddenly, she emerged from the kitchen, and her feet pounded up the stairs. Panicked, I scrambled into my room and dived under the covers.

My bedroom door flew open, spilling light across my bed, but I lay motionless, feigning sleep even though my heart was pounding. The bedclothes were yanked away from me and Molly leapt into my bed.

She grabbed me to her as Dad turned on the light. 'He's going to kill me!' she screamed. 'He's going to kill me like he killed his first wife.'

Molly held my arm in a vice-like grip, so I sat frozen with shock, not daring to say a word. Even though she'd told me countless times, to my knowledge, she had never made that accusation in front of my father before.

Dad stood motionless in the doorway with Molly's words hanging between us and in that moment, I believe everything changed for him. I saw the anguish in his eyes as he looked at me, searching my face for any sign of shock or disbelief at Molly's accusation and not finding it. He must have wondered how long I had carried this terrible secret. The room was silent as Dad struggled to process what she had said and how little I'd reacted. I watched understanding dawn in his eyes as pieces of a terrible puzzle clicked into place. He swallowed hard, looking aghast. He must have thought about my questions about my birth mom's death, the whispered conversations he'd caught fragments of, and the many incidents where Molly tried to wedge distance between him and his children. I began sobbing as Molly squeezed and twisted my arm under the bedclothes. I'm saddened now thinking he may have mistaken my tears for fear of him.

'Sarah, you know I did nothing to hurt your mom. I loved her very much,' he said, looking straight at me pleading for understanding.

He looked devastated – I'd never seen him look so upset. He didn't realise I'd been listening to that claim for years.

'Molly, come on,' he pleaded. 'Let Sarah sleep. Let's go to bed.'

He wanted to get her out of my room, but she responded by gripping me harder and shrieking louder when he came closer.

I saw the fight drain out of Dad. He slumped in the doorway, looking defeated as he realised the depth of the chasm between him and his wife. He couldn't come any closer to me without her screaming.

I watched something fundamental break in my father. He had just realised the full scope of Molly's betrayal and the extent of the psychological warfare she'd been waging in his family.

Something pivotal in their relationship also shattered that night. I believe that Molly realised she had let her mask slip too far and revealed far too much of her true nature. I saw a new resolution forming in Dad too. I believe that was the moment he gave up entirely on his marriage. His constant efforts to muddle on ended that night and that was when he decided, for my sake and Jack's, that he had to leave her. He had known for some time that his marriage was ending, but that was the incident that sealed it for him. Leaving her became an urgent matter. The decision to leave would ultimately save my brother and me, though Dad could never know how steep a price he'd have to pay.

'Okay, good night, Sarah. Molly, we'll talk in the morning,' he said, his voice heavy with resignation and new-found knowledge as he switched off the light and shut the door behind him.

Molly told me to get to sleep. She pulled out some blankets and slept on the floor.

When I woke in the morning, the blankets were on the floor, but she had gone. I looked out, and her car was gone too. I went downstairs, following our dog's whines to be let out. But my mind raced, replaying Molly's heated words and Dad's shocked expression.

I was angry and confused. I always took Molly's side in an argument, but not this time. I was mad that Molly had brought me into their row. I knew my dad was incapable of hurting anyone. But I vowed I wouldn't talk to either of them that day.

The basement door squeaked open and Dad emerged, his eyes bloodshot and red-rimmed with either tears or exhaustion. He looked at me pleadingly and a lump formed in my throat.

'Sarah, you need to know I'd never, ever hurt your mom, and I'd never hurt Molly.'

His worn and raw expression melted my heart, and I ran to him, sobbing. Kneeling on one knee, he held me in a bear hug and I realised he was crying, too. It shocked me. I'd never seen my father cry before. He was distraught, apologising over and over, 'I'm so sorry. I'm so sorry about everything.'

Molly didn't come home until late that evening. She didn't talk to anyone – she went to her bedroom and shut the door. We knew we couldn't disturb her. We all lived in unnerving silence for the next few days.

CHAPTER 5

VICTIMS

Your Honour

The charge they now accept is voluntary manslaughter. I've seen my father's bloody handprint on the door of his bedroom. There was nothing voluntary about his death. I know in my heart he tried to leave that bedroom. He didn't choose to leave us; he was taken from us. HE was the victim.

Courtroom 6, Davidson County Courthouse
Day 2: Tuesday, 31 October 2023
When we entered the courtroom on the second morning, we could see the baseball bat and the brick paver used to beat my father to death laid out as exhibits. I had no warning, no chance to avoid seeing them. The fluorescent lights cast a harsh glare on them, making the dents on the metal bat impossible to unsee. My breath caught as I saw the paving stone, stained red-brown with Dad's blood.

The weapons, casually displayed on brown paper bags by the defence, prompted a rush of awful images into my mind. I tried not to think about the injuries they had inflicted on my dad's head. I faltered for a second with an urge to flee the room, but I fought that urge with my determination to see this hearing through to the end.

Glancing at Jack, I realised with relief that he was distracted and hadn't spotted the table. So, I stayed silent and moved with him to our seats. He didn't need to start his day by being confronted with those weapons. But the courage and motivation I had felt singing in the car that morning had vanished. The second day hadn't even started and I felt sick to my stomach.

As Judge Hall opened proceedings, Molly's counsel let us know the spotlight was turning to Tom's wife Sharon and the statement she had made to police on the night of the killing. The prosecution had not been able to compel her to appear in the original trial, so we hadn't heard her statement before. I was more than curious to hear what she had said about that night.

Sharon was in the courtroom. She had been ill for some time, having undergone treatment for ovarian cancer, and she looked a lot older and more gaunt than I recalled.

I can't remember when I saw Sharon and Tom Martens for the first time, but they became a regular presence in our lives after we moved to America. Molly and her mother spoke nearly every day, and the couple visited us in North Carolina frequently. We also went to Tennessee to see them, making the five-hour car journey on some weekends.

We called Molly's dad 'Grandpa Tom', but Sharon refused to be called 'Grandma' or any variation of that because she said it made her sound old. Instead, Jack and I were told to call her 'Seekoo'. I don't know what the name means or where it came from.

Grandpa Tom attempted to relate to me as a child and read me a bedtime story when we stayed in his house. Seekoo, however, was not a nurturing, grandmotherly type. I was more fearful than fond of her, finding her cold and critical.

'Show Seekoo your new dress,' Molly said after her parents arrived at our house one day.

Obediently, I ran to Seekoo, beaming with delight, and held out the billowing skirt for her approval, spinning for good measure.

She scanned me from head to toe, and I still remember her reaction as clearly as yesterday. 'You look fat in that,' she said.

Her words instantly deflated all the joy I had felt. Looking back, I feel sad for that insecure little girl, seeking a bit of praise and approval.

But Sharon prided herself on her say-it-as-it-is attitude. Like many people convinced that 'just being truthful' and 'not sugarcoating things' is admirable, she didn't care about leaving hurt feelings in her wake – not even those of a small child.

The defence introduced Sharon's statement by painting her as another victim of my dad's killing. Sharon had apparently hoped to enjoy retirement from her career as a maths professor but, instead, had to spend her time visiting her husband and daughter in separate jails while battling cancer. The defence told us the appeals process had also cost the Martens dearly, forcing them to sell their $600,000 beach holiday home.

As I listened, I thought about how my family had killed no one. Yet, we had faced a far greater financial drain between custody, guardianship and estate battles with the Martens, and the costs of attending all the pre-trial hearings, the trial and the appeals.

Sharon's statement to Detective Nathan Riggs of the Davidson County Sheriff's Office told how she and Tom had arrived at our home around 8.00 p.m. on Saturday, 1 August 2015.

I remembered that day perfectly. The sky had been brilliant blue from early in the morning and we knew it would be another hot summer's day. Dad went out to mow the lawn before it got too hot.

He only had a manual push mower despite the fact we had the largest lawn in Panther Creek Court and were surrounded by neighbours with ride-on lawnmowers. Every time we were in The Home Depot, Dad lingered around the gleaming displays of ride-on mowers. He liked to run his hand along the contours of the shiny machines, settle into the padded seats and grip the steering wheel. I think he always imagined cruising across the lawn, but Molly had insisted that pushing a manual mower was exercise for him.

Beads of sweat ran down Dad's face as he worked and the temperature soared. I ran to him with water tumblers, most of their contents slopping out before I reached him.

'Thanks, Sarah, I really appreciate it,' he'd say each time before winking at Jack, who delivered him full glasses.

Before he finished, Molly and I left for horse riding and, when we returned in the late afternoon, I ran straight to Dad to tell him all about it. He was sitting across the road having a beer with our neighbour, Dave Fritzsche.

Molly changed into cut-off denim shorts and a tank top, and then she and Dave's wife Michelle joined the men. The four sat in a semi-circle of lawn chairs in the shade as I played with the Fritzsches' younger child, Danny.

Meanwhile, Jack went to the tenth birthday party of his school friend, Jay Sams. Molly knew his mother, Melissa Sams, a family-law attorney.

Later that evening, as Molly went over to our house for something, Dad said, 'When you're coming back, can you bring another beer, hun?'

Molly looked over her shoulder and replied, 'Yeah, if my parents can come over.'

That was the first we knew that Tom and Sharon were visiting. Before her words had time to sink in, Grandpa Tom and Seekoo's car wound down the road. They pulled into our driveway just after 8.00 p.m.

'Oh, what a great surprise!' I remember Michelle saying.

Sharon had only left our house in the previous forty-eight hours, so I hadn't expected to see her or Tom again so soon. The police officer never asked, and Sharon never explained why she and Tom changed their dinner plans at the last minute, and drove five hours from their home in Knoxville, Tennessee, to ours. They said they were coming before 'the kids' returned to school but we were not due back to school for weeks.

Nor did the interview explain why she and Tom had exchanged thirteen phone calls with Molly that day. Tom had placed the first call to Molly at 2.21 p.m. He then tried to call Dad at 2.36 p.m. but was cut off after six seconds and forwarded to his messaging service. Four minutes later, Tom made two further calls to Dad. The first didn't connect and the second lasted thirty-seven seconds and was forwarded to my dad's messaging service. We don't know the content of that call, which was around the time Molly had taken me to horse riding.

Phone records show that Molly and Sharon had also exchanged a dozen more calls, the last of which was at 7.28 p.m., shortly before they pulled up to our house. We have never discovered the reason for this flurry of phone calls.

Sharon told Detective Riggs that Molly and Dad were constantly fighting, but that her daughter told her it was always verbal, not violent. 'Molly knew I would be hysterical if I knew he was hitting her,' she said.

But she claimed that Jack and I told her we had witnessed physical violence. Sharon told the investigator that she was so concerned about it that she had trained us to call her at a number and on a phone she had hidden in our house. That latter statement was true, at least.

She had given us secret codewords and told us to use them in an emergency. Mine was 'Peacock' and Jack's was 'Galaxy'. If something 'terrible' had happened or Molly and Dad were fighting too much, she'd told us to call her and Grandpa Tom, say our codeword and 'help would come'. She had never said what kind of help but, as a child, I knew Grandpa Tom was an FBI agent, with all the influence and connections that entailed.

Sharon had written her phone number on the underside of a Russian doll set and stowed it under the bed in the guest bedroom. Alongside it, she had placed an old landline phone that was plugged in and working.

Even as children, the secret password scheme seemed peculiar. And looking back now, it seems even more bizarre. Most parents train their children to call the police or fire services in an emergency. The Martens lived a five-hour drive away from us.

What was the point in calling our grandmother, who may or may not have heard the phone and answered?

In court, we also heard Sharon's explanation for her whereabouts on the night of the killing from the officer's statement. She told him she'd been woken by a commotion on the morning of 2 August.

'I could hear the dogs barking, and I could hear Molly screaming,' she said. 'Tom got up and said he was going to tell them to calm down or he was going to call the police.'

Then, Tom grabbed a baseball bat and ran from the room and up the stairs. She said the noise had stopped after a few minutes, and she'd fallen asleep again. She hadn't woken again until a policeman entered her room.

Assistant DA Marissa Parker rose to tell the court that Sharon only ever made that single statement, and the prosecution had no opportunity to cross-examine her. If she'd had the chance to do so, she would have liked to ask Sharon about her admission that she 'wasn't aware of any physical violence' in the marriage.

She also said she didn't think it was credible that a mother, awakened by her daughter screaming and seeing her husband rush upstairs with a baseball bat, would turn over and go back to sleep.

If Marissa Parker understood how close Sharon and Molly were, she would have thought it even more incredible. Sharon doted on Molly, even sending her 'half-birthday' cards every six months despite her daughter being over thirty.

She asked Judge Hall not to give any weight to Sharon's statement as the state had been given no opportunity to cross-examine her.

During the Martens' original trial, Assistant DA Alan Martin for the prosecution also insisted that it wasn't credible for Sharon to have slept through an event where two people had beaten a man to death. He claimed that Tom kept Sharon out of the narrative that night because two people could keep a story straight more easily than three.

After listening to the statement Sharon had given the officer, the courtroom heard evidence surrounding a so-called 'fingernail dig'. This was a faint red mark discovered on Molly's neck on the night of the killing.

The defence showed the courtroom a hugely magnified photo of this fingernail mark and spoke for an entire hour about a line found on Molly's neck.

They submitted written testimony from John Guard, a chief deputy from Pitt County Sheriff's Office and an expert witness in domestic-violence incidents. Guard claimed that the fingernail mark found on Molly's neck was consistent with someone having been strangled. He said he'd watched the complete video of Molly's interview with Davidson County Sheriff's Office after Dad's death and said that she was rubbing her neck area and spoke with a raspy voice, which he said can signify she was a victim of strangulation.

I had to stop myself from sighing aloud in frustration. No one had mentioned the statement from Deputy David Dillard of the Davidson County Sheriff's Office that contradicted this. He had been tasked with observing Molly while law enforcement was investigating inside our home on the night of the killing. His statement says he noticed no obvious injuries on Molly.

He reported that she 'was making crying noises, but [that he] didn't see any visible tears. She was also rubbing her neck … It wasn't a constant. She would do it and stop and do it and then stop while continuing to make the crying noises'.

Nor did anyone mention the officer who had photographed Molly to document her physical condition on the night of the killing. He testified that she 'continually tugged and pulled on her neck with her hand'.

We would soon hear Detective Lieutenant Wanda Thompson asking Molly to stop rubbing her neck during a video interview recorded hours after Dad's killing.

After Molly had spent three hours chafing at her neck, the defence had found a tiny fingernail mark and said it was consistent with being strangled by my dad.

To make matters worse, Judge Hall said he agreed with the expert testimony. In his experience, he said, rubbing the neck area was consistent with strangulation. My eyes rolled.

During the hours of the hearing, we sat behind the prosecution, but could have no contact or interaction with them. However, they had given me a small notebook and pen, saying I could write down any questions I had and discuss them with the team afterwards. They may have regretted giving me that notebook. I took notes constantly in court and presented them to the Assistant DAs immediately after the judge had ended the hearing or first thing in the morning. I became exasperated at some stages of the hearing because there was so much evidence that they could have presented but didn't. I couldn't understand why.

I constantly approached Alan Martin, asking him, 'Why aren't you saying this?' or 'Why aren't you asking that?' I was persistent but not rude. They knew how to do their jobs, but I wasn't yet aware just how hamstrung they were regarding the plea deal. They never admitted that the plea agreement prevented them from raising many issues. Their default reply was, 'Don't worry, that will come up later in the closing argument.'

Anytime we spoke to the prosecution team about a failure to present what we considered significant evidence, we heard the same thing – that they would deal with it in the closing arguments. As the days went on, it became harder for me to stay polite.

The second day's proceedings had begun with Sharon Martens and ended with a screening of her husband's ninety-minute interview with detectives from Davidson County. Tom's interview began at 6.31 a.m. on 2 August, some three and a half hours after he killed my dad.

In the interview, he sat, arms folded and legs crossed in an orange striped polo shirt and dark shorts, chatting amiably with detectives who were about to interview him. He quickly signalled his law enforcement credentials by saying he had been an FBI agent for thirty-one years. Tom was skilled in interviews as he had trained FBI agents and Drug Enforcement Administration personnel about how to interview suspects. He was also a law graduate from Emory University in Georgia, so he was keenly aware of what to say during a police interview.

I noticed how quickly he established himself as a colleague rather than a suspect, helpfully advising the young detective across the desk from him that he consumed more caffeine than was good for him and urging him to cut down on energy drinks. Tom's polo shirt was drenched in my father's blood as he sat there drinking coffee. Yet, he could have been chatting with a couple of pals in a canteen.

When he had established the crucial details of his background and built rapport with the investigators, he took control of the interview.

'Perhaps it would be helpful if I just kind of launched into the story because it will contribute to my state of mind.'

His state of mind played a big part in this sentencing hearing.

The grounds for his defence started straightaway as he implicated my father in my birth mom's death in his first sentences.

Tom said that Dad was an Irish citizen. 'He was married in Ireland. He had those two children and his first wife died in mysterious circumstances. The finding was that she had an asthma attack in his car. She died of asphyxiation.'

He continued: 'Molly saw an advertisement for a, what you call it, a babysitter, and it might sound too sugary, a nanny, and so she answered that ad to work for Jason in Ireland, and they subsequently got involved in a romantic relationship, and he got transferred here to Winston-Salem to a packaging plant.'

Tom then painted a picture of my dad as a boorish, drunken Irishman.

'He [Dad] sat in the driveway and drank all afternoon. So, when we got there, he was clearly under the influence,' he told police.

Judge Hall didn't hear evidence from the medical autopsy report, contradicting this claim. The report showed just 20 mg/dl of alcohol in Dad's blood. The current drink-driving limit in Ireland is 50 mg/dl and in North Carolina at the time it was 80 mg/dl.

However, the report did find the powerful sedative Trazodone in Dad's system. The drug had been prescribed for Molly three days before she killed Dad. No one presented evidence about the presence of the drug to Judge Hall either.

Tom said that, earlier in the evening, he had been woken by an argument in Dad and Molly's bedroom. 'I heard arguing and thumping. It sounded bad.'

Tom said he had left the basement with the bat he had brought for Jack, gone upstairs, opened their door and had seen Dad choking Molly.

'I opened the door and, Jesus Christ, it was a horrible scene,' he said in the video. 'He was holding her in front of himself. I was afraid that I was going to hit her. I said, "Let her go." He said, "I am going to kill her." I am scared to death. I hit him with the bat. I was scared to death that he was going to kill her.'

He then said Dad had lost his grip of Molly and had grabbed the bat from Tom. He said his glasses had been knocked off in the struggle.

'I got the bat back from him,' Tom said. 'I can't tell you how many times I hit him. I can't tell you how many times he shoved me. I can't tell you because it was a battle. And then he goes down and we call 911.'

Tom then described Dad as a big man who had training in martial arts and boxing. That was one of those moments when you're in an awful situation, and all you can do is laugh. Dad watched golf and played it occasionally. He played soccer sometimes and trained children's softball, baseball and soccer teams. He had never trained in martial arts or boxing. As the sound of stifled laughter came from our row of seats, Molly's defence attorney, Kingsbery, glowered at us.

Despite Dad's martial-arts training, Tom said he overcame

him with the bat. 'I had a few years on the street [with the FBI]. I can't tell you how many times I hit him. Then he goes down … He was wild. I cannot believe that alcohol is the only thing in his system. I hit him [with the baseball bat], and it was like turning on a switch. I was scared to death he was going to kill me. I know it sounds like an excuse, but the guy was crazy. It was not sloppy drunk.'

Tom remembered so much detail of that night but could not shed any light on the heavy brick paver soaked in Dad's blood. Asked if he knew anything about a cement landscaping block on the bedroom floor, he replied that he didn't. He hadn't seen it and didn't see Molly using it.

Tom described Dad as 'cruel, abusive and controlling', but even he admitted he never saw him being physically violent to Molly.

'He was abusive. To my knowledge, not physically abusive [before this night]. I don't think she [Molly] told us everything. She didn't talk to me. She would talk to her mother. He [Dad] was very controlling.'

Judge Hall asked to handle each of the weapons – the baseball bat and brick paver – that were used to kill Dad. Using gloved hands, he cupped each item and turned them over and over, assessing the weight of each. My stomach rolled as he did, and I looked away.

In the interview, Tom said that he had brought the black-and-red Louisville Slugger baseball bat and a tennis racquet from Tennessee, intending to give them to Jack and me. Because they had arrived so late, he had decided not to give them to us that night.

We knew that this was not the truth, and we tried but failed to get the prosecution to raise it in the hearing. The tennis racquet Tom said he had brought was never found by investigators.

'I have probable cause to believe that the baseball bat used to assault Jason Paul Corbett may have come from the sports equipment bag used by Jack Corbett and stored in the garage,' Detective Lieutenant Wanda Thompson wrote in a report.

Tom admitted that he had never liked Dad and claimed he would go into the basement of his home or play golf when we visited his Knoxville home. His dislike of Dad wasn't a secret even to me as a child. Tom and Sharon had never been pleasant to Dad.

Tom had always used the hard-drinking Irish stereotype to try to provoke Dad, accusing him, and his friends or family, of drinking too much. But Dad always responded with implacable humour and politeness.

I never felt comfortable at the dinner table when Tom and Sharon were around. I watched and listened, and even though Dad continued to nod and smile, I knew the conversation was strained. Tom had always found it hard to disguise his contempt for Dad or maintain a veneer of civility around him.

After he had killed him, Tom had free rein to paint my gentle Dad in any manner he wanted. The Martens' defence teams introduced slivers of 'evidence' – like the faint mark on Molly's neck and Dad's first wife dying in 'mysterious' circumstances – and magnified them in the courtroom. They had to turn Dad into a drunken, violent wife abuser and potential killer to keep their clients out of jail. I couldn't believe they were talking about the man I had watched trap spiders between a sheet of paper and a cup before releasing them unharmed in our garden.

The prosecution's rebuttal was brief, drawing attention to the perfect condition of Tom's glasses, after saying he had lost them during the fight.

'All this fighting and all this aggression, but there are no tears, rips or even stretches in their clothing,' Marissa Parker said. 'Molly Martens' clothing is perfect.'

As convicted felons, Molly and Tom were in the courtroom to be sentenced for their crimes. Yet, most of the courtroom time was spent portraying them as innocent victims of my 'abusive' dad.

Not only had Tom and Molly stolen his life but, with the help of this sentencing hearing, I was watching their intent to steal his good name too.

CHAPTER 6

THE NIGHTMARE

Your Honour
The Martens made me an orphan. They took away my father, my only constant, the only loving parent I had. On 1 August 2015, I said, 'Goodnight, Daddy, love you' – and when I woke up the next morning, he was gone forever ... My dad used to tuck me in every night. He would do 'as snug as a bug in a little tiny rug'. He'd leave my bedroom door cracked so I didn't get scared at night, and he was always there to take care of me when I had a nightmare.

Panther Creek Court, Meadowlands
Saturday, 1 August 2015
After Tom and Sharon Martens pulled into our drive, we said goodnight to the Fritzsches. Dad crossed the road to help take their luggage from the car and bring it to the basement – as usual they were sleeping in the 'blue room', which was directly below Dad and Molly's bedroom.

We sat in the garden as daylight faded, and Molly made mojito cocktails using mint that Sharon had brought from her garden in Tennessee. She had ordered Domino's pizzas for dinner even before her parents had arrived.

Later, I went inside, and Dad woke me on the couch around 10.00 p.m.

'Time for bed, Princess,' he said, reminding me to say goodnight to Seekoo and Grandpa Tom. I hugged Tom goodnight, and Dad said Seekoo was downstairs. She was in her dressing gown, bent over the side of the bed, putting on her slippers. I hugged her and said goodnight.

Dad encouraged us to hug everyone and say 'I love you' before leaving the house or going to bed. 'You never know when it might be the last time you see someone,' he said.

Molly gave me tablets before I went to bed, telling me they were for a yeast infection. The Martens' late arrival disrupted our nighttime routine, so I had no bedtime story from Dad that night. He still had to collect Jack from the party at Melissa Sams' house too.

Dad was standing with Tom in the living room as I went upstairs. He shouted after me, 'Goodnight, Princess. I love you.'

'Goodnight, Daddy, love you.'

I never spoke to him again.

Sometime later, I jolted awake, panicked, my heart beating fast. The glow of my nightlight revealed something on my bedsheets was moving. The sheets were printed with magical fairies. I had those sheets for as long as I can remember but the fairies had suddenly become a writhing mass of spiders and lizards. They were crawling all over me.

Stricken with terror, I tried to get out of bed but felt a leaden heaviness. I half slid out, my foot hitting the floor with a thud. In hindsight, I believe whatever tablets I'd been given had affected me. The room swayed like a moving boat and, as I stumbled to the door, I realised someone had closed it. My door was never shut. Darkness terrified me, so I always had a nightlight and the door was kept ajar.

I opened the door and made for the stairs. My legs felt so unsteady that I clung to the banister, descending one tentative step at a time. Moonlight or streetlamps cast shifting patterns through the front-door glass panels and onto the floor.

At the last step, I saw a shadow of someone standing outside, gazing in. Overwhelmed with fear, I dropped to my knees and crawled past the solid wood in the lower half of the door. I'll never know whether the figure was real or imagined.

Summoning what little courage I had left, I got to my feet and staggered, sobbing, to Dad and Molly's bedroom door. I knocked once and Molly appeared instantly, wearing one of Dad's white T-shirts. She positioned herself in the doorway, one foot on the carpet and the other on the wood threshold. I caught a glimpse of Dad behind her. He was asleep, his back turned to me, the bedclothes pulled to his shoulders. My dad snored loudly, but he wasn't snoring that night. He didn't stir or move even though I'd knocked on the door.

Usually, if I got scared at night, Molly and Dad brought me to their bed, and I slept between them. But Molly spun me around by the shoulder and shut the door behind us. She steered me to the kitchen.

I told her I wasn't going back to my bedroom because spiders and lizards were crawling over my bed.

'You had a nightmare, Sarah,' Molly said, sitting me on the counter.

She stuck her head in the fridge and mixed a drink for me that included water and cranberry juice. Molly told me I had to drink it all to make me better. I felt so dizzy that she had to help me return to my bedroom, where she whipped off the fairy print bedsheets.

'See? There's nothing here,' she said.

Then she tucked me into my bed, turned off my nightlight and shut my door, leaving me in terrifying darkness. My instinct was to cry out and follow her, but I felt paralysed, too heavy to move and overcome with sleep.

Earlier, Molly and Dad had collected Jack from Melissa Sams' house. Jack remembers that Molly had also given him two pills before he went to bed, but he had returned downstairs to say goodnight to Dad. Jack had heard Molly in the basement talking with her parents while Dad watched Japanese golf on the small TV in his bedroom. He told Tracey and David afterwards that he had seen a large holdall with some of his and my clothes in it standing on the floor of Dad and Molly's bedroom.

David checked the TV schedules in the weeks after Dad's death and confirmed what Jack had seen on the television, but no suitcases ever appeared in the crime-scene photographs taken only hours later.

Jack had hugged Dad goodnight and had never seen him again.

I had woken once more that night, disturbed by muffled voices in the hall. I had heard Tom and Molly downstairs; their voices were low but seemed to be charged with anger. I had tried to listen, but their voices were hushed, and I fell asleep again. The next time I woke, Corporal Clayton Stewart Dagenhardt of the Davidson County Sheriff's Office was at my bedside.

CHAPTER 7

THE SWIM COACH

Your Honour

Molly Martens tried to destroy me and my family. She turned me and my brother against each other ... making us compete for her love. Her way of punishment was starvation – she just wouldn't feed us if we did something wrong like, for example, not swimming fast enough in our heat. She would stop speaking to us or turn to violence.

Courtroom 6, Davidson County Courthouse
Day 3: Wednesday, 1 November 2023
I glanced across the courtroom and my eyes locked with Tom Martens'. He may have been trying to catch Tracey's or David's eye, but I looked his way instead, so he fixed me with an unwavering stare. I refused to flinch or look away, and returned his stony gaze. No member of the Martens family was going to unnerve me. *You people don't scare me,* I thought. *If anyone should be scared, it's you.*

The Martens still saw me as eight-year-old little Sarah. But I had grown up and become pretty smart, and I remembered much more than they thought I did. They had no idea how much I remembered. But when I read my Victim Impact Statement that would become apparent.

Tom's gaze continued to bore into me from across the aisle. He was willing me to look away, but my resolve grew with every ticking second. Our silent battle of wills continued for what seemed a long time but was probably only six or seven seconds. Then, I had the pleasure of seeing a flicker of annoyance, or maybe unease, before he broke eye contact first. I wish I could have recorded that interaction. It felt like a minor victory – like the balance of power subtly shifted a little in the courtroom. We never locked eyes again.

Molly was the focus of the third morning of the sentencing hearing. We had avoided making any eye contact for most of the hearing. She even angled her chair away from Jack and me, so her gaze rarely fell in our direction. Our eyes met only once, and that was accidental because she looked away immediately. I can't know why she avoided making eye contact, but I did it to prevent negative feelings from being stirred up. Whenever possible, I avoided looking at her or thinking about her.

Molly had exercised her right not to testify at her original trial; only her written statement was introduced into evidence. The interview she gave in the sheriff's office hours after she killed Dad was never played to jurors, so we had never seen it.

Her questioning began in Interview Room 2 of Davidson County Sheriff's Office at 6.45 a.m. on 2 August. Tom's interview was ongoing almost simultaneously in another room. Detective Lieutenant Wanda Thompson, the head of the Criminal

Investigations Division, sat opposite Molly in the windowless room.

Jack and I had met Lieutenant Thompson that August morning. I was gazing bleary-eyed out the basement window when I heard footsteps approach. Lieutenant Thompson's arrival punctured the bubble of silence in the room. Jack and I followed her, as instructed, out the basement back door and down the side of the house. Police radios crackled and the air felt thick with activity. The lights of police cars and an ambulance continued to flash. I could see the silhouettes of the Emergency Medical Technicians and police officers standing around. I trembled with growing anxiety. It had been hours since they had woken Jack and me in our beds, and no one had told us anything.

'Why is there an ambulance here?' I asked her.

'Oh, someone got hurt, but it's okay,' Lieutenant Thompson had replied.

I resented her for a long time afterwards because I had believed her. I'd thought everything would be 'okay'. As she led Jack and me across the road to our neighbours' house, I'd thought, *Mom and Dad are waiting for us in the Fritzsches' place!* However, inside the door, we only saw Molly sitting on the edge of the couch.

'My babies!' she cried, lunging for Jack and me and wailing. 'I'm so sorry, but I had to do it!'

I had no idea what she was talking about. I looked around. Police officers stood in the room with Molly, and I saw Dave and Michelle Fritzsche standing in the far corner of their kitchen as if to distance themselves. I could see no sign of Daddy or Grandpa Tom.

The small room where Molly sat was almost dark, there was just the light cast by a single lamp and the kitchen lights. I felt unsettled and afraid watching Molly. She continued to sit hunched on the edge of the couch, rubbing her neck and rocking back and forth in a frantic motion. She was no longer wearing my dad's T-shirt but had changed into sleeveless turquoise pyjamas. I saw rusty brown spatters on her pale face and thought they were mud streaks. I look back now and am grateful for my innocence. It was much later when I learned that those streaks were my father's blood.

Nobody was telling me what had happened. Molly kept repeating, 'I had to do it' without explaining what it was she'd had to do. All the police, the ambulances and the way Molly behaved frightened me. I wanted my dad more than ever. But the lieutenant said that someone had got hurt, so perhaps Dad was getting plasters or stitches. Or maybe Tom had got hurt, and Dad was helping him. Maybe Dad had fallen down the stairs and broken his leg, just like his sister Marilyn had done. Worries, hopes and questions had rolled around my head, but I didn't think anything serious could happen to my dad. He was invincible in my eyes. I'd thought of everything that could keep him apart from us, but Daddy being dead never entered my head.

Sometime later, the lieutenant had sat opposite Molly in an interview room of Davidson County Sheriff's Office. In the grainy footage, we saw Molly huddled in a big black fleece, her arms wrapped around her body. She stated her name as 'Molly Martens Corbett', then listed her occupation as 'swim coach'.

Swimming was Molly's 'thing', and she trained our local team at Meadowlands' outdoor pool from May until September. In winter, she coached another kids' team in a community YMCA. Jack and I were on both teams, which meant Molly trained us year-round.

Swimming became a pivotal activity in our lives because it was important to Molly. The schedule was so vital that we ate dinner in the car to get straight into the pool after school. But when Molly was in her competitive supermom mode, she was obsessed with 'healthy' plant-based food. Our dinners rarely varied then from fried kale and carrots with plain pasta.

Molly had ambitions for us to qualify for the Junior Olympic Games. She wanted us to get scholarships in prestigious swimming colleges like the University of Duke and Clemson. She distributed leaflets to advertise her coaching, claiming to be a former member of the prestigious Clemson University swim team. But Molly had dropped out of Clemson in her first term and was never on the team. She also liked to tell people she nearly made the Olympic team.

Most outsiders looking in would have regarded us as a super-active and athletic family. Dad also coached different teams – baseball and soccer – and we played lots of sports. At first, I loved swimming, but Molly's training became more intensive and obsessive. I trained in the pool every night after school when I was six. When I was seven and eight, we did yoga with a qualified teacher and worked out in the gym. During the summer holidays, we were in the pool from before the gates opened to the public until it closed late at night. Training was vital to our success, and Molly insisted that everything in our lives be dedicated to making us faster, stronger swimmers.

I had tried at first. Everyone wants to make their parents proud.

I knew if I trained harder than everyone else, ate all the carrots and won all the races, she'd love me – and she'd reward me.

But as Molly's training regimen intensified, my love for the water faded. She drained away my passion for the sport with each lap she added. The gulf widened between Molly's ambition and dedication, and my enthusiasm. I started to dread the pool. However, success was essential because it was a reflection of Molly's coaching skills. It was crucial to her that we won everything. We were her display trophies, and she thrived on the attention and praise that came with our achievements. She was always happy when we won.

Jack was a phenomenal athlete, and he thrived in a competitive environment. He became the star swimmer in the family, and Molly was ecstatic.

But her mood turned foul when we lost, and I felt Molly's wrath after unsuccessful swim meets. I made a mistake by swimming butterfly style instead of front crawl during one important race. I had to commit to butterfly when I'd started or I'd be disqualified. I put in an immense effort and secured second place. However, when I left the pool, I saw Molly gritting her teeth with fury.

She yanked me aside at her first opportunity. 'What do you think you're doing?' she hissed. 'How could you be so *stupid*? My God, you are such an embarrassment to me out there!'

I caught sight of Dad a few minutes later.

'I'm sorry – I messed everything up. I'm so stupid,' I cried.

He reacted with astonishment. 'What are you talking about, honey? You came second. You should be so proud of yourself. Why are you crying? You made a mistake, and you still did great!'

Molly lashed out at me when I failed to win – and when I didn't win, I didn't eat.

'Dinner? You didn't earn a dinner,' she said. 'You might think about that the next time and swim faster.'

She embarrassed me before the entire swim team.

'If you act like a baby, you're going to swim with the babies,' she said, putting me into the infants' swimming class for weeks as a punishment.

My peers and all the teenagers thought it was hilarious, and Molly said she was setting an example as the swim coach. She said she was making it clear that she didn't have favourites. But I knew Molly was punishing me for not winning. She'd lash out, humiliate me and make me feel small when I failed to please her.

She presented a charming image as a supportive mother and enthusiastic swim coach in public, but Jack and I faced relentless training, control and manipulation behind closed doors.

Whatever about the summer, what I dreaded most was winter training in the YMCA complex. Despite its indoor heated pool, Molly often exposed us to the frigid air and icy waters outdoors. She loved her winter competition – the Polar Bear Challenge – where the team had to dive into the outdoor pool. I still remember the bone-aching cold as we shivered in our swimming togs, frost crunching under our bare feet and our breaths forming steaming clouds around us.

Anyone who managed a full lap of the pool was a polar bear, but we were shrimps if we scrambled out. Some kids refused to jump in, but I didn't dare refuse because I feared Molly's temper more than plunging into the liquid ice.

As soon as I hit the frozen water, however, the shock and pain stole my breath. It felt like a thousand needles stabbing me at once and I hauled myself out to escape the pain as fast as I could. 'You're a shrimp, Sarah! A useless shrimp,' she'd yell poolside, wrapped in her oversized jacket. I was always a shrimp; Jack was a polar bear.

Stress knotted my stomach every time I entered the pool. So, I worked up the courage to tell Molly that I wanted to train with the baseball team, which Dad coached. I wouldn't escape swimming entirely, but I might swim less. I'd hoped she would see it as an easy switch, leaving her to concentrate on Jack's training, but she reacted as if I'd stabbed her through the heart.

She became hysterical. 'So, you'd prefer to be with your dad instead of me?' she cried. 'How could you hurt me like this after everything I've done for you? Do you not love me?'

I hadn't even begun the school day but I was tearfully apologising and reassuring Molly that I loved her more than anyone. I told her it was a stupid idea because I loved swimming. She didn't talk to me for days after that and I never dared suggest leaving swimming again. She controlled me easily, but I didn't recognise that for years.

Incidents like that impacted my relationship with my dad. We never spent as much time together as we wanted. He may have thought I was a mommy's girl who clung to Molly a lot, but the truth was that I was compliant, a people-pleaser, and she was a master at manipulation. She kept me close to her and apart from Dad.

As we watched Molly's interview in court, it became clear from the start that Molly could manipulate the police officers too.

She addressed Lieutenant Thompson in sweet Southern style as 'Ma'am'. I watched as the police detective responded by speaking kindly and assuring Molly that she was not under arrest.

'If you want to stop this or you want to leave, all you need do is tell me,' Lieutenant Thompson said.

As I watched the video, it struck me that Molly, like her father, was treated with kid gloves. It was hard to believe they had just beaten a man to death.

When asked about who was staying at 160 Panther Creek Court that night, Molly replied 'my children' and her visiting parents. She put her head in her hands when the detective asked to describe what had happened.

'We were fighting,' she said, yanking at her neck.

When asked who was fighting, she specified, 'My husband.'

Asked if there was a history of domestic violence in the house, she replied with a whisper, 'Forever.'

Throughout the interview, Molly pulled at her neck, leading the detective to ask, 'Why do you keep rubbing your neck?'

'I'm sorry. It hurts,' she said. 'He choked me because he wanted me to shut up, and I screamed.'

When asked if Dad had ever attacked her in other ways, she replied, 'He might have elbowed me in the face.'

She also said she had a condition in her foot where veins pressed on a nerve. (She'd told me she had a tumour in her foot that could kill her at any time.) She said when Dad was angry, he stamped on it 'accidentally on purpose'.

When asked why she never called the police over domestic violence, Molly said she couldn't tell anyone because she feared if she did, Dad would take us away from her.

Molly confirmed to the detective that she had been in a relationship with Dad for seven years, and that they had been married for four years. She admitted for the first time that Jack and I were not her biological children and that we were Irish citizens. But, by then, we were in the back of her brother's car and would soon be living with the people who had killed our only living parent.

The authorities put us into the custody of killers, and no one seemed to regard that as a matter of concern. We would remain in the Martens' custody for the next fourteen days.

In the interview, Molly then claimed that my actions had ignited the fight that night. She said I'd woken with a nightmare, thinking the fairies on my sheets had turned into insects and spiders. She'd got up, changed my sheets and the row with Dad had begun when she returned to their bedroom.

'She woke up, so he was angry that he was woken up. And then a dog barked, and he was angry that the dog barked. I said she'd just had a nightmare. He choked me, told me to shut up. I screamed.'

The lieutenant asked Molly where she was in their bedroom when Dad began to choke her. In statements Molly changed what her position had been from lying on the bed to sitting on it and then standing at the end of the bed.

Molly's voice rose as the detective became more insistent about the exact location in the bedroom. 'Sitting down and standing up. I don't know. Can we stop? Please stop.'

Molly removed her black jacket for the police photographer, who had arrived to document any injuries. The photographer took a shot with her head thrown back to expose her neck. Her bare arms were also outstretched and displayed for the camera. No mark was visible on the photo, which captured a delicate chain bracelet dangling from her wrist. It was still intact after an apparent battle for her life with my father.

Molly continued with her account of what had happened that morning. 'We were fighting. He was just angry. He started choking me … in the bed. I could not breathe. I thought I was going to die.'

She said she had screamed when Dad eased his grip a little. 'He put his hands on me – with his arm. He put his arm around my neck. I told him to stop. He let go for a second, and I screamed really loud.'

She said that's when her father appeared at their door. 'He [Tom] had a baseball bat, and he hit Jason or tried to hit him, and Jason got the baseball bat, and he tried to hit my dad, I think … he might have missed, and I hit him on the head.'

'You hit him on the head with what?' said the lieutenant.

'With the brick on the nightstand,' she replied.

That was the first time we heard the words from Molly's mouth that she had used a concrete paving stone to help kill my father.

'You have a brick on your nightstand?' asked the officer. 'What was that for?'

She said it was for an arts and crafts project she'd planned to do with Jack and me.

Molly didn't say that she had bought the pavers weeks earlier. Some neighbours had used chalk paint on similar pavers and had used them as decorative edging around trees and flowerbeds. We had planned to do the same, but Molly never got around to starting the project.

We'd left the pavers in a pile outside our house under the back porch. However, on 1 August, she'd asked Jack to carry one to her bedroom. We did all our projects on the kitchen island, but Jack had to pass the dining table, kitchen and living room to bring it to her bedroom. Jack took it to her, and she placed it on her nightstand. A day later, she used it to kill Dad.

When the detective asked how many times she hit Jason, Molly answered, sobbing, 'I don't know.'

Like Tom and Sharon, she tried to portray Dad as a heavy-drinking Irishman who liked 'all kinds, mostly expensive beer'. When asked if she thought Dad was drunk that night, she replied, 'Yes, he was drunk.'

She said he had been drinking for almost six hours with a neighbour and had consumed more than eight beers. She also claimed that his drinking was 'not uncommon', adding the 'big drinking' had been worse when they'd lived in Ireland, where she said he'd gone on 'binge-drinking sessions'.

Throughout the interview, Molly was agitated, crossing and uncrossing her arms, hugging herself, rocking back and forth, rubbing her neck, and wailing and wringing her hands. When the detective left the room, she rested her head on the table and lay motionless until the interviewer reappeared – then all the frantic activity began again.

It was strange to watch this interview from the morning of Dad's killing, but I'd seen that behaviour countless times in our home.

The last time Molly had seen Dad, the paramedics were working on him in the back of an advanced life-support ambulance outside our house.

In the interview, the lieutenant asked Molly if she realised her husband hadn't survived his injuries.

'I didn't think so,' she said.

I was shocked at the seeming indifference of that reply.

She claimed that she and Dad had discussed funeral arrangements and that he'd wanted a cremation. 'Yes – he would like to have a service in Ireland, and he would like to have his ashes scattered by the coast of Clare,' she said.

(Tracey had to sign a legal guarantee to underwrite all of Dad's funeral costs in the US and Ireland before Molly agreed to allow Dad's remains to be buried in Ireland.)

However, when Lieutenant Thompson asked about breaking the news of Dad's death to his relatives in Ireland, Molly began to sob. 'What if I am scared of his family?' she said. 'Because they will try to kill me because he is not alive.'

I shook my head upon hearing this. It wasn't enough that she had tried to portray Dad as a killer, but she then tried to paint his family as potential murderers too. Yet, the only killers were in her own family.

She added, 'I am scared they will take the kids. They are his children. They are not citizens.'

The lieutenant replied, 'Then that's a real possibility. I anticipate there is a distinct possibility that either his family or [their mother's] family will probably try to fight for custody of the children.'

'But I've raised them,' Molly cried.

The only emotion Molly displayed was in response to the suggestion she could lose custody of Jack and me, never over the loss of her husband. Within forty hours of Dad's killing, Molly took immediate legal action. She filed and was granted an ex parte order, expressing her concerns that Tracey and David could pose a threat to our safety. She also filed for guardianship, custody and adoption rights over us, as well as claiming our father's life insurance in the US and Ireland.

Molly never phoned Dad's family. Sharon Martens made the call in the end, using Molly's phone to ring Wayne in Ireland on the evening of 2 August. She said Molly and Dad had got into a fight and that Molly had pushed Dad, who'd fallen, hit his head and died. Wayne asked to speak to Molly, but Sharon hung up. The call lasted about fifteen seconds.

Tracey had called Sharon back and asked if Molly had been cautioned or arrested, but Sharon's response was to hang up on her too.

Wayne had to tell his elderly parents that their youngest child was dead. That was about all the information Dad's family had until Tracey rushed back from a holiday in France and, together with Paul and Marilyn, flew to North Carolina days later. David followed two days after.

Molly also voiced another concern during the interview. She wanted to know who would clean up the bloody crime scene before she returned to the house. The lieutenant told her there was a lot of blood and it was not the sheriff's responsibility to clean the scene.

Within forty-eight hours of Dad's killing, a sanitation firm had arrived to scrub the house at Panther Creek Court from floor to ceiling. Molly spent $5,000 from her and Dad's joint bank account to pay for a forensic deep clean that left the property spotless.

At the end of the interview, the lieutenant reassured Molly that her story about fighting off a brutish Irish husband was credible. 'At this point, after talking to your dad and talking to you, I think this is going to be self-defence,' the lieutenant said. 'I don't think there is going to be any issue with that.'

It would take another seven weeks before Tracey and David got any confirmation that Davidson County Sheriff's Department was becoming sceptical of the Martens' argument of self-defence. By then, they had received the pathologist's report, which indicated the considerable brutality involved, and the toxicology findings. The Martens' story did not tally with the evidence.

This prompted investigators to hire a blood-spatter expert, Dr Stuart James, to get his assessment of what had happened on 2 August. He said in his evidence that he believed the first blow to Dad's head happened when he was lying in bed and that some blows were made as Dad fell to the ground. He proved Dad had also been hit when his head was on or near the floor.

The Martens' version of events began to fall apart.

In 2018, as part of their appeal process, the Martens said expert testimony about blood splatter on the Martens' clothes should have been inadmissible because it was not based on reliable data.

When Molly's hour-and-a-half-long interview video concluded, Judge Hall called a ten-minute recess.

Something must have happened or been said to Molly because, a minute later, she had a meltdown. She pushed away her uncle Mike Earnest as he tried to soothe her before she tore down the courthouse hall. It was a brief glimpse of the volatile Molly we'd had to live with.

Tracey and I had already left the room and gone for a walk because we couldn't bear to listen to or watch Molly anymore. At one stage, Molly's sniffles filled the courtroom and she rested her head on the desk in front of her in a display of abject despair. Kingsbery played a supportive role, patting her heaving shoulders with a comforting hand.

I felt like throwing my hands up in despair at her story of my dad getting angry because I'd woken him. Dad never got angry when I woke up in the night. He just bundled me into the bed between him and Molly. That night, he didn't have a chance to do that because she'd stopped me from entering their bedroom.

Assistant DA Marissa Parker also gave the state's view about why the evidence presented by Molly's lawyer, that painted Dad as a violent man, should not be given great weight. She warned that Molly had 'struggled with and has had a very complicated relationship with the truth'. *'Complicated' was a very deferential way to describe it*, I thought.

CHAPTER 8

DRAGONFLY

Your Honour

I was an orphan, eight years old and totally lost. I said what I was instructed to say. Now those words have helped the Martens escape a murder charge and helped Molly pretend she's the victim. I was used by her. All I have ever been is a piece on her chessboard. I am in therapy, learning how to live with the fact that I lied and helped their case.

Lexington, North Carolina
Thursday, 6 August 2015

The reception for Dad's memorial mass in North Carolina four days after his death and what happened afterwards remain vivid in my memory. Jack and I stood in an overheated and sunlit room surrounded by people wearing black, holding cups and saucers, and eating canapés and tiny sandwiches.

Flowing chiffon curtains separated us from the world outside where the summer sun was beating down. I longed to go outside, but knew I had to stand obediently beside Jack.

The mass at the Church of Mary Immaculate in Lexington would have been more memorable if Dad's coffin had been there. But Dad was not in the church nor were any of his family, who had been told they were not invited. As a precaution, Molly had even hired off-duty police officers who were meant to protect us from Tracey and David. She had painted them as villains and said they were planning to kidnap Jack and me. Molly had ensured we were scared of them, while also gaining the public sympathy she craved.

No one even placed a photograph of Dad in the church or honoured him during the mass. Without the coffin or any personal mementoes belonging to Dad, it was like any Sunday mass, but it was Thursday, four days after he died.

The absence of a coffin or any palpable sense of grief made it easy to cling to denial. Surely, if something terrible had happened, people would have been upset. If my daddy was dead, wouldn't there be more tears and sadness? It felt like the Martens took us to mass, and we had sandwiches afterwards.

The adults talked about their kids and the weather. No one spoke to us. Looking back, it seemed like Jack and I were two exhibits in a room with tea and sandwiches.

We had first learned that Dad was dead early in the morning of 2 August, hours after he had been killed.

Lieutenant Thompson had led us back from the Fritzsches' house after spending a short time with Molly. The lieutenant left us back with Sharon in the blue room. Sometime later, Tom and Molly had arrived together to see us. It must have been between

5 a.m. and 6 a.m., just before police took them to Davidson County Sheriff's Office to be interviewed.

I looked expectantly behind Tom but was disappointed to see no sign of Dad. Tom shut the door and stood leaning with his back to it. Molly sat on the edge of the bed with Sharon.

She took a deep breath as if composing herself and then addressed Jack and me. 'Okay, guys, I need to tell you what happened,' she said. 'Your dad and I got in a fight. And I pushed him, and he hit his head and died.'

They were her words, as I remember them. Jack, who was sitting behind me, let out a terrible wail and began crying hysterically. I just stood in disbelief, staring at her. *That's not true*, I thought and didn't respond.

Molly thought I hadn't understood what she had said, so she repeated everything. It didn't matter. I still didn't believe her.

'We've packed you a few things, and Uncle Bobby's outside,' she said. 'He's going to bring you to his house.'

In my head, I screamed, *No! I'm waiting for Daddy!* But still, I said nothing.

Jack cried inconsolably. 'I want to see my dad,' he sobbed.

This can't be real, I thought. My father was my comfort blanket and sense of security. When I was sick or I fell, I ran to Dad first. I felt so frightened at that moment that I needed him more than ever.

Sharon walked us outside to where Bobby was waiting in his car. I looked back, still expecting Dad to appear at the door, beckoning us. But there were only police officers standing outside the home I'd never enter again.

Bobby said, 'Hop in', so Jack and I got into the back seat in stunned silence.

We were to stay in his house, and Molly never said when she'd see us again.

Bobby turned the radio up as he drove, listening to music and humming. I stared out at the landscape, whizzing past. Jack grabbed my hand to squeeze it, and I held on until we got to Bobby's house, an hour away in Monroe.

Bobby's wife Ellie's family was there from Puerto Rico. Kids were playing ball and splashing in the pool, and Bobby and Ellie's daughter Gabby was playing in the treehouse with a cousin. Adults were lazing on the couches, watching TV and eating chips. I heard the birds singing. No one appeared to have told them what had happened, and everyone was enjoying the sunny summer morning.

It all felt surreal. How could people have fun after saying my father was dead? I had a ball of anxiety the size of a fist in my throat.

That day passed in a haze of confusion. While I was in denial, Jack responded by shutting down and being silent.

Tom and Sharon arrived later with Molly. I remember her hunkering down and opening her arms so we could run to her. Hugging us, she squealed with delight. Molly seemed so happy, but I felt adrift.

Her smile disappeared when I tried to ask about Dad. So I stayed quiet in the face of her anger and the Martens' silence. I went along with it, but still didn't believe Daddy was dead. Nothing about the memorial service for Dad four days later changed my mind.

When the memorial service reception ended, Molly, Sharon and her sister-in-law Mona ushered us into the car. They drove

Jack and me to The Dragonfly House, a children's advocacy centre in Mocksville, North Carolina.

A social worker had already called to Bobby's house the day after Dad was killed to interview us. Molly explained we now needed to talk another woman. We had to tell her the same thing we had told the first social worker – about how mean Daddy was to her.

'You guys did brilliant the last time, so you just tell this lady everything again,' Molly told us. 'Remember, you tell them that Daddy hurt Mommy, and Daddy hit Mommy. You say you really love Mommy and don't want to go anywhere else. Just tell the truth.'

During the ninety-minute drive to Mocksville, Jack and I were reminded our aunt and uncle from Ireland were going to kidnap us and take us away from Molly and all our friends. They would take us from school and everything we knew.

While in the car, Molly gave me her old iPhone for a while. I remember it because she'd never given me her phone before, but she had just bought a new one. She gave me earphones and told me to listen to her iTunes music. I listened to a song, 'Bright' by Echosmith. I saw her pass her new phone back to Jack. Years later, I learned that Tracey and David were on the phone to Jack – the first time they had got to speak to either of us since Dad died.

The three women brought us to eat at the fast-food restaurant Chick-fil-A.

'Listen to Molly,' Sharon warned me at the table. 'Pay attention and don't make any mistakes. You can't mess up. If you mess up, they'll take you away and you'll never see us again. They will split you and Jack up too.'

I remember feeling terrified by the time we reached Dragonfly House. My dad had been taken away from me and they said I'd never see him again. Now, another threat to my safety and security loomed. I could lose Molly and Jack now too.

We pulled up outside a wood-sided, one-storey building with a tall pointy gable in the centre. I can still see it in my head because, to my eight-year-old self, it looked like a giant dog kennel. We entered a place with fluorescent lights, and hard plastic and steel chairs. Random splashes of colour from cartoonish images only highlighted its grim, institutional nature.

Heart pounding, I entered the interview room where a social worker was waiting. I could hear Molly and Sharon talking and laughing outside. They were so nonchalant, joking with the receptionist. It was hard to believe Molly had killed her husband just days earlier.

The social worker introduced herself and pointed out the cameras recording us. She tried putting me at ease and gave me a pad to colour and draw on. She asked if I knew why I was there, and I said, 'Yes, because my daddy's dead.' I could say it, but I didn't believe it.

When asked about Dad and Molly fighting, I said, 'My dad was always the one who started it. Say if the lights were on in the bathroom, he would get really angry with Mom.'

I said he got angry 'every day or most likely twice a day'. I also told her that Dad called Molly all the time and, on one occasion, he had called her mobile phone forty-seven times. When asked how I knew this, I said that Jack had scrolled through Mommy's phone and saw the missed calls. But Molly never let us near her phone.

The social worker asked if Dad would hurt Mommy. They

were very interested in his drinking. They never asked did Molly drink or did Molly hit us. Yet Dad was the one who was dead?

I said he didn't, but added that I'd seen him step on her foot. I said that it 'might have been accidental, but I don't think so'. Molly had reminded me to say that earlier in the day.

The social worker followed up by asking, 'So when you said that he would fight with her and he would hurt her, you said you didn't really see it. How would you know about it?'

'Because, um, my mom told me,' I responded.

I told her that, when I was six, Molly had told me, 'Your dad isn't that good of a dad.'

This social worker asked me similar questions to those asked by the first social worker. 'Did your mom and Dad fight a lot? Did your dad drink a lot?' They were very insistent about his drinking.

I told her that he drank beer. Asked if he drank every day, I said he didn't – he only drank beer with friends or at a party. I said he had some beers with his neighbour that day before he died.

Dragonfly House's Medical Services log noted that: 'Sarah does not disclose witnessing [domestic violence].' The social worker's notes also said: 'Sarah states her father screams and yells and states when her mom and dad go into the room, her dad hurts her mom. She stated her mom told her.'

They also noted in their report that I used the exact phrases Molly also used in her interviews.

The video also showed that I spoke naturally about my friend Ashlyn or my school, but I sounded much more cautious when discussing anything related to Molly and Dad.

Jack also identified the source of the information by saying, 'My mom told me.'

The interviewer said that she had asked all her questions, and I handed her the drawing I had been doing while we spoke. I wanted her to like me and tell Molly that I'd done well. She asked me to stay in the room while she went out. I panicked. *Could they hear me the whole time? Did I say everything right?*

When the social worker brought me out, Molly was beaming. 'Oh, hi, honey. Well done. She said you did great, sweetie.'

The social worker said, 'Remember, you don't have to tell your mom or anyone what we discussed.'

'Of course,' Molly said.

I didn't realise the worst part of the day was yet to come. They led me into a small, sterile white room where two medics confronted me. They wore full protective gear – full-length gowns with their hands encased in latex gloves. Surgical masks obscured their faces, so I could only see their eyes, while disposable caps concealed their hair. I'd never seen people as scary-looking as these medics before. (This was years before Covid-19 struck.) Terror gripped me instantly.

The room was filled with the sharp scent of disinfectant and contained a metal cabinet and two exam tables covered in white paper sheets. A window on the opposite wall offered a tantalising glimpse of green foliage and a blue sky.

The main doctor was a woman with blue eyes that had green flecks. That's all I saw of her. She moved my body parts around like I was a mannequin rather than a scared child. She issued instructions but offered no reassurance.

'We're going to do this now.'

'Lie this way.'

'Stand here.'

The examination was forensic, involving far more than a regular checkup. Armed with a bright light, they scrutinised every square inch of my anatomy. Their investigations were not just invasive but painful as they prodded me with instruments and examined areas of my body that I was always told were private. The process was efficient, hygienic and heartless.

I only have to think about their rustling gowns for my heart to beat faster and my stomach to churn. I remember lying back, frozen and powerless, looking out the window at the blue sky with a few wispy clouds and thinking, *Please get me out of here.*

I've only spoken about this in recent years with Jack and discovered he underwent a similarly invasive exam. I can't fathom why they subjected us to this trauma when we presented no evidence of child sexual abuse. They carried this out without consent from a legal guardian. And I don't remember anyone asking permission to carry out such an invasive examination. I left The Dragonfly House in shock, feeling upset and distressed. For years, I refused to see a gynaecologist even when I needed one.

No one was interested in the medical that day. Instead, Sharon and Molly gave me the third-degree in the car on the way home. 'What did she ask you? What did you say? Did you tell her you don't want to go to your aunt and uncle?'

I felt isolated and frightened rather than loved or supported by those around me. More than anything, I wanted a big, comforting bear hug from Dad. I still expected him to appear around a corner or be there when I woke up. Meanwhile, I had to pretend he never existed, just like everyone else around me was doing.

CHAPTER 9

BIG LITTLE LIES

Your Honour
Molly used words I said out of fear against my dad and my family to get out of jail, and now they are using them to get a reduced sentence. Can you try and understand the effects that can have on a girl growing up?

Courtroom 6, Davidson County Courthouse
Day 3: Wednesday, 1 November 2023
Molly's police interview had dominated the third morning of the hearing. After lunch, we returned to listen to more lies – this time Jack's and mine.

The defence team could barely contain their excitement as they prepared to unveil their trump card: the video recordings of the interviews Jack and I had given at The Dragonfly House. The tapes had become a linchpin in the Martens' appeal against their murder sentence, a fact that upset Jack and me deeply.

The judge in the 2017 trial had excluded the statements and the recantations of those statements we had made months after returning to Ireland. However, the defence had successfully argued that our words supported the Martens' self-defence claims. The appeals court had been swayed by the argument and found that the trial should not have excluded our statements. No one mentioned the duress that we, as children, had been put under.

I felt an overwhelming sense of powerlessness and frustration about the showing of these videos.

Throughout the years of the winding legal process, I had repeatedly implored the prosecution to allow me to take the stand. Each time, they had told me that I must be patient, compliant and trust the system. Instead, I had to watch recordings of myself as a frightened eight-year-old girl giving testimony – a child who repeated what she had been told to say by those she considered to be her mother and grandparents.

I had watched myself on The Dragonfly House video for the first time when I was around fourteen years old, and I had been upset and ashamed of what I'd said about my father. I remembered most of it. It was like rewatching a movie – I knew what was going to happen. Even though I had reconciled the fact that I had been a child when I had done the interviews, I felt angry and disgusted at myself. *How could I have said those things when I knew they weren't true?*

I had never seen Jack's Dragonfly video. The recordings were our secret shame and they were private. But now they were about to be played for the media, the Martens, the general public, and everyone in the courtroom and beyond. Molly had consistently exposed our vulnerability and was about to reopen our childhood wounds.

Dean put his two hands on my shoulders in the courtroom as the defence started to play my video. 'We know the truth, Sarah,' he said.

It was just what I needed to hear from one of my brothers. But I think I was more worried for Jack than me that afternoon. Jack was so private, so I felt very protective of him being exposed like this.

As the video played, I was immediately struck by how small I was. I turned to Tracey and whispered, 'Oh, my God, I just want to give myself a hug.' I hadn't appreciated just how young I had been. My instinct was to pick that small girl up and say, 'Come on. We're leaving. No one is going to put you through this.'

I had done a lot of therapy since I'd last seen the video, and this had enabled me to be more objective when I watched the recording in the courtroom. I could more easily forgive that eight-year-old child. How could I expect her to have known what she was doing?

I knew I had not been motivated to speak the truth in that video. Everything I'd said had been motivated by my wanting to keep Molly and Sharon happy, and to ensure that Jack and I stayed in America. I had to go home with those people after the interview, and I was convinced I'd live with them for the rest of my life. It was in my interest to lie. I'd been in survival mode when I'd given that interview. I was also isolated. I discovered much later that Molly had denied Dad's family's request to see us in the aftermath of Dad's death. She wouldn't even let them see us for a supervised visit.

For years after, everyone said, 'Sarah, you were just kids. It's not your fault or Jack's.'

Tracey had pointed to my godfather Paul's child Elena once and said, 'Look at Elena, she's about the age you were doing that interview. Would you judge her?' And of course, I wouldn't.

But as much as I told everyone that I knew it wasn't my fault, it still felt like my fault. It felt like being trapped in a nightmare, watching a version of myself that I no longer recognised speak and being unable to stop what was happening.

These recordings were shown in that courtroom as 'evidence' of Molly being abused. If the judge had listened, all he would have heard was me saying that Molly had 'told me' she was abused. 'Mommy told me Daddy hit her.' It showed a subtle and insidious pattern, and only in recent years have I come to recognise it as coercive control.

But Jack and I had been completely dependent on Molly's approval. Our survival had depended on it – sometimes we didn't get fed if we didn't please her. She had exerted complete control over us, even telling us what to believe. Molly had told us a version of events and then urged us to 'tell the truth' to social workers, which meant repeating what she had said even though it wasn't our experience or the truth. I was overly dependent on Molly and told the interviewer she was 'my best friend'.

Regardless, the defence played the recordings of two scared children and presented the videos as black-and-white evidence of Dad's 'brutality'.

As my video played, I remember glancing around at the rows of media, and every single reporter was either fiercely scribbling, gazing at the screen or staring at me. My heart sank. I was worried how the recordings would be received outside the courtroom. I've always advocated for my dad and the Justice for Jason campaign. *What will people think now? They would ask how can we believe what she says?*

At one point, I watched myself tell the social worker, 'Sorry, I lost my place' or 'I got that bit wrong'.

'You're such a bad liar!' Tracey said in my ear.

And I was. It was so obvious that I was trying to work with a script. I still don't know how the social worker or a judge couldn't tell.

When I was being interviewed, I had no idea that Molly had used a paving stone in the killing of my father. In response to a question about the brick paver, Jack had explained why the stone was in Molly and Dad's bedroom.

'We were going to paint it so it would look pretty, and that ... it was in my mom's room because it was raining earlier, and we already ... we were going to paint it. We didn't want it getting all wet. So we brought it inside and my mom put it at her night stand.'

My father had been cutting the grass in the baking sun that day, and the adults had sat in the garden for hours drinking mojitos. If anyone had bothered checking, they would have discovered that it never rained that day.

Watching the Dragonfly House tapes was awful. They were hard to listen to as they felt like a terrible betrayal of Dad. But I was much more forgiving of myself than I had been in the past.

It was a frustrating experience. I wanted to go up and swear on the Bible and tell the truth. I wanted our retractions presented to the judge. In 2021, when I was about fifteen, I'd recorded a seven-hour statement with Davidson County Sheriff's Office, detailing everything that went on in our home, but they wouldn't play any of that either. They would only listen to me as a scared eight-year-old whose dad had just died, with my father's killer and her mother sitting outside, waiting to bring me home with them.

At one point during the Dragonfly interview, the social worker quizzed me on my feelings for Tracey and David. I said that Tracey was all right, but that I didn't really like Uncle David. Right on cue, David nudged me. 'I never really liked you either.' It was one of the few moments that made me smile that day.

CHAPTER 10

FAMILY

Your Honour

I am so lucky I have a loving family that will go to the ends of the earth for my brother and me. We are lucky and grateful for what Tracey, David, Adam and Dean have done for us. Not only were we provided with a home by them, but they loved us like their own from the day we were reunited. They have supported me when I have completely broken down. And they have cheered me on when I have had successes, especially Tracey, my mom, the only real mother figure I have ever known. She has let me be myself, learn about the world and form my own opinions. That is family, and that is love. That is what my dad would want. He loved me unconditionally.

Winston-Salem, North Carolina
Wednesday, 1 November 2023

Tracey, Jack and I went for a walk to clear our heads after the court day ended before returning to our house. The Dragonfly tapes had made it a long, stressful day, and the fresh air and soft light of a November evening in Winston-Salem brought some relief. The autumn leaves had fallen, so warm hues of russet, gold and deep maroon carpeted the neighbourhood. We felt the satisfying crunch of maple and oak leaves beneath our feet, and the air carried a hint of smoke and earthy scents of decay.

We hardly spoke until we spotted a rabbit and a hedgehog in the hedgerows. I breathed in the magic of this autumnal scene and lost myself in my thoughts. I had to give myself a pep talk some days. I felt immense anger about what had happened in the courtroom. My body felt the strain, and I felt jumpy and anxious. I felt pushed around by forces out of my control. I reminded myself we were listening to words, not reality. The words were often twisted justifications for an unjustifiable act. And they were as hollow and sickening as the principles of the people uttering them. But they were empty words in the end.

But I knew those words could affect the outcome of this hearing and I was powerless to do anything about them. Crying is an emotional release for me, but I tried not to cry during the days of the hearing, especially in public. And when alone, I was careful not to slide into self-pity. Emotions were building up, but I couldn't afford to open the dam or they could overflow and overwhelm me. I had to stop the words said in court getting into my head. It always helped to have a cuddle with Tracey in the evenings. We're unbelievably close. I tell her everything – more than I should at times.

Mostly, however, going to court became a grim lesson in resignation. What they said hurt, but I told myself, *Look, you have to return to the courtroom tomorrow. Pull yourself together and deal with this another day.* I had to accept that I needed to let go or I wouldn't be able to face another day in that room. My belief in justice, however, began to crumble.

Shortly after we returned from our walk that day, I asked David to pass me something in the kitchen. His nose lifted with a haughty sniff.

'Why should I?' he replied. 'You said you don't like me. You're not getting anything from me.'

Everyone laughed. The simple act of smiling can bring light to a black day. Even in our darkest hours, we found pockets of silliness, and we all needed that after the toxic environment of the courtroom.

Most in our Winston-Salem house had been through this before. That sentencing hearing wasn't their first rodeo. My dad's twin Wayne has always been part of this crew, travelling back and forth for every trial and appeal date. So has Dad's sister Marilyn and now her partner, Sharon. Everyone there had been there from the start – for the guardianship battle, the trials, the appeals. My godfather, Paul, went to America when his daughter was two days old to help in the custody battle for Jack and me.

After Dad's death, Jack and I remained oblivious to the heartache and struggles my family endured to get custody of us. I had resigned myself to living with the Martens forever. However, two weeks after Dad's passing, a large black van turned up on a quiet Sunday afternoon and changed everything.

A vehicle with tinted windows pulled up outside Bobby's house as I played in the front garden with his daughter, Gabby. As a vaguely familiar woman stepped out, I ran inside to tell

Bobby. He looked out and immediately told me to close and lock the garage door.

I hurried to comply, trying to close the garage door from inside. However, the woman from the van slipped under the descending door and strode past me with a casual, 'Hi!' I followed her into the house, filled with uncertainty and apprehension.

She strode straight up to Bobby and Sharon's brother Michael Earnest, who were both federal agents, and flashed her identification. I saw Bobby go outside to Molly, who was in the pool teaching his toddler Natalia to swim. Then, everything went wild. Molly started shrieking hysterically, 'Please don't take my babies! Please don't take my babies!' I watched in shock, thinking the woman was taking Natalia.

But then Jack and I became the topic of conversation. Everything moved too fast for me to comprehend as Molly took us upstairs. She flung a bag at me.

'Pack your things,' she said as she yanked out clothes for Jack and me.

I wondered why she was angry at me.

The woman from the van hurried us out, shepherding us before her. The Martens followed as the woman secured us in the back seats. A driver smiled back at us while waiting behind the wheel. But no one said goodbye or explained what was happening. By now, Molly was wailing and hyperventilating on the pavement. I needed her to comfort me, tell me I'd be okay and reassure me she'd come and find me. Instead, she collapsed on the grass verge, and the woman slammed the van door shut. I screamed as the van pulled off, but the Martens were too busy attending to Molly.

Molly warned that Dad's Irish relatives would kidnap us, and now we had been taken by strangers in a black van. My heart beat with terror, not knowing what was happening and if I'd ever see my mom again. That journey seemed to happen in slow motion, dragging on forever. It was like the horror night my dad disappeared, when we waited hours in the blue room.

We finally pulled into an empty car park in front of a bleak brown building. The place looked like an abandoned warehouse. Few were working that Sunday afternoon.

Inside, the woman left us in a room set up as a playroom. I found a doll and sat on the floor to play with it.

The woman was Shelly Lee from the Department of Social Services. She had brought us to Thomasville Division of Social Services (DSS) offices on foot of an order from Brian Shipwash, the Clerk of the Superior Court for Davidson County, to remove us from Molly's care on 16 August.

We had been the subject of a custody case in which Tracey had spent five hours in a witness box, pleading her case to be our guardian. Dad's will, lodged safely with his Limerick solicitor, had been central to the custody hearing. His wishes stated: 'I appoint the said David Lynch and his wife Tracey Lynch (my sister) to be guardians of my infant children.'

My family is eternally grateful to Brian Shipwash for agreeing to my late father's wishes. I don't like to think about our lives if he'd left us in Molly's care.

Tracey and Dave had also engaged a Winston-Salem attorney, Kim Bonuomo, to fight for our custody. Her name is also sacred in our house. When someone raises her name it's followed by, 'Thank God for Kim.'

While playing with my doll, I heard the door open and I remember turning to see Tracey standing there. Of course, I recognised her because she had been a visitor to our house so many times. We had also stayed at her Raheen home. Tracey and David had always been present in our lives, but I felt no strong emotional bond with the couple. However, I worshipped their younger son, Adam, six years older than me. Even though I was the youngest cousin on my dad's side, he always included me in their games. 'Come on, Sarah, you stick with me.'

However, Molly had warned me about Tracey, saying she would take us back to Ireland from everyone and everything we knew. So my heart sank as my aunt hunkered down beside me. She had come for me, just like Molly had told me she would.

Then Tracey spoke.

'That's a lovely doll,' she said, and instantly her soft but distinctive accent resonated with me. She spoke like my dad, and hearing her voice made me relax. Everything about her struck a chord of fond recognition and connection to Dad. Then Tracey asked if she could hug me, and even though I was suspicious, I nodded my consent.

As Tracey embraced me, something extraordinary happened – the fear I felt dissolved, and suddenly, I melted into her arms. I realised she hugged me just like my dad, and I sank into her with relief. I exhaled during that hug, feeling safe for the first time in a long time. Something deep inside me told me she would not let anything happen to me. Almost subconsciously, I knew she had flown across the world to hug me.

Tracey and David brought us to the most enormous hotel room I'd ever seen, with a vast carpeted sitting area. They had booked a massive suite with separate bedrooms, so we didn't feel overcrowded. They wanted us to have space until we were comfortable around them.

Jack and I found a Gideon Bible inside a bedside drawer as we went to bed. I'm not sure what possessed us because we were not religious, but Tracey found us on our knees, hands pressed to the Bible, reciting the 'Our Father'. We were scared kids who, in a world turned upside down, reached for a lifeline in a hotel drawer. The emotional exhaustion of the previous two weeks must have hit us because we slept for sixteen hours straight. Tracey and David, concerned that there was something wrong, had to wake us the following day.

Guardianship had been awarded the previous day, but we could not leave because we had no passports due to a pending custody hearing. Tracey and David were doing their best to get Jack and me home. As they worked on that, my godfather Paul and Aunt Marilyn looked after us. Paul endeared himself to us forever because this forty-year-old man jumped on the beds and play-wrestled with us all day. I stopped wondering what would happen to us and became a kid again for those hours.

In the following days, I noticed Tracey and David focused everything on Jack and me. With Molly, I felt I always had to please her. But suddenly, I had adults checking in with me, asking what I needed and wanted. I still had the occasional tantrum where I demanded to go home to 'Mommy', but Tracey and David responded with such kindness and patience that I ended up feeling guilty about making a scene.

When we landed at Shannon Airport and reached the arrivals hall on 20 August, I saw hundreds of people waiting for us. They applauded and photographers were snapping, and I saw a blur of smiling faces. The air was cooler and crisper, and everyone seemed to speak like my dad. I clutched one ear, distressed that I'd lost an earring from a set Dad had given me. The first person I recognised was my granda, John Corbett, standing quietly in the crowd, and I went straight to him.

'I'm so happy you're here, love,' he said, and he had just enough time to hug me before searching in vain for my earring. The sights, sounds and smells of a country I barely remembered surrounded me, but I felt wanted and welcomed from that first day.

I didn't know that Jack was going through entirely different emotions. When we reached the arrivals hall, he eagerly scanned the crowds, desperately hoping to spot a face he loved. He told us years later that he secretly believed that Dad would be waiting when we landed in Shannon so was heartbroken on arrival.

I called our guardians Aunty Tracey and Uncle David for the first year in Limerick. Then they became Tracey and David. As I got older, I had to stop myself calling them Mom and Dad. My reasoning was complicated. I thought it wouldn't be fair to Adam and Dean because Tracey and David were their parents, not ours. It seemed like I was trying to usurp their place. I berated myself. You can't just take someone's mom and dad because you don't have one.

Also, I didn't want to call them 'Mom and Dad' without Jack. I feared he might see it as a betrayal – that I had moved on to a new family. I was fourteen when I started calling Tracey 'Mom'. At first, I started calling David 'Dad' by accident, and then I gave up trying to stop myself.

When Jack and I moved to Ireland, Dean was already living with Kelly, now his wife, but the sibling bond was there from the start. He opened his arms wide and let Jack and me walk into his life. Adam never resented our arrival either. He hugged me when I woke upset from a nightmare in the middle of the night. Sometimes, I didn't want to wake Tracey and David, so I knocked on Adam's door, and everything was okay again.

Being in America for the sentencing trial was stressful and grim, but I left with lovely memories of my family. I remember Dean, Adam, Jack and me in Tracey's and David's bedroom in our pyjamas, laughing and chatting about nothing and everything. That sense of togetherness was like being wrapped in the warmest embrace. When I was with them, I felt protected, like nothing could touch me.

The daily routine between us all during the hearing in North Carolina became a comfort too. Almost immediately, everyone knew the drill. Most mornings, we woke at the crack of dawn because of jet lag. I'd go to Tracey and David's room and launch myself into their bed because, in my head, I was still twelve years old. Tracey and I went through our wardrobe to pick out our clothes. We were in court to represent Dad and support the prosecution. It felt important to dress in a way that conveyed gravity and respect for the process. Paul was the short-order cook who plated up eggs, bacon, sausages and toast for everyone.

When we returned to the house every evening, it was like we removed our courtroom coats and left them outside the door. No one was angry or sad, we were just in the moment. The day in court was the past, and we tried not to worry about the following day. David and Paul went shopping and made dinner. The rest of us just unwound and caught up on everything and everyone we missed at home.

The house was old, but everybody had space. When I needed to recharge, I ended up with Adam. We stretched out on two couches and chatted and watched TV. Then, one by one, everyone gathered in the living room and when the couch space was filled, I sat on the floor. Dean set up a trivia game on Netflix, and we split into teams. We drank coffee and Shirley Temples.

We arrived in Winston-Salem in time for Halloween when the neighbourhood was decked out in carved pumpkins, fake cobwebs and plastic skeletons. Our accommodation, a historic timber clapboard house, was perfect for the spooky season. Marilyn and Sharon thought an antique wooden crib among its furnishings looked particularly scary. On Halloween night, we carried the cot to their room, made a baby shape with blankets and left it in the dark. Everyone roared with laughter, hearing their shrieks and the women dragging the cot across the floorboards that night. We never forgot to laugh even after a bad day.

But everyone felt the loss of Dad more acutely being in North Carolina. We had returned to the place where he had been taken from us. Yet, our spirits never stayed low for long because we were such a tight team.

When we talked about the case outside of the courtroom, it was brief. We never spent time overanalysing what had happened. Tracey, David and the other 'adults' probably limited the post-courtroom analysis to give Jack and me time to decompress. We were all adults, but some were more adult than others, and everyone in my family protected Jack and me. We're 'the kids' and probably always will be.

Our time in America for the hearing made me realise how fortunate I am. I may have lost my parents, but I hit the family jackpot with the people who have surrounded me since. We're the closest-knit family anyone can imagine. Tracey, David, Dean, Adam and Jack are my lifelines, and I'll be forever grateful for Dad's foresight in providing an amazing safety net for his children.

Walking into that courtroom, I had Tracey clutching my hand, and I had Dean or David's protective arms around me in court. I had Paul to laugh with and Adam by my side. Meanwhile, Jack and I exchanged supportive glances and squeezed each other's hands. I remember leaving the courtroom one day, and the Martens started filing out just as we did. I immediately tensed. I didn't want any contact with them. But suddenly, Adam was behind me, at my elbow, like a buffer, making sure no one could reach me. I never felt safer than that week in North Carolina. Everybody in that group had my back, and I had everyone else's back. Everyone was there to support my dad and each other.

Tracey and David are the bedrock of our family. They are the most incredible mom and dad. Tracey isn't just my mom; she's my confidante, someone I trust and can share anything with. Their love for each other and us is so strong, it could power a small city. She and David are also the most intelligent and hardworking people I've ever known.

Dean and Adam are my older brothers whose constant presence speaks volumes about their love for Jack and me. Dean, sixteen years my senior, has been our guardian angel since we returned to Ireland. From the start, he has showered me with big-brother wisdom and unconditional love. He is always there to catch me when I fall. He left his one-year-old baby in Ireland to stand by our side in North Carolina. When Tracey and David were in America for the Martens' trials and appeals, Dean stepped up to care for us.

As Adam grew older, Dean passed the baton to him. Adam is not only a brother but a built-in best friend. He is willing to move mountains for his family too, clearing his schedule and uprooting his entire life to be there for my dad's sentencing hearing. I've adored Adam since I was a toddler, and that will never change.

Together with the rest of Dad's friends and family, we form this incredible support system of strength and softness. I feel so fortunate because there's nothing quite like knowing you've got a family like mine in your corner.

CHAPTER 11

THE SPY AMONG US

Your Honour

What kind of mother hides recording devices all over the house? I remember those recordings and those events. I remember what happened before. I remember what my stepmother did. I remember my dad bringing her flowers. He was caring for her, trying to bring her to the bedroom out of our earshot when she had another meltdown. These recordings have been orchestrated and selective just like my words and my brother's words were coached and doctored when the Martens made us lie about our father. I did it out of love and fear. I now understand how both can exist alongside each other.

Courtroom 6, Davidson County Courthouse
Day 4: Thursday, 2 November 2023
Molly made a secret recording in our kitchen six months before she killed Dad that became the focus of the fourth day of the sentencing hearing. The recording featured a row between Molly

and Dad, one of many in our house in the weeks and months before she killed him.

Molly had sought legal advice from our neighbour and family law attorney, Melissa Sams, in January 2015, seven months before she killed Dad. Molly had said she was considering divorcing Dad and related the usual tale about Dad being abusive. She told Melissa that she didn't want to leave the marriage without custody of Jack and me.

Melissa had advised her that she needed to demonstrate that Dad was a domestic abuser, a drunk and a danger to his children. If she could document that behaviour, she could apply for an emergency custody order for us. Molly had decided to set up covert listening devices around the house. At that time, what Melissa or anybody else didn't know was that Molly had been covertly recording Dad as far back as 2013.

As the defence began playing the tape recording in the courtroom, I thought I recognised the row. The one I was recalling was when Dad had arrived home with a colourful bunch of flowers for Molly. She'd beamed with pleasure, delighted with the gesture, and had put the bouquet in a vase on the kitchen table.

Dad had casually moved the vase to one side as we sat for dinner – it had been like flicking a switch. Molly had stared at the empty spot on the table where the flowers had been. Then she'd gone berserk, screaming at him, her stool screeching against the hardwood floor as she rose furiously to her feet. 'Who gave you the right to move those flowers? Why bring me flowers and then ruin it like that?'

She'd grabbed our full dinner plates, food flying as she did, and flung our dinners in the bin, plates and all. Then, she'd stormed off to her bedroom. We sat there, looking at each other, shaken and confused by what had happened.

Of course, Molly would never have played the tape of that row in the courtroom. The District Attorney's office estimated that Molly had made 150 hours of covert recordings with all the devices around the house. They only received three hours of tape despite requests made under discovery.

'This may be one bad instance out of a hundred and fifty,' said Assistant DA Alan Martin that day, adding that Molly had made the tape recordings to 'manufacture evidence'. He said the remaining tapes were never produced because they didn't suit Molly's purpose to prove Dad was abusive.

One hundred and fifty hours must be a gross underestimation. We thought that she had only started recording Dad in 2015, but at least one of Molly's recordings in evidence was labelled as 2013. She'd used her phone to record Dad secretly long before she bought multiple recording devices.

The Martens' defence played the 'pancake recording' that day in the sentencing hearing, so-called because it took place on Pancake Tuesday in February 2015. Dad liked to ensure that we experienced the traditions he'd grown up with in Ireland, so he rang Molly and asked that we all have a family dinner that day. It was snowing, and Molly had brought us sledging. Meanwhile, Dad had had a tough day because the snow had upset the plant schedules. When he arrived home, he discovered Molly had already fed us, which was of course all part of her gaslighting Dad so the family dinner he'd wanted would not happen.

You can hear anger and frustration in Dad's voice on the tape.

'I work twelve hours a day and I couldn't have dinner with my family because you ignored me,' he said.

As the tape played, no one in the courtroom could miss Molly rocking back and forth in her chair, furiously dabbing her eyes.

During the recording, there was a loud bang that the defence claimed was the sound of Dad pounding his fists on the table. There was no truth to this. The sound came from Dad's chair falling to the ground. The stretcher between the front legs was at an odd height, and when your leg calves hit it, the chair toppled backwards. It always happened with visitors who weren't used to the chairs. The bang was Dad's chair falling as he stood up.

I could even hear Jack on the tape saying, 'Dad, be careful. They're $100 chairs.'

And Dad replying, 'I know. I paid for them.'

I also heard myself butting in and shouting at Dad at one point. 'You are not talking, you are screaming!' I yelled, jumping in to defend Molly.

On the tape, I heard Dad asking for the results of my blood tests, saying the doctor had left a message days earlier. Molly claimed she had phoned the doctor.

'Show me where you called on the cell phone,' Dad insisted.

Molly used this as proof that Dad was controlling and would check her phone. It only showed that he could no longer trust anything she said. 'It's Sarah's medical!' he said.

I was sad to hear him shout, 'You have made it very clear you want to separate me from my kids.'

The recording wasn't Dad's finest moment, but neither did it show the violent monster Molly hoped to portray. Her solicitor Kingsbery said the tape was evidence of an angry, abusive and controlling husband who was frightening his wife and children.

But he had never frightened me. I'm recorded shouting at Dad, which proved that I wasn't scared of him.

All of Molly's 'incriminating' evidence amounted to Dad raising his voice. The pancake tape is all the defence presented to the court despite her recording hundreds of conversations and exchanges in the house.

It was also missing the end of the recording Molly made of that evening, but I've listened to it all since. Near the end of the recording, I had gone to my bedroom and Dad had said that he was going upstairs to speak with me. 'By the way, don't have a whispering session with my son or daughter again,' he said. 'When I go up here, I don't want any whispers about anything. I'm not stupid, Moll.' It's clear that Dad had realised that Molly was conspiring with us behind his back.

After Dad had left the kitchen, the sound on the tape got loud because Molly and Jack had started to use an electric mixer to beat pancake batter. Then, as I listened closely, I heard Molly whispering to Jack, 'Go listen to what he's saying to Sarah.'

It was classic Molly. Her whisper is so quiet that no one would have heard it. *'Go listen to what he's saying to Sarah.'* I thought I was her only little spy in the house, but that single recording showed she'd used Jack in the same way to monitor Dad. I wonder if the prosecution even realised it was there in evidence?

Molly had ensured she always knew what was happening in our house, and I'd often help her with that. When anyone from Ireland arrived, Molly sent me to their room to look through their luggage.

I remember entering the guestroom, leaving the door slightly ajar one day. I knew I needed to be quick. After glancing around, I headed for the suitcase lying on the bed. I lifted the layers of clothes and felt around the case edges before unzipping a large make-up bag and rummaging through its contents. Paul and his wife Simone had arrived from Ireland and were in the garden with Dad. However, as I crouched to unzip a holdall, the door creaked, and I saw Simone standing in the doorway.

'Sarah?' she said, her tone wary.

I snatched a T-shirt from the holdall and stepped back from the bag. 'I thought this was really pretty,' I said, beaming, holding up the garment.

Simone raised an eyebrow, and I felt my face grow hot. But I didn't dare tell her the truth – that Molly had sent me to root through their belongings.

'See if they brought anything for you,' Molly had said. She put a finger to her lips, but I already knew my mission was a secret.

I'd open guests' bags, rifling through each before fixing everything back to how I'd found it. Then, I'd return to Molly and tell her what I'd seen. I never figured out what she expected me to find.

On another occasion, my cousin Kate walked in on me while I was going through her things. I was holding her hair extensions when she caught me. She'd been eighteen then and reacted with outrage. 'What are you doing going through my stuff?'

I spluttered some excuse that I'd left something in the room – nothing that explained why I had taken hair extensions from her bag.

Of course, Molly's monitoring had kicked up a gear before Dad died.

We discovered that Molly was recording us one weekend in summer 2015 when Dad offered to pay Jack to clean his car. Jack did a thorough job because he came in with a shiny silver gadget, saying he'd found it under the driver's seat. He'd thought it was a gaming console or a phone. It looked like a TV remote, only smaller, with a little screen and buttons. Dad had examined the device and told Jack and me to leave so he could talk to Molly. I'd assumed my usual position by the bookcase at the top of the stairs.

'What's this?' he said.

Molly didn't sound fazed at all.

'I just don't trust you anymore,' she replied.

'You're recording me in the car?' he said in disbelief.

'Yes, I don't trust you.'

'Why would you record me?'

The conversation went around in circles, with Molly claiming she didn't trust him and Dad sounding like he was in utter shock.

The following day, he tried to talk to her as she went for a shower without realising she was still recording him.

The 'shower' recording was one of a handful of tapes that Molly had either handed to the defence or that had been unearthed by a prosecution subpoena to access information from her phone. This and the other tapes were never aired as part of her defence. We only received them for the first time in January 2024 when they were released by the District Attorney after the case was closed.

'Just yesterday, I found a recorder in my car, and I'm concerned about it. Extremely concerned about it, to the point that I can't trust you,' Dad said.

He wanted to check her phone to see if she had other recordings of him and us, but Molly refused to let him check.

'I don't want us to break up, but you're saying no. You're saying you'll record if you like,' he said.

Molly replied, 'No, I'm saying if you want to give me your phone, and I'll go through all your Facebook stuff, all your internet and emails.'

'It's not a debate. I've no problem with you going through any of my stuff anyway.'

Molly seemed anxious about the recording device Dad and Jack found the previous day. 'You have proof of the recordings … You said you lost my recorder since yesterday when you found it.'

'I don't know where I put it. I'm still in shock,' he replied.

Molly seemed to suspect he was deliberately holding on to it. 'But you saved the recordings?' she asked.

'No,' he said.

'Well, that's what you said.'

'I did not say that.'

'So, you were lying about that?'

'You don't believe anything I say anyway,' Dad said. 'I, on the other hand, have believed a lot of what you say … This is why it is not going to work out, hon. Because I do feel betrayed about the recordings, okay? I came home, and I thought it could be okay. I thought you would prove there are no more recordings there – and I asked could I look at your phone to prove there are no more recordings there … Your attitude is [that I've] done so many wrong things, so I'm not doing that.'

Molly replied, 'My attitude is I'm going to retain that little bit of privacy.'

During the same row the day after Jack found the recording device, she also complained about him 'cussing' and a 'Facebook affair'.

'I don't know what affairs you might have had. You refuse to let me see,' she said.

'I don't know what kind of affairs you may have had!' Dad replied.

'I've never had an affair.'

'Neither have I.'

'Well, you have!'

'Well, I haven't, actually,' Dad said.

'Okay, you had a Facebook affair … an internet affair, whatever you want to call it.'

I don't know what this 'Facebook affair' is about. I asked Tracey and she explained that my dad had been in contact with someone on Facebook when Molly had been working as the au pair. I think this was most likely what she was referring to.

Molly continued to argue that Dad didn't give her access to his Facebook account because he was having an affair. All we know is that she had friended Dad on Facebook, so she already had access to his profile and shared content.

Molly also accused him of threatening divorce and taking us away.

'You told me I was never going to see my kids again,' she said on the recording.

'That's just the fundamental part,' Dad said. 'We are husband and wife, and you—'

'You threaten to divorce me every week for five years,' she said.

'We are not even married for five years,' he said, sounding worn out.

'I've been with you past five years, you've been trying to get rid of me for the past five years, every week,' she said.

'You've done things to me every week for five years,' he replied. 'Acting like you're scared and—'

'I can't help being scared.'

'Acting like you're scared of me like, you know, like I'm some kind of demon.'

'I don't act like you're some kind of demon,' she said.

'You don't think that has some psychological effect on me? That that doesn't affect? Of course, it does.'

'I'm sorry that I've been scared! I can't help being scared,' she shouted.

I know Dad might have taken her accusations more seriously if he'd known that she was recording that conversation.

But Dad had clearly listened to the tape Jack had found in the car and heard things on the recording that she'd never intended for him to hear, because he continued to question her. 'Is there anything else you want to talk about or discuss that I might not know about?'

'No, there's nothing else. I'd just like to take a shower.'

'Okay, in terms of talking in front of Sarah, about me doing something that I didn't do,' he said.

Dad must have overheard her accusing him of things on the recording, but Molly redirected him and went off on another tangent instead of replying.

On Monday, 3 August – the day after Dad had been killed – Molly's uncle, Mike Earnest, had phoned Dad's workplace several times, looking to collect his personal effects.

Dad's colleagues were unaware of the circumstances

surrounding his death and had handed over Dad's effects to Molly on Tuesday, 4 August. What was Molly's urgency about getting Dad's personal effects? I often wonder if she was concerned about finding the recording that Dad had said he'd lost.

Dad's colleagues also questioned the haste.

'What I remember most is that he [Mike Earnest] was particularly aggressive [in tone],' said Dad's MPS colleague, Melanie Crook.

Mike Earnest had worked for a US federal law enforcement authority called Special Inspector General for Afghanistan Reconstruction. His employers confirmed they were investigating him after Dad's colleagues had alleged that he'd identified himself as a federal agent when trying to access Dad's office. Mike vehemently denied claims that he had used his position as a federal agent to gain access to Dad's office. He later said the investigation had cleared him.

Whatever was on the tape Jack found in the car, we never heard it because the recording was never found. The shower tape was heartbreaking to listen to. I could hear Dad trying to make things better. It wasn't unreasonable for her to show him her phone and prove that she didn't have any other recordings of Dad or us. I'd never fully understood how much he endured until I heard that recording. I could almost hear him giving up. He was at his wits' end, struggling to find a solution weeks before she killed him.

Another of Molly's secret recordings is from her and Dad's bedroom, though we don't know when she recorded it. Because she was recording these conversations, Molly was calculated and strategic in her responses to Dad, choosing words and actions that presented her in a more favourable light and Dad in a poorer one. At best, their bedroom row presents a distorted image of the usual arguments I heard, where she normally screamed a lot. But it certainly doesn't paint Dad or her in a good light and shows a complete breakdown in communication between them. It was an end of a marriage. She sounded like she hated my father and he sounded tired of her.

Another of Molly's covert tapes was labelled: 'Jason comes home late. Dec. 2013'. I couldn't believe it when I saw that date. It showed that she had been secretly recording Dad for at least two years.

It's a brief three-minute recording that starts with the sound of Dad outside the front door, trying to turn the key to open the lock.

The front door of our home was rarely used. Dad and Molly always entered the house via a door and keypad in the garage. He must have already tried that door, found it locked and come around to the front door. It was another of Molly's gaslighting tricks that I was familiar with: leaving the doors unlocked when we went out so he would find the house open on return from work, and locking the doors when he didn't have keys so he couldn't get in.

On the tape, he tries the keys for twenty seconds before he realises the front door is also locked from the inside. That's when he starts ringing the bell repeatedly. I can hear Rory, our dog, barking furiously at the disturbance. Dad continues ringing the doorbell for forty seconds.

Bear in mind that this is all taping on Molly's phone, which means that she must be recording nearby. She deliberately leaves him ringing the bell to provoke him and capture an angry reaction.

'What are you doing?' she says, arriving to answer the door and feigning astonishment.

'What are you doing locking the door?' he says.

'I'm sorry,' she says.

'You never mean to do anything, do you?' His tone is angry.

She says, 'Please, please.' It makes her sound as if she's cowering in fear.

He doesn't respond to this. It's as if he doesn't hear it, but he clearly believes she locked him out deliberately.

'Yeah, yeah, whatever. Fuck you, husband,' he says. 'As usual it will be like, "I'm sorry, I didn't realise. I didn't know. It was an accident. I didn't realise I locked you out of my house. It's no big deal."'

The bickering continues, and he says, 'Didn't mean to, didn't mean to, didn't mean to. That's okay you just cry.'

That is the last we hear of Dad in the recording. We don't hear his footsteps in the hall or his voice or any sound or movement. It's like he disappears.

But then Molly wails, 'It's just too hard!'

There's a sound and she cries out dramatically. Then, we hear the sound of four similar sounds that could be interpreted as 'slaps'. They happen in silence, with no reaction from Molly and nothing to indicate that Dad is there.

Seconds later, she sobs into the phone, 'I hate you.' Then the recording crackles for a few seconds, and Molly sobs into her phone for a few seconds, before the recording ends.

It's a strange recording.

Molly tried to present this to the media as an example of Dad's violence towards her. The recording should have been gold for a defence team that desperately wanted to portray Dad as a violent abuser. For some reason, however, it was never presented as evidence in the court.

I am not aware that any of Molly's recordings were subjected to audio-forensics analysis to confirm their authenticity.

I believe it had been edited and that my dad was not even present for part of it. Perhaps the attorneys also found it not to be credible.

All recordings kept by Molly capture moments when Dad was angry and upset, and, as she planned, show him in a negative light. Yet, the only recording played by the Martens' defence team was the 'pancake tape' excerpt. Despite her best efforts and attempts to control the narrative in the recordings, she does not emerge much better than Dad. What the tapes really demonstrate is a marriage in crisis with high levels of stress, frustration and hurt. It pains me to hear his frustration and his willingness to try to placate Molly, all while she was surreptitiously recording him. The last weeks of his life were desperately sad and lonely.

Not long after Jack found the device in the car, I started seeing more of them. Molly could be obsessive about things, but not housework. When she was home, she was often propped on her pillow, flipping the pages of her latest novel.

She delegated much of the housework to Jack and me, writing separate lists to assign us our cleaning chores. As I polished one day, I found something attached to the underside of a side table in the living room. It came off when I pulled it, and Jack and I realised it was another recording device attached to the table with black Velcro. We quickly reattached it.

After searching, we found many more devices. They'd been left underneath the living room couch, in the guestrooms and bathrooms. I spotted something under the pool table, in the office and even in the room where Molly's parents stayed. She had also planted several in her and Dad's bedroom: under a large standing jewellery cabinet, under Dad's chest of drawers and yet another on their bed frame. Jack's room and mine were the only places we didn't find one.

I never told Dad about the devices. I was complicit in many of Molly's gaslighting and schemes against him, and it makes me feel so guilty. I loved her but also feared her too much to tell Dad. If there had been recording devices in the bedroom on the morning of 2 August, they were never found.

Tracey and David had found empty packaging for a recording device and industrial-strength Velcro in a box after Dad had died. Molly had left the empty boxes on the bed where they used to stay when visiting Dad and her at our Panther Creek Court home. Tracey and David believed the packaging was placed there deliberately and interpreted this as a message that she had recordings of them in the bedroom. In addition to the packaging, she left a book on emergency care. They submitted the packaging into evidence for the 2017 trial.

Despite all Molly's efforts, she was never able to record evidence of any of the 'abuse' that she needed to prove to gain custody of us. But I believe that she uncovered information that Dad planned to leave her instead.

A week after my dad's killing, Paul had given a statement to the Davidson County Sheriff's Department. He said that Dad had called him from his car in the weeks before he died, saying he was leaving Molly and taking us back to Ireland, but he needed to arrange his departure secretly. Had Molly placed another device in his car? Did she hear this conversation? Only she knows that. When Paul made this statement, he knew nothing about the recording devices. No one except Molly, Jack and I knew about them at that stage.

Paul's statement of 11 August reads:

He disclosed to me his fears about leaving the US to come home and the fight he would have for the kids ... he was led to believe from [Tom] that, in the US, Molly had as many rights as Jason did after they got married concerning the kids. Jason was aware of her father's profession and was really worried about this. [Jason] told me on numerous occasions that Molly and her family were putting huge pressure on him to allow Molly to adopt the kids. Jason told me, 'I would need to be on a plane before [the Martens] even knew I [had] left.'

This was also echoed in a conversation Dad had with Tracey and Dave. Other events and discussions also signified that Dad was planning to leave Molly. However, he would have left far sooner if I had told him what was happening under his own roof and about all the other recording devices around the house. And that's something that I must live with.

CHAPTER 12

THE BONDS THAT BIND

Your Honour

When I got home to Ireland, Molly posted images of me on Facebook and went on the radio to tell people to find me. Molly Martens took notes I wrote for her when I was younger and pictures of me as a child and shared them all publicly on social media for everyone to see. She betrayed me again and again – and even shared a note I left with her the last time I saw her. And she did all this to get publicity for her lies about my father. There was nothing I could do to stop her. I was trying to start a new life in Ireland, but she stalked me.

Courtroom 6, Davidson County Courthouse
Day 4: Thursday, 2 November 2023
Childhood is supposed to be a time of innocence, but Jack and I had a crash course in survival instead. We sat through stressful interviews, trying to recite the lines Molly had taught us. Months later, my brother would reach out to the person who had

orchestrated our lies, and she would use this to betray him in the media and now in the courtroom again.

The day after Molly had killed Dad, she'd sat Jack and me down, her expression solemn as she'd clutched our hands. She'd told us a lady was coming to talk to us, and it was very important.

'You guys need to tell her the truth: Daddy was very mean and he hit Mommy and hurt her all the time,' she said. 'You must tell her you love Mommy very much. Do you understand? If you don't tell the truth, they'll take you away from Mommy.' I remember being so confused. Here was my mother telling me to lie and calling it a 'truth'.

The day after playing our Dragonfly tapes in the courtroom, the defence called the social worker who had interviewed us the day after Dad's killing. Sheila Tyler testified that she made an 'unannounced' visit to Bobby Martens' house on Monday, 3 August 2015. She was there to carry out a welfare check for the Union County Department of Social Services. This interview took place three days *before* the Dragonfly interviews, which were on 6 August.

I have clear memories of her visit because I was so apprehensive about it. The stakes had been higher than any swim-meet medal – this lady would take me away if I couldn't remember the correct answers.

When she'd arrived, Sheila Tyler chose the dining room inside the front door to interview me. If she had explored Bobby Martens' house further, she would have seen that the entire ground floor was open plan. The dining room had no door and the kitchen was behind the wall. The social worker couldn't see anyone, but

I knew Molly and Sharon were listening in the kitchen and could hear everything.

Sheila Tyler had taken statements from Jack and me that were similar to the ones we would give in The Dragonfly House. We answered all the same questions they would ask later in the week, and we gave similar answers. I said my dad 'is angry on a regular basis'. I still spoke about Dad in the present tense, and 'on a regular basis' is not a typical phrase for an eight-year-old.

Tiredness had weighed me down throughout the interview. I had been stressed and worried all day, waiting for her visit. I'd just wanted to go to bed. I've seen the department's reports, and they state the social worker didn't arrive until 5.45 p.m.

Sleep became my refuge after Dad died. I couldn't wait for the day to end. I just wanted to go to bed. And every morning, I'd wake with the same desperate wish: *Please, let Daddy be here. Please, let it not be real.* But the waking nightmare continued, no matter how much I yearned for it to be different.

Sheila Tyler believed she arrived at Bobby Martens' house unannounced. The Department of Social Services also said her arrival was unannounced. The Supreme Court emphasised this when it overturned the Martens' murder convictions. They said the Martens couldn't have coached Jack and me because the visit was unexpected.

However, official call logs from the Department of Social Services showed their beliefs were incorrect. The social services in my home county called Bobby Martens to tell him that a social worker from his county would be calling to interview us. The call logs also verified my clear memory of that day. When I finally saw the logs, the paperwork confirmed calls to the Martens began at 11.00 a.m. on 3 August.

The documentation also stated that social services told the Martens that they were about to arrive. The social worker had turned up that evening, thirty-nine hours after our father had died. The Martens had plenty of opportunity to coach us but, in reality, Molly had been coaching Jack and me for years. It appears to me there was a communication error between the two counties. Union County sent social worker Sheila Tyler at the request of Davidson County, which is located hours away. Union County did not announce the call. However, Davidson County informed the Martens multiple times, as reflected in the DSS records.

At the sentencing hearing, the prosecution reminded Judge Hall that we had recanted the allegations about our father made to social workers after we'd returned to Ireland. Assistant DA Alan Martin also said that my brother and I made fresh statements to detectives in 2021, recanting our allegations again. I spent seven hours recording that statement, which has yet to be heard.

Jack was reminded of Molly's cruelty when her attorney Douglas Kingsbery introduced a screenshot of missed calls from him to Molly after we'd returned to Ireland. He tried calling in early 2016, by which time Tom and Molly had already been indicted on second-degree murder charges. Jack had tried to call Molly from a friend's mobile phone. When he couldn't reach her, he left a voicemail: 'Hi Mom, this is Jack. This cannot go public. I miss you, and I still love you. Keep fighting really hard.'

People might think it odd that he sent a secret message to the woman who had shattered his life. But I had no problem understanding it. It was simple: Jack was eleven years old and he missed her. Tracey and David had been careful to shield us from all the details of Dad's killing. Jack's dad had just died and, despite what he endured living with her, Molly was the only mother he'd known. He'd worshipped her as a child and felt a deep emotional bond with her.

Contact with Molly and North Carolina had ended abruptly, but our attachment bond had remained strong and persistent. He'd urged her to 'keep fighting' because he needed to feel that someone in his old world cared enough to want him. Like me, Jack was feeling a range of conflicting emotions, including love, confusion, loyalty, dependency and, especially, homesickness. He missed his home, especially his friends, and life with Dad and Molly in North Carolina. I understand all the mixed feelings that drove his desire to reconnect. I had experienced them myself. My father was buried close to our house in Ireland, but memories of him were still in North Carolina.

It was difficult for Jack to hear his message in the courtroom because it was deeply personal, and it had been years since he'd sent it. And a special kind of pain comes from betrayal by those who are supposed to love you. He realised how little he'd meant to Molly that she could betray his trust as a child and air a childish plea to keep fighting for him. He'd felt more comfortable making his Victim Impact Statement after that. Even today, he still feels guilty about trying to contact Molly. He feels like he betrayed his father and his family.

I'd lied in an effort to stay with Molly, and Jack had attempted to reach her many months later. I'm sure a professional could better explain what had motivated us, but our actions showed the lasting nature of a child's attachments. Day four of the sentencing hearing was a stark reminder for Jack and me that children often seek comfort in the familiar, even if that familiarity is toxic.

The efforts to reconnect were not all one-way, however. Weeks after we had arrived back in Ireland, and Jack and I celebrated our ninth and eleventh birthdays respectively, Tracey received a call from a company at Shannon Airport. They said Molly wanted to charter a plane and fly a banner over our new school in Limerick. It would read: 'Jack and Sarah, Happy Birthday, Love Mommy.'

The company carried out their due diligence before accepting the contract and realised it wasn't appropriate to involve two minors at the centre of a recent custody battle.

The Martens also tried to place half-page adverts in the local newspaper, *Limerick Leader*, but the newspaper also refused to accept their business. Molly still, unfortunately, was given airtime on a live radio show in Ireland when she was 'a person of interest' in the investigation into my dad's killing. The general public responded by flooding social media with complaints and urging listeners to boycott the show.

Molly continued trying to reach us on social media, even sending friend requests to classmates to try to glean information. She left her phone number and contact details on social media for us. In one message, she wrote: 'I will never stop loving you. I am sorry that we do not share our genetics. We shared our lives and I was the person chosen to be your mom. I was the person you called "Mom" for eight years. You will always be my children. You are my heart and soul.' To be clear, Molly was in my life as an au pair, then as my father's girlfriend and then mother figure over a total of six years.

I had no phone, but Molly contacted a girl who sat beside me in school. Jack's classmates were targeted. Other families and teens in our area received unsolicited 'friend requests' from North Carolina.

Gardaí considered placing us on their Child Rescue Ireland alert system, a rapid response system for children at risk of abduction. An undercover detective carried out a security screening at Tracey and David's home. Everyone felt more secure when Molly was finally charged with second-degree murder and her passport was removed.

CHAPTER 13

TRUTH ON TRIAL

Your Honour
Who is the victim here? The Martens made my pain so much worse by trying to have the world think my dad was a bad person.

Courtroom 6, Davidson County Courthouse
Day 4: Thursday, 2 November 2023
The defence had more testimony from Department of Social Services investigator Sheila Tyler – this time what Molly had reported to her about Dad. Little that the Martens' defence team raised in the hearing could shock me after growing up with Molly. Their words upset and frustrated me because their depictions of my father as a violent wife abuser were being broadcast to the world. But I had heard versions of Molly's twisted allegations years before her legal team ever aired them. She whispered them constantly to me as a child.

Molly had told Sheila Tyler that our dad would force her to have sex and would place his hand over her mouth and nose so that she couldn't breathe and would pass out.

It was hard to hear this on the most public of stages, but Molly often told me stories about Dad choking her. One of my first disclosures for the District Attorney was sent by email, and the opening line reads: 'I couldn't say the words so [I] wrote them down and asked Tracey to send them ...'

Telling vile allegations to a child was part of a continued narrative where she cast Dad as a dark villain in our house. Yet, everything I saw contradicted what Molly said. She said he beat her too, yet I never saw bruises or any evidence of physical abuse inflicted on her. And she never seemed to fear Dad – instead, she screamed so much that he walked on eggshells around her. We all did. The strongest response I ever recall was when she beat his chest in anger in front of Jack and I. Dad would hold her two hands to his chest, pleading with her to calm down and stop.

Yet, her terrible tales of victimhood continued. One day, I saw blood on the bathroom seat in Molly's ensuite and spotted used sanitary pads in the waste bin.

'What happened?' I asked, appalled. I knew nothing about periods, so all I saw was a chaotic, bloody scene.

'Your dad raped me,' she said. 'He does it all the time.'

I didn't understand the word 'rape', so she explained it was when someone stuck a knife into a woman and cut their insides. She once used a carrot to demonstrate what it was to me. I was six. I knew Daddy wouldn't do that, but the blood seemed like evidence. The unwavering conviction with which she told these tales and the vivid details she shared unsettled me. She made me second-guess myself and my dad and doubt the evidence of my own eyes. I never knew what to believe.

I believe she was trying to isolate me from my dad and make me more dependent on her. She did a good job of it. But my world warped and shifted according to her moods and manipulations, often leaving me disoriented. As a child, I was frequently trapped between Molly's persuasive tales on one side and gut instinct and evidence on the other. The latter won out, and I never believed what she said about Dad. I hoped Judge Hall would see the evidence and feel the same.

Sheila Tyler's evidence about Molly's choking claim was vital because it dovetailed perfectly with the narrative that her counsel had already outlined: that our birth mom had died in mysterious circumstances and strangulation was 'a possibility'.

The defence produced Molly's statement to Sheila Tyler claiming she had been choked. Tom claimed he had seen Molly being choked. To complete a perfect trilogy of choking scenes, they needed to prove that my father had choked and murdered his first wife – or at least, they needed to prove that Tom and Molly had reason to believe that he had.

The state responded with an expert to refute the defence's narrative that Dad had killed my birth mom. Jack spent a lot of time trying to get our mom's 2006 medical files and post-mortem report from University Hospital Limerick and the Limerick coroner. However, all our efforts to get them to America backfired.

Even if the defence couldn't shock me, the state evidence did.

My mom's recorded cause of death was 'an acute cardiorespiratory attack following a bronchospasm in a known asthmatic'.

The state expert, Dr George Nichols, a former chief medical examiner from Kentucky, appeared via video link on the afternoon of the fourth day and his evidence was incendiary.

He shredded the post-mortem report that we'd sent from Ireland and said the doctor who had carried out the post-mortem was 'completely wrong'. He insisted that my birth mom's respiratory system was not thoroughly examined, nor were her eyes, mouth, throat or neck.

'There is no cause-of-death evidence here at all. There is nothing we can go on that has killed this woman. There is no determined cause of death.' He also said there was 'a whole bunch of stuff missing' from the post-mortem.

When the defence put it to Dr Nichols that my birth mom's death could be homicide, he answered, 'Correct'. He said he couldn't rule anything in or out.

There was a loud intake of breath when he said this, and I sat there stunned, knowing it was farcical.

He did add the important caveat, 'It is possible, but it is nowhere close to probable.' But his clarification didn't matter to my dad's good reputation.

As soon as Dr Nichols had said there was a 'possibility' of homicide, the defence had a ball that they could run with.

Dad wasn't able to defend himself and the prosecution didn't counter the evidence with witnesses. The defence had also sent the post-mortem and medical reports to their experts, who were due to give testimony in the following days.

However, a prosecution witness saying my birth mom definitively did not die of an asthma attack was a great bonus to the Martens' defence team. Dr Nichols' evidence captured all the headlines and news reports that day and the next. Dad emerged as a potential killer instead of the reality – a heartbroken widower left with two small children.

We were fully aware that this representation of my birth mom's death was ludicrous and easily refuted. Both the defence and the prosecution were well aware of it. Yet, no one mentioned that my birth mom's sister had witnessed the tragedy unfolding that night. This crucial evidence was never raised before Judge Hall, the assembled media or anyone in the courtroom. We sat there saddened and exasperated but powerless.

'Why?' I asked the prosecution, during the lunch break. I wanted this nonsense about my birth mom to stop. As part of a plea-bargain agreement, the state could only produce evidence with the agreement of the defence. And the truth didn't suit the defence's preferred depiction of events. Aunt Catherine had lived with my dad and my birth mom and was there on the evening when my birth mom died. She was willing to travel to North Carolina to testify but her testimony was never requested. I believe that if the defence had known she was willing to testify, it would have undermined their plan to suggest that my dad killed my birth mom.

I sat in the courtroom mute, knowing the truth but unable to say a word. My birth mom had asthma – Jack and I have inherited the same condition. My parents were only three years married when my birth mother had her severe attack, which caused respiratory failure and her heart to stop on the evening of 21 November 2006.

My aunt Catherine was woken by Dad looking for help. However, when an inhaler and nebuliser had failed to improve my birth mom's condition, she must have had an inkling of her fate. Struggling to breathe, she'd told Catherine that she feared she was about to die.

Dad was on the phone to emergency services, but they were slow to arrive. To hasten medical help, he'd helped my birth mom into the car and sped to an agreed meeting spot with the ambulance crew. Catherine had remained behind, looking after me, a newborn, and a sleeping two-year-old Jack.

Mom had continued to deteriorate and she collapsed in the car. Dad had revived her with CPR, and she was alive when the ambulance crew rushed her to Limerick Regional Hospital. My father gave chase in his car. However, all the care and haste were in vain because she stopped breathing again in the ambulance. Grim-faced medics at the hospital delivered the news that my mother had lost her battle for life at 2.00 a.m. on 21 November 2006.

Friends and family gathered with my dad in the hospital, united in disbelief. I've been told that my father's anguish was heartbreaking to witness. No one, not my mom's family, not the doctors, nor the coroner, ever considered her death as anything but a tragedy. Those who knew Dad best said a light left him that night. He was never the same again.

Tracey said she knew she could find Dad in Castlemungret Cemetery most lunchtimes. She remembers him leaning against Mom's headstone, eating his lunch, reading the newspaper to his late wife and filling her in on all the latest news about Jack and me.

Dr Nichols' opinion, and those of the other supposed expert witnesses, will never change what I believe. I know my birth mother died as the result of an asthma attack. She suffered from asthma, and she'd recognised that she was having an asthma attack. My father had recognised an asthma attack. Her sister Catherine had recognised it. The ambulance doctors and a coroner had agreed that it was an asthma attack. None of the so-called experts who claimed otherwise ever met my mother and none was present that night.

Contrary to Dr Nichols' assertions, I'm also confident the Irish doctors involved in treating my mother and carrying out her post-mortem were also perfectly competent. If there were bruising or markings on my mother's neck, gardaí would have been notified.

However, the defence's version of events dominated the news cycles. We were devastated by this, but so were my birth mom's family back in Limerick. That weekend, the Fitzpatrick family made a statement, refuting all suggestions that Dad had been involved in her death.

Their statement also rubbished a claim that Tom Martens had tried to introduce in his 2017 trial about my birth mom's father. Tom said he 'was approached by Michael Fitzpatrick [since deceased], the father of Jason Corbett's first wife … [saying] he believed that Jason has caused the death of his daughter, Margaret'.

Tom initially said that this approach had occurred at Dad and Molly's 2011 wedding in Tennessee. However, my grandfather never attended that event. My grandfather went to a solicitor and made a sworn statement before he died. He said he had never discussed his daughter or her relationship with Dad with Tom. He branded Tom's statement as 'totally and utterly untrue and mischievous'. The judge ruled that Tom's statement concerning my grandfather was not admissible in the trial.

The statement from the Fitzpatrick family also maintained their firm belief that my birth mom had died because of asthma. They said they missed my dad and said he had been a part of their family for a long time, even after they lost my birth mom. They described Dad as a warm and kind person who had loved my birth mom with all his heart, and that they had always welcomed him into their home. I loved how they ended their statement: 'No amount of lies will tarnish the love Jason and Mags had for one another.'

> This week has been an extremely difficult time for all our family especially our mother, Marian. The last eight years since Jason was brutally killed have been unimaginable for our family and all the Corbett family.
>
> It has been difficult for everyone who knew Mags and Jason to hear the lies that the people who killed Jason are saying about him as a person. They are wildly inaccurate and untrue – especially the lies about how our Mags died.
>
> Mags suffered with asthma all her life. She would always have to keep her inhalers close by. She also had a nebuliser in her home and had to use it when feeling unwell.
>
> On the night she died, she used both her inhalers and the nebuliser, but they weren't helping.
>
> Mags' sister Catherine was living with Jason and Mags at the time of her death and was present the night she passed. Jason woke Catherine and he also rang an ambulance.
>
> Jason put Mags in the car and rushed to meet the ambulance on the way. Jason revived Mags before he met the ambulance.
>
> He did everything he could to save the person he absolutely adored, and our family have always been grateful for how he tried to save her.

A TIME FOR TRUTH

Previous to our father's death in 2016, our family were informed that the killers were going to state that our dad said something to them about Mags' death, which he never did. Our father, Michael, went to a solicitor to write an affidavit to set the record straight on their lies. Firstly, Michael Fitzpatrick never said what they claim he did and, secondly, he was never alone with that person to have ever said it.

We were heartbroken when Mags died. She was the rock in our family, the one we all turned to. She was a great daughter, wonderful sister, loyal friend and a loving wife and mother. We will always miss her, but we are extremely grateful to have so many great memories with Mags. We also miss Jason dearly, who was a part of our family for a long time, even after we all lost Mags, and he was always welcomed into our home.

Jason was a warm and kind person who loved Mags more than anything else in life. We want to set the record straight and let the world know what the truth is. We know how much Jason loved and adored our Mags. We hope the facts and truth will speak for themselves, and no amount of lies will tarnish the love Jason and Mags had for one another.

My grandmother, aunts and uncles – Marian, Michael Jr, Catherine, Sean, Thomas and Sarah Fitzpatrick – all signed the statement.

CHAPTER 14

SPANISH POINT

Your Honour
He was supposed to watch me grow up. He was supposed to be there when I felt like nobody else was.

Winston-Salem, North Carolina
November 2023
My fondest memories with Dad surfaced as I worked on my Victim Impact Statement. Being with Dad on Spanish Point beach in Clare one wet day was a favourite memory of mine. We came back to Ireland twice the year before he died. I vividly recall how my hair had whipped around my head as I faced the headlong winds. My small hand was clasped in Dad's larger one. The gusts were armed with darting spikes of rain and the waves crashed hard onto the shoreline. The beach stretched before us under a vast expanse of steel grey sky, and it was deserted. It was just Dad and me.

'Do you want to head back, Sar?' Dad said, glancing down at

me. But I wanted to walk further, enjoying a rare opportunity to have Dad to myself.

I was seven and *The Little Mermaid* was my favourite movie then. I pretended the seaweed on the beach was the film's evil witch, Ursula. Each time I stood on seaweed, she trapped my foot. The only way to get free was for Dad to lift me out. *Whoosh!* He swept me up, freeing me from Ursula's clutches, and I squealed with delight.

Large figures approached at speed through the drizzle and sea haze. Several horses, their powerful forelegs churning up the wet sand, galloped towards us.

'Look, Dad!' I said, transfixed at the unfolding scene.

The jockeys were crouched low and the horses' nostrils snorted with exertion. They passed us with a thunderous pounding of hooves that shook the ground. My heart raced with exhilaration at the experience, and my eyes shone with a new light.

'Dad,' I said, full of wonder. 'I want to do that. I want to ride like that.'

'Well,' he laughed, 'we'll have to look into lessons when we get home.'

My gaze was still following the shapes disappearing into the distance. I've never forgotten the thrill of those horses galloping on Spanish Point beach, and the sight ignited a passion for horses that still burns in me today.

That entire holiday to Ireland with Dad was magical. He had only told Tracey that we were coming home, so we arrived on a surprise visit. I still remember walking into Nana's house and seeing tears start to roll down her face.

'Am I dreaming? Are you real?' she cried.

Molly didn't travel with us, making our stay relaxing and peaceful. Dad, Jack and I exhaled and enjoyed every minute of the holiday with Dad's family.

Dad held many fond memories of the beach at Spanish Point. All his family spent their summer holidays there. Whenever we came home from America, we visited and relived some of his favourite childhood days.

He and Mom got married in Our Lady Star of the Sea church nearby and had their reception in Spanish Point. They brought me there on my first holiday. We have a photograph of Dad holding me at four weeks old in a summer house they'd rented that overlooked the beach. Dad hoped to instil in his children the same love of the area that he had in his children – and he succeeded.

Dad never liked to sit around. Even though it was raining that afternoon, he wanted to get out for a walk, but no one wanted to go to the beach apart from me. After we saw the horses, the sky darkened even more, and fat droplets of rain fell. The shower intensified into a real downpour. We spotted dark openings in the weathered rocks bordering the beach and ran for shelter in a cave. Inside, we found an old couple already sheltering with their little Yorkshire terrier.

In the musty scent of dripping seaweed and stone, Dad and I chatted with the couple and ruffled the dog's wet fur until the rainstorm cleared. Afterwards, we headed back to the holiday cottage, where we changed out of our rain-soaked clothes. I told everyone about our adventure with the horses and the cave.

That afternoon may have been one of the first times I'd got to hang out with my dad without feeling bad for doing it. I could relax without getting dark looks from Molly for going with Dad rather than staying with her. That afternoon is one of my most cherished memories of spending time alone with Dad.

Later that year, Tracey called Dad on my mother's anniversary, 21 November, to let him know she was thinking of us. Dad was feeling homesick, and Tracey told me she cajoled and coaxed him into considering returning. Shortly after, Dad announced we were returning to Ireland for Christmas. Molly came too this time. Every Christmas was great, but it was an extra treat to celebrate with all the family in Ireland, especially my grandparents.

Christmas 2014 – our last with Dad – was extra special to me.

I bounded down the stairs in Tracey and David's home on Christmas morning with no idea that I would soon spend every 25 December with them. The fire blazed, and my dad was happy, surrounded by his children and family.

When we opened our gifts, I tore through the wrapping paper, and there, nestled in tissue, lay a black-velvet riding hat.

Molly had started bringing me to riding lessons in America so, by the end of 2014, I'd become obsessed with horses, and begged for a pony every birthday and Christmas. (I was fourteen before I realised it would never happen.)

But there were more gifts, a large box containing a pair of polished, black-leather riding boots. They were several sizes too big for me – Dad had made sure I wouldn't grow out of them in a hurry, and I was twelve before they did fit me. I didn't care. I pulled them on under my Christmas dress and placed the riding hat on my head. Dad told me I missed something in the box. I squealed as I found a riding crop with a red-leather handle. It matched the roses on my hat. Dad had gone to a saddler and bought all the accessories for my riding lessons.

We have a photograph taken at Tracey and David's house with me on their coffee table, wearing my horse-riding gear. Tracey and I were singing karaoke – 'Poker Face' by Lady Gaga. In the photo, I can see Dad laughing in the background. He was always happiest when he was with family.

That was the last time Nana, Granda, Tracey, David and the Corbett family, apart from Wayne, saw Dad.

When Tracey and David brought Jack and me back to Ireland, they were aware of my obsession with horses. They took me horse riding in Clarina in Limerick soon after I arrived. They didn't bring me specifically for equine-therapy classes, but horse riding became a form of therapy, nonetheless.

Just being around horses was calming. I only had to catch the scent of the horses and the sounds of their hooves and snorts to relax. Resting my head against a horse's velvety muzzle and stroking it was like a natural tranquilliser. Even grooming the horses – working the curry comb in small rhythmic circles across a horse's coat – made every worry melt away.

As soon as I swung into the saddle, I had to focus on posture, reins and aligning myself with the horse's rhythm. My head had no space to think of anything else. By the time I finished a lesson, I felt transformed and any anxieties that had plagued me disappeared. I left those riding lessons with a restful affection for my horse, whether it was Lizzie, Ruby or my favourite, Millie, a big, white, beautiful Connemara pony. I forgot about everything when I got to the stables.

My biggest hero is JP McManus, not only for his altruism but also for his beautiful horses. I was honoured to sing for him and meet him a few times, including once when I had dinner with Tracey in Adare. While we were there, he spoke to me, and for once in my life, I got completely tongue-tied. I had just completed a project in school where I chose him as the subject. Horses continue to be a passion of mine.

From that day on the beach with Dad, it became a dream to ride a horse on the sandy shores of west Clare. I wanted to splash through seawater shallows, kicking up the waves, and feeling the wild freedom that I imagined those jockeys had felt that day. Tracey helped me fulfil that dream for my thirteenth birthday.

Spanish Point remains a special place for all the Corbett family. Recently, Tracey and I stayed a night in the same hotel where my parents had had their wedding reception. Mom and Dad were the first couple to marry in the Bellbridge House, a family-run hotel overlooking the Atlantic Ocean.

While there, I went for a stroll while Tracey was on a work call. Gusts whipped across the wet beach and dark clouds threatened overhead. A few surfers rode the crashing waves, but otherwise, the beach was empty. As I walked, the memories of being with my father came rushing back.

The rain started pelting down, just as it had done that day with Dad. Concerned for my earphones, I ran for shelter. I spotted several dark openings in the rocks and went for one.

As my eyes adjusted, I realised I was standing in the same cave that I'd sheltered in with Dad all those years earlier. I had been to Spanish Point beach many times since and never found it again until that day. As the rainstorm ended, I went to leave, and an old couple with a Yorkshire terrier walked past.

I looked towards the sky, smiled and said, 'Hi, Dad!'

My mom and dad, Mags and Jason, on their wedding day – Dad framed this photo for me and it sat on my bedside table when I was a child.

Dad was loving, kind, gentle and always did everything he could to make us smile – he really loved being a dad.

We moved to North Carolina when I was four years old – the hot summer evenings and the sound of crickets outside my window took a bit of getting used to!

It was so important to Dad that we kept my birth mother's memory alive – here, Jack and I are releasing balloons on her anniversary, an annual tradition. Dad said she was always watching over us.

Losing Dad was incredibly difficult for our whole family. Jack and I were very lucky to be brought to a safe, loving home with them in Ireland – Dad's absence is constant but there have been happy times too.

Since returning from North Carolina, I have had to learn a lot about how to process grief and trauma – Tracey has been there for me every step of the way. Because of her, I now know what it's like to have a loving mother.

Writing has been such a gift to me over the years, always encouraged by Tracey, helping me to process many complicated feelings. My aim with my book, Noodle Loses Dad, *was to help other children like me who had experienced grief and loss and I was really lucky to appear on The Late Late Show to spread the word about it.*
(Credit for image [l]: Liam Burke/Press 22)

I have discovered remarkable communities in my hometown of Limerick and in County Clare, feeling embraced by those places and supported by my family. In 2019, the same year Noodle Loses Dad *was published, I received the Limerick Person of the Month award, followed by a National Garda Youth Award, which marked a truly proud moment in my life.*

Returning to North Carolina was difficult each time, but we always made time to remember Dad when we were there, an important part of healing for all of us. Here's me and Jack in 2020 with the memorial plaque placed by my dad's colleagues outside his former workplace.

And at the balloon release ceremony we held in Lexington in October 2023, I was able to meet Clay Dagenhardt again, the police officer who shielded me from the horrific scene and carried me downstairs. I can't thank him enough.

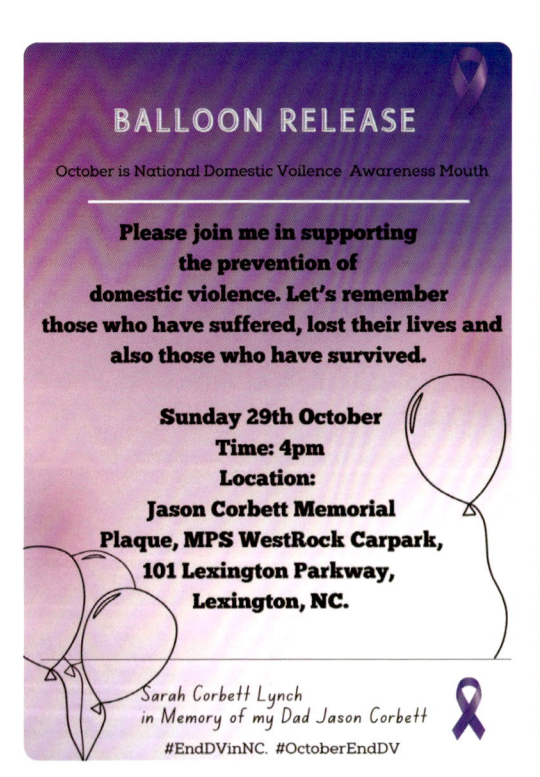

I lost my passion for swimming as a child due to the pressure that surrounded it but since leaving the US, I've gradually fallen in love with it again. Here I am in Kilkee having just enjoyed a refreshing swim in the sea.

And my rediscovery of swimming has turned into a love of diving! Big thanks to a fantastic group of people in Kilkee – especially Joe, Ger, Phil, Mary and Cillian – who mentored and trained me. In November 2024, I achieved my qualification as a commercial and surface-supplied diver with An Bord Iascaigh Mhara. (Credit: Cillian Gray)

Jack and I have been through so much together, and we're lucky to have two older brothers in Adam and Dean who are always ready with support and advice. And Tracey and David are such loving parents – they have taught me the true meaning of family. Here we are at David and Tracey's vow renewal in 2018. (Credit: Dermot Culhane)

And our family is growing! Here's us celebrating Christmas in 2023 with Dean's wife Kelly and my nephew Max.

CHAPTER 15

LADIES' DAY

Your Honour

I would like to give you an example of how our truth is being twisted. When Ms Shannon Grubb testified about the park incident where I had no shoes going to school, there was no fight with my dad. My dad had already gone to work well before we got up for school. Molly had beaten Jack again, and that is why I was hysterical ...

I know what Molly Martens is capable of – I remember. I remember I was encouraged to be disrespectful to Dad, to call him fat, but I still felt comfortable enough to shout and express myself at my dad because I did not fear him.

Courtroom 6, Davidson County Courthouse
Day 5: Friday, 3 November 2023
Molly's friends dominated day five of the hearing, telling tales of whispered confessions, tears and brutality. Together, the five women tried to depict Molly's life as one of fear and martyrdom.

They spoke about how she lived under the tyranny of an abusive husband and suffered a troubled marriage for Jack's sake and mine.

The prosecution pointed out that investigators had taken fifty statements from Dad and Molly's neighbours and friends. Only five of these fifty witnesses were called by the defence – and all were Molly's women friends. They were also the only people to question the detectives' accuracy in taking statements. According to state counsel, four of the five women had requested changes to their police statements after they had made them.

Shannon Grubb, our neighbour in Meadowlands, was one of the five women. Two weeks after Molly had killed Dad, Shannon had also testified for Molly during the guardianship hearing for Jack and me, describing her as a 'supermom'.

The house that Shannon and her husband Charlie had lived in when we first moved to Meadowlands was diagonal to our home. They had two children, Ashlyn and Cassidy, who were the same age as Jack and me. Shannon told how we often carpooled together to sports events, like swimming and gymnastics. Our two families even holidayed together.

Shannon was Molly's ride-or-die pal. Dad also regarded Charlie as a trusted friend, so it felt like a complete betrayal when Charlie didn't stand by Dad. It hurt to see him sit on the Martens' side in court. Dad and Charlie had been close. I couldn't have done what Charlie did if I were to lose a close friend.

Shannon testified that she saw Molly pulling a bloody tissue from under the brim of a beanie hat, and Molly told her she and Dad had been in a fight.

'I said that this cannot continue,' Shannon recounted. 'She's going to get hurt or worse than that if this abuse goes on. She said she would not leave the kids.'

The pertinent words throughout her testimony were 'she said'. Molly said a lot of things, and as the state counsel pointed out that day, a lot of what she said was untrue.

From watching court scenes on TV shows, I'd always believed indirect evidence was known as 'hearsay' and was inadmissible in a court case. However, we heard a lot of hearsay from Molly's friends that day.

Shannon said they'd hired a limo one time for a social event and, when Molly got out on one side of the limo, it seemed to anger Dad.

'He grabbed her and yanked her to the side, and there was a disagreement about something. I asked what it was about and [Molly] said he felt that she got out of the car to the side where other men would be noticing her in her dress. He was just very jealous.'

Once again, we heard those significant words 'Molly said'.

Shannon had also received a call from Molly's phone at 1.01 a.m. on 12 October 2014. She heard Dad and Molly screaming and yelling and Molly crying, 'Stop, please don't do this to us.'

Shannon thought it might have been Jack or me calling. She said she and her husband debated whether or not to call the police, but whoever was calling hung up after four minutes. To me, it indicated what they heard didn't concern them that much. The following day, she called Molly, who said she was embarrassed Shannon had overheard the incident.

'I just said she needed to get some outside help,' she said, agreeing with the defence counsel that Molly didn't want to leave Jack and me.

Neither Jack nor I called the Grubbs that night. Even if we wanted to, we were never allowed near Molly's phone. So I have to wonder, who else in the house wanted Shannon to hear that altercation?

Shannon related a story to the court about how Molly rang her one morning, tearfully asking for a pair of her daughter's shoes for me to wear. Molly said she had fled from Dad after a fight in the house. She was afraid to return home for my school shoes.

'When I met her in the park to give her the shoes, Sarah was hysterical, crying. She didn't want Molly to go back home without her,' she said.

In the courtroom, I shook my head vigorously and mouthed, 'That's not true.' I didn't care if the judge saw me.

I could recall every detail of that morning. Molly was in one of her rages, screaming at Jack and beating him. Suddenly realising she had to get me to school, she grabbed me by the arm and shoved me in the car. As we were driving towards the school, Molly saw I was still in my socks. I had been too afraid to say anything.

Just as Shannon said, Molly rang her, asking her to bring her daughter's shoes. We met Shannon in the park, where she was waiting with pink ballerina shoes that I discovered were two sizes too big for me.

Molly spun her story about fighting with my dad even though Dad had left for work hours earlier. Shannon accurately described me as hysterical. However, she misinterpreted my tears. I didn't want Molly to return home without me, but it had nothing to do with Dad. I feared what Molly would do to Jack if I wasn't there.

The story was another example of Molly's deceptions. She used Shannon and the other women to lay a breadcrumb trail of supposed domestic-abuse incidents.

Molly also told Shannon that getting up to look after us at night had led to arguments with Dad.

'He would say he didn't want her getting up, and I think the word he used was "coddle". He didn't want her coddling the kids. They would fight about it,' Shannon said in court.

Yet again, we heard more of the 'Molly said' testimony. Dad 'coddled' us often, and I never once heard him object to Molly doing the same.

In cross-examination, Shannon admitted that she had changed her original statement. Assistant DA Marissa Parker put it to Shannon that she hadn't been aware that Molly would get to read her police statement.

Marissa Parker said that Molly, enraged by the Grubbs' statements, had told a mutual friend and neighbour that Shannon was 'naïve'. She also said Shannon's statement 'made no sense'. Molly had then confronted Shannon, accusing her of being on 'Tracey's side'.

We have never heard what Shannon said in her original statement that annoyed Molly so much. However, Shannon and Charlie contacted detectives to say that they wanted to change their statements. Shannon insisted she only changed her statement because of errors in her original statement, not because of pressure from Molly.

Under cross-examination, Shannon said she never saw Dad hitting Molly. She also denied hearing Molly abuse Dad in social situations, calling him 'fat' and 'Meatloaf'.

The last party Dad attended before he died was at Shannon and Charlie's house in Meadowlands. The Grubbs had moved from beside us to a larger house further up the road. He only had thirty-six hours left to live when we all went to the Grubbs' new house on the estate on Friday, 31 July 2015.

In the months before Dad was killed, the atmosphere in our house was tense. Things were particularly icy in the last days, especially after Molly jumped into my bed and accused Dad of murdering my birth mom. But Molly linked her arm with my father's outside the house and, as usual, they walked in smiling as if nothing was wrong.

Even after a marathon blazing row, when Molly's voice became hoarse from shouting, a remarkable transformation often took place, and they could suddenly morph into a vision of marital bliss. Molly would nudge herself under Dad's arm, and they'd arrive to friends' homes with arms draped around each other or they'd walk in somewhere, holding hands.

People in the neighbourhood often got together for barbecues and Super Bowl or 'corn hole' parties – a game where players aimed bags of corn kernels at a hole in a plank. We holidayed with neighbours at Myrtle Beach one time.

Every time, Dad and Molly portrayed the perfect image of a happily married couple. We all wore a mask when we left the house. Outside, it was like the arguing never happened and we became the picture-perfect family.

I liked it when we were out in public. In front of friends, colleagues and neighbours, the Corbetts *were* the perfect family. I liked it. Appearing like a normal family for a while was nice, even if it was all fake.

But Molly couldn't always keep the mask in place and often humiliated Dad in public. It was usually a jibe about his weight.

'Maybe leave a few burgers for someone else, Jay,' she might say.

Or she'd quip, 'Look at Meatloaf piling his plate again!'

She hurled these barbs as a joke, and Dad brushed them off good-humouredly, but the comments were unnecessary. I felt bad for Dad, and they made other people feel uncomfortable.

That Friday, we entered the Grubbs' new house as the perfect family. Our neighbours had a vast open-plan kitchen and a games room with a darts board, pool table and shuffleboard. The garden was enormous and strung with atmospheric fairy lights.

All summer, I had been swimming with Molly, so I was relieved to run around with other neighbourhood kids for a change. We played games like Marco Polo, hide and seek, and bulldog takedown. We also drank a cherry soda drink called Cheerwine, a real Southern favourite. Jack joined the older kids playing EA Sports video games inside.

I saw Dad playing shuffleboard with the guys for a while and Molly chatting with the other women. Later, when I found Dad and Molly, the smiles and all the happy pretence had disappeared. Dad's expression was emotionless, and I heard him say, 'Stop, just stop. We can talk about this at home, Mol.'

A neighbour wrote to Tracey shortly after Dad was killed and said Molly had made nasty comments about Dad and his weight in front of their friends. 'She was belittling him, calling him a fat ass, saying that he must have taken all the nutrition from his twin because he looked like he had eaten for two.'

The neighbour said Dad 'seemed down, not like himself'. She added that Molly and Dad's marriage was one of the topics of conversation at the party. 'Some had heard that Jason had asked for a divorce three weeks before,' she wrote.

We left the Grubbs' party early, with Dad carrying me on the short journey home.

'Isn't your dad such a big meatloaf, Sarah?' Molly said when we were outside. 'Doesn't he look like a big meatloaf?'

My head was on Dad's shoulder and I pretended to be asleep so that I didn't have to answer. Dad just kept walking with me back to our house. He said nothing. I don't remember Molly coming home with us so she may have gone back into the party.

Molly often tried to persuade me to be disrespectful to Dad. She liked to sing 'our' special song about him all the time. She sang it to the tune of a jingle for an auto-shop company advert that played non-stop on radio.

But her lyrics went: 'Big fatso, meanie weeny, just won't stop until he's auto shot.' She liked to sing it in the car and urged me to do to same.

'Sarah, join in!' she'd say.

Or she'd pause for me to complete the lyrics. 'Big fatso ... Sarah, come on. What's next?'

To my shame, I did join in. I had little choice, but the memory now is upsetting. She never sang this within earshot of Dad – it was 'our' private song. I'm just relieved Dad never heard it or the disrespect his wife tried to instil in his child.

During the hearing, Shannon denied ever hearing Molly's abusive remarks about Dad at her party or elsewhere.

Marissa Parker continued her cross-examination of Shannon by questioning Molly's credibility. She said that Molly had made a series of untrue statements. However, Shannon said that she was unaware of any lies. She insisted that she never saw the flyers distributed around Meadowlands on which Molly had claimed she was part of Clemson University's swim team.

Molly did indeed secure a place at the prestigious college after high school. She can be seen in Clemson University's yearbook as a freshman in 2003. However, former college friends said she failed her social-studies classes and never returned after the Thanksgiving break in the first semester. In media interviews, Molly said she'd dropped out because she was suffering from mononucleosis (glandular fever).

Marissa Parker told Shannon that Molly had invented a sister who died from cancer during that semester in Clemson. In media interviews, Molly's co-ed housemates recalled how she kept a photo of this 'sister' who had died from leukaemia. However, a student who went to stay at the Martens' Knoxville home soon discovered that Molly was an only girl. When dorm friends inspected Molly's photograph, they realised it was a stock photo that was sold with the frame.

Molly continued to propagate the lie about her non-existent dead sister. Six years later, she spoke about this sister again in an email to Dad after what she claimed was a betrayal on his part.

'Other than my sister's death nothing has ever devastated me so much,' she wrote. Her email was included in the prosecution's investigative records.

Her fellow college students noticed other odd behaviour. In these interviews, a student recalled returning to their shared dorm to find Molly, fully clothed, eating chips under a running shower.

They remembered Molly calling their dorm months after she had left college, claiming to be attending the University of Tennessee, saying she was on the cheerleading team. She also said she had travelled somewhere with the team, and it had rained. Several students were on the call and, while she was still on the phone, they started googling her claims.

'I remember that vividly because we even checked the weather for the day she was talking about, and there was no rain,' one former student said. 'We looked up the cheerleading team squad pic and she wasn't on it.'

Marissa Parker detailed more of Molly's lies, including her claims on another occasion to have been the editor of a magazine in Ireland. She also claimed that she had once been a foster mother, and told my father when he hired her that she was a qualified Montessori teacher who had been vetted as a foster parent.

State counsel told the courtroom that Molly had claimed she was my birth mother. We learned during investigations before the Martens' 2017 trial that Molly had regaled her Bible study group with stories concerning her pregnancy with me. Neighbours in the Bible study group, who knew that Jack and I were not Molly's natural children, had been stunned to hear her talk about her stretch marks and an episiotomy. The women had eyed each other nervously, but no one had raised that red flag with Dad.

The Assistant DA told Shannon that Molly had even woven a web of deception for her bridesmaids in 2011. Dad's friend Paul overheard a bridesmaid gushing about how Molly was fulfilling my birth mom's last wish. He was stunned and asked what she was talking about. The bridesmaid explained that Molly and Mags were pen pals and that, before dying, Mags had asked Molly to look after her kids. The bridesmaid thought Molly's story was romantic, but it shocked Paul who knew my birth mom did not know Molly at all.

For this and many other reasons, Paul tried to dissuade Dad from marrying Molly. Even afterwards, when my dad was leaving with his new bride, Paul reminded Dad of his happiness when he had married Mags and how miserable he looked after marrying Molly.

'You don't have to get into that car – you can just walk away,' he said.

Dad replied, 'It's too late', adding that he wasn't willing to take a second mother from his children.

Any time that Assistant DA Marissa Parker even mentioned Molly in the courtroom, Molly sniffed loudly in response, dabbing her eyes furiously. I never actually saw any tears, but she certainly seemed to exhibit great distress.

Marissa Parker concluded her cross-examination saying to Shannon, 'She invented a sister who died from cancer. In Bible Club, she lied about how complicated the birth of her daughter was. She claimed she helped care for Jason's first wife. She claimed Mags told her she was dying and she wanted Molly to take on the role of mother to the children. So, all those were lies. Do you have any concern for Molly's truthfulness?'

Many in the courtroom rolled their eyes when Shannon replied, 'I do not.'

Marissa Parker's loaded questions that day proved one of the most powerful rebuttals of the defence's claims. The state showed Molly had fabricated and exaggerated details and told stories that contradicted previous ones. Thankfully, the plea agreement entered into by Tom and Molly gave prosecutors the ability to attack her credibility by pointing out any of several false statements she had made.

They exposed lies piled upon more lies until they had painted a troubling portrait of someone whose relationship with the truth was tenuous at best. Yet, even after hearing all the evidence of Molly's lies, Shannon still could not recognise that she was just another pawn on Molly's chessboard.

None of the other ladies who followed her could be drawn on Molly's 'very complicated relationship with the truth' either.

CHAPTER 16

SECRETS

Your Honour
There were many times where I had to drag Molly off Jack, she was hitting him so much. One time, she was hitting him so hard that I jumped on her back, using all my body weight to pull her off him, but she grabbed me, threw me to the floor and started screaming at us both. I am telling you this to demonstrate the power and control she had over my life.

Winston-Salem, North Carolina
November 2023
Our time at the sentencing hearing brought Jack and me closer. As a very private person, I knew Jack found it more challenging to be thrust into the spotlight than I did. Suddenly, we were both under a microscope, with our personal lives dissected and twisted in a public courtroom. Yet, day after day, he walked into that courthouse with his head held high. I can't count the times I proudly thought, *That's my brother.* He insists that Mom and Dad would've been proud of me too.

I feel fortunate that we have a better relationship now because, as children, Molly was like a wedge between us, fostering competitiveness and undermining our bond as siblings. She believed in divide-and-conquer parenting, picking favourites and keeping us apart.

Oddly, she never seemed to like us playing together. She stormed into my room one day, yelling at Jack to get back to his room. Then she flung around the toys we'd been playing with and ordered me to bed when it was still daytime.

I had to be peeled from Molly as a child – we were never apart – but, as I got older, things changed. I was her golden child one day, and Jack basked in her adoration the next. On days when he was winning at swimming, he could do no wrong. When I was no longer her number-one child, I hugely resented Jack. I became the telltale who got him into trouble when I could.

Molly instilled mistrust between us with her wildly swinging affections, pitting us against each other for her love and attention. After years of Molly's emotional tug-of-war, Jack and I are picking up the pieces of our fractured relationship. We're forging the bond we were always meant to have.

We both vividly remember feeling the brunt of Molly's rages. Dad never realised what went on when he'd left for work. Jack was the target of Molly's physical abuse, and he was beaten often. He bears the physical marks to this day. She never hit me, but I bear other scars that will never fade.

The only time I didn't fear Molly was when we were in public. She always liked to play the devoted mom when we were with other people. I still knew to behave, however, because I would suffer the consequences when I got home if I didn't.

I have a vivid childhood memory of hiding in the dark from her, terrified. I was crouched in the back corner of a long, narrow walk-in wardrobe in Jack's bedroom. I concealed myself between a cream fur coat, a brown fur and a scattering of dusty suitcases. Molly was screaming for me.

'Where are you? Where are you, Sarah? I know you're here!'

My breathing was so heavy and my heart was pounding so hard that I feared they would give me away. It was summer, and it was sweltering in the dark of that wardrobe. I don't know where Dad or Jack were, but neither was home. I trembled, tears flowing silently, feeling scared for my life.

Even though the memory of cowering in the wardrobe remains vivid, I don't recall what prompted it. All I remember was feeling like Molly was hunting me and terror and isolation. I felt so alone.

However, the dynamics between Molly and Jack were even more fraught, probably because he wasn't as compliant or dependent on her as I was. She enjoyed being the number-one parent, with both of us conspicuously reliant on her, clinging and needy. When Dad suggested doing anything with me, she usually said, 'Sarah has plans with me.' When Dad's friends or family held my hand or sat me on their knees, Molly would tell me that I needed the bathroom or to help her in the kitchen. When Dad's friends or family from Ireland went on day trips, Molly would whisper, 'You don't want to go.'

'I want to stay with Molly,' I would dutifully parrot, even though I longed to go with my cousins.

Her manipulation was less successful with my brother, who asserted his independence and wasn't so easily tied to her apron strings. He wanted to go golfing with his father and go on day trips with our Irish visitors. But Molly worked hard to break his spirit and wear him down over the years. Dad's friends and family got a few brief glimpses of Molly's rages with Jack.

My birth mom's close friend, Lynn Shanahan, and her family came to visit Dad one summer. Jack got cheeky with Molly outside a restaurant in Winston-Salem.

'You're not my real mom!' he said.

Molly lost control, screaming at him on the street. She turned on Dad, then, demanding that he do something. Embarrassed, he had to walk Molly away from Lynn and her husband to calm her.

One summer afternoon, Jack and his cousins started a water fight in the garden. Amid lots of laughter and shrieking, Jack splashed Molly. He made the mistake of laughing when Molly scolded him. She picked him up, carried him inside and thrust his face under a powerful tap in our kitchen.

'Do you like that?' she demanded. 'Do you like that now? Not so much fun now, is it?'

Jack struggled and spluttered, suffocating in the relentless torrent gushing down his throat and nose. Some of his cousins cried out, and Dad, suddenly realising what was going on, leapt from his seat and ran into the kitchen. Everyone followed and saw Molly trying to hold Dad back with one hand, as she held Jack under the tap. Dad wrestled Jack from her grip as David, Marilyn, Tracey and our cousins stood watching in shock. After Dad had calmed Jack, he disappeared to his bedroom after Molly. David passed by the bedroom a while later and saw Dad, sitting alone at the edge of his bed, with his head in his hands.

However, the adults weren't always around to protect Jack from the worst of Molly's ferocious temper. While Jack was Molly's little ray of sunshine some days, there were many other days when the mere sight of him seemed to trigger something deeply hostile within her.

She once threw a sports trophy down the stairs at Jack, which struck him in the stomach. I remember gazing at Jack in shock as blood spread like a dark map across his white T-shirt – he still has a scar. She often pinched him when we were in company or underwater when he performed poorly in training. He said his eyes watered with the pain, but he knew not to make a sound. He never dared react or cry out because he knew he'd be in bigger trouble when he got home.

One day, I heard panicked screaming in the kitchen. I ran downstairs and stopped abruptly at the end of the stairs, paralysed at the scene. Jack was flailing around on the kitchen floor with Molly standing over him, mercilessly punching him. I stood frozen to the spot until Jack uttered the words, 'Sarah, please!'

Jack had never involved me or called for help before that day, but this time was different. She had lost all control. Something about his anguished cry triggered me and cut through my panic. I knew I had to protect my brother. I ran and leapt at Molly from behind, encircling her neck with my arms, trying to tug her off him.

Molly was filled with too much fury. She reached behind her, grabbed my arm and flung me to the ground beside Jack. I braced myself for punches to rain down on both of us.

Instead, she began screaming. 'Do you wanna see what your dad did to me? Do you? Do you?'

I cowered on the floor, expecting a blow or a kick at any minute as she continued to rant about Dad. Nothing she said made any sense to me.

Then it was all over and she stormed off abruptly, slamming

her bedroom door shut. I staggered shakily to my feet, but Jack continued lying curled on the floor for some time afterwards. We hardly dared exchange a word between us for fear she might hear.

Jack guards his privacy closely, but he gave me permission to tell this part of his story. It helps illustrate some of what he meant in his Victim Impact Statement when he wrote: 'I was abused by Molly Martens in every way you can imagine, and then some.'

Despite occasions like this, neither of us told Dad she was beating Jack. When Jack had cuts or bruises from Molly's beatings, he'd shrug off his injuries, telling Dad that a ball hit him or that he'd fallen and cut himself while playing sports.

I wish we had told him. If my dad had known that Molly was physically beating Jack, he would have swept us up and left her, never to return. Our lives would have been so different.

Many factors ensured my silence about what was happening in our lives. Partly, I feared what Molly might do if I betrayed her. While she never physically struck or beat me, the fear of her violence was a factor because I'd seen what she had done to Jack. Her unpredictability was what scared me the most about her.

Molly filled up every room she entered, so I was always conscious of her. Pleasing Molly and reading her moods were always my priority. I was watchful, learning that specific behaviours and routines often indicated her emotional state. I needed to be careful if Molly was in her bedroom and had shut her door. She brought me with her most of the time, and when that changed, it meant trouble. The sound of a running bathtub was not a good sign, either. She was either very sad or angry.

However, I also feared the consequences for our family if Dad found out what was happening. Like most children in troubled marriages, I sensed our family life was precarious and could easily be upended. I lived with a dread that betraying Molly might cause irreparable harm and change our family dynamics forever. Family life was on a knife edge, and telling Dad would provoke more rows and arguments between him and Molly. I didn't want to cause our family to break up.

It's hard to remember good times because so much trauma has overshadowed them, but Molly was the only mother I knew in early childhood. She and Dad were my sources of security, love, affection, support and guidance. Both Jack and I loved Molly and had strong emotional attachments to her. I felt protective of her and loyal to her and never wanted to cause her trouble.

But I was too young to grasp a lot of what was happening. Even if I'd had someone to confide in outside my immediate family, I didn't recognise the problem or know how to articulate what was happening.

Molly normalised everything and made us feel as though we deserved her punishments. I never felt resentful or angry when she yelled at me for not winning a race. Instead, I felt ashamed for failing to reach her expectations and for causing her embarrassment. Life in Panther Creek Court was my normal.

Yet, I knew something was off at home. Molly was on edge and deeply unhappy. It seemed my life and the lives of my father and brother were spent tiptoeing around her. It was accepted policy that we all did what Molly wanted. We could never fully exhale.

This tightly wound, strained existence was the only one I knew. What would I have without Dad, Molly, Jack and my princess bed in Panther Creek Court? They were my world and I wouldn't jeopardise any of it.

CHAPTER 17

MOLLY SAID

Your Honour
Molly took everything I loved away from me ... everything.

Courtroom 6, Davidson County Courthouse
Day 5: Friday, 3 November 2023
Molly's friends continued with their statements, and it was tough listening, especially as so much of it was spurious. The women often related second-hand evidence – Molly's version of events – rather than anything they had witnessed themselves.

Billie June Jacobs was another of Molly's defenders on the fifth day of the hearing. I had a confrontation with Billie June while attending the pre-trial hearing in March 2022 – my first time attending court proceedings in America for Dad.

I had just seen Molly for the first time in seven years, when one of the women accompanying her doubled back. I had recognised her as soon as she emerged from the lift with Molly. Billie June was a neighbour who became friends with Molly less than a year before Dad died. They often power walked together through the park.

Billie June approached me in the hallway of the courthouse, her head cocked to one side, a look of concern on her face. I was crying and didn't want to talk to her, but she began chatting about her daughter, a girl I didn't know. Tracey asked her to leave us alone. Afterwards, I felt angry that Billie June had thought it was okay to approach me.

'I don't want to talk to any of them,' I said.

'You don't have to,' said Tracey. 'You have a voice.'

When we entered the large courtroom, I spotted Billie June on a bench behind the Martens, and I crossed the aisle from our bench to reach her.

'I wanted to see how you were,' she said. Her expression seemed to be a picture of sympathy.

Somehow that made me more furious. 'I don't want you to speak to me ever again,' I said. 'If you want to support killers, do that, but please don't speak to me.'

Her eyes widened in response. Molly's other friend, sitting beside Billie June, went to interject. She looked vaguely familiar.

It was an empowering moment for me in the courtroom – one of very few. I was setting boundaries and was no longer that polite child whom Molly had led by the hand, dressed up and pushed around. I was an adult who could say no. I didn't want to speak to anyone who had anything to do with the Martens. And I certainly didn't need their 'sympathy'.

I once heard a great analogy explaining the difference between sympathy and empathy. Sympathy is looking down at someone in a hole, shaking your head and saying, 'Oh, that must be terrible.' Empathy is more than acknowledging someone's pain. Empathy is when you find a ladder, climb into that dark hole and say, 'I'm here with you, and I'm going to help you out.' There's a vast difference between empathy and sympathy, and the last thing I wanted was sympathy from Molly Martens' friends.

Tracey later told me that the other friend with Molly and Billie June that day was Shannon Grubb, but she had changed so much in seven years that I hadn't recognised her. Those two women were here again, centre stage again for the Martens' sentencing hearing.

Billie June gave evidence that Molly had *told her* that Dad was physically, mentally and emotionally abusive towards her. Molly had *told her* that her husband would yell at her, pull her hair, pinch her and step on her foot.

'I knew that someone would get hurt sooner or later,' Billie June said. 'It was going to come to a boiling point.'

She testified that she and Molly had confided in each other as they power walked. She said that, when they were out walking, Dad would keep calling or texting Molly, wanting to know where she was, who she was with and when she was coming back.

Dad and Molly rowed often because she never answered the phone. In the 'pancake' tape, he complained that the doctor had tried to call her with my medical report three days earlier, and she hadn't answered or called them back.

Some days, he arrived home and found the house unlocked and deserted. He returned from a work trip in April 2015 and took a video of the garage door wide open, the access into the house and the back door left unlocked. The fan was left on whirring away with lights ablaze in the mid-afternoon. The video that he recorded that day gave a glimpse of the disarray and chaos we often lived in. Other days, Dad came home to find us alone, with no sign of Molly. His attempts to call her went unanswered. He wasn't happy that she had left us unattended but he also worried about her. He was aware that she had mental-health issues that made her erratic, but he didn't know the full extent of what went on when he wasn't at home.

She often deliberately kept him in the dark about our movements. He loved to attend all our sports days and competitions, but then he started missing big swim meets and other events. On one occasion, I won a swim meet and felt particularly hurt he didn't turn up.

'Where's Dad?' I asked Molly. 'He said he was coming.'

Molly sighed. 'I don't know. He just hasn't bothered showing up again.'

He explained later that he had got the wrong date, but I was upset. Jack was also hurt when Molly told him Dad didn't bother coming.

We didn't know until later that Molly was deliberately withholding schedules and giving Dad the wrong dates or times for events. I overheard the rows, but we didn't realise what Molly was doing. Sometimes, Dad learned about our events at the last minute and arrived late and frustrated.

'Don't try to blame me when you forget your own children,' she said.

She looked like the responsible parent, the long-suffering wife of someone neglectful of his children.

We discovered, after Dad's death, that he had to email Molly in her official capacity as the team swimming coach to insist that he receive the schedule that she had sent to all the other parents.

'It is with great sadness that I now have to resort to email for communication regarding our kids,' he wrote on 25 May 2014. 'I would also like to be included in school events ... since you will not or forget to tell me, maybe copying me on email might help.'

Billie June may have heard Dad calling her repeatedly, but I wonder if Molly ever answered.

Molly had also told her that, during sex, Dad would put a pillow over her face and strangle her. 'She was afraid that what happened to Mags ... that she would not wake up one morning,' she said.

Billie June said my birth mom's name as if she had known her and had great sympathy for her. She spoke as if there was no doubt about what had happened to my birth mom in her last moments. Bringing my birth mom into the courtroom became one of the hardest things I experienced during the hearing. People who had never met her and had never known her spoke as if they cared about her. They spoke as if they were authorities on how she had lived and died seventeen years earlier. I wanted to scream at times.

Billie June said she had been a victim of domestic violence, and she knew the signs of abuse. She said she could see it in Molly's eyes, so she knew everything Molly had told her was true. Even though she'd urged her friend to leave, Molly had insisted she would not go without Jack and me.

If Billie June was so perceptive, Jack wondered, how did she not see fear in his eyes and mine? He was right. Why didn't she notice how I jumped with every command from Molly? Did she never question why everything I did revolved around pleasing Molly and seeking her approval? Did she never notice how Jack flinched at Molly's sudden movements?

Melissa Sams, a family law lawyer who lived in Meadowlands, was another witness for the defence. She was more of an acquaintance of Molly's than a friend. They were in a book club together, and Jack went to school with Melissa's sons. Dad had collected him from a birthday party in her house a few hours before Tom and Molly killed him.

Melissa said Molly had called her in January 2015 and said she was considering divorcing Dad. She said he was physically and verbally abusive towards her. Melissa said Molly had claimed Dad used the threat of losing Jack and me 'as leverage for control over her'. Molly had said she could not leave Jack and me as she regarded us as her own.

Dad was missing when we got home from swimming a few times.

'Where's Dad?' I asked one night.

'I didn't want to tell you, but your dad's having an affair,' Molly said. I didn't know what an affair was, but she assured me it was a terrible thing and that she was very upset that Dad was being so mean to her.

Weeks later, I heard Dad talking to a friend and discovered he was part of a new soccer team. He'd been going to training after work as part of his new fitness regime. Molly had insisted that he lose weight and frequently criticised him about being too heavy. Yet, she continued to tell me how cruel he was and that he had removed his wedding ring and gone to bars after work.

Melissa said her advice to Molly had included documenting

Dad's 'abuse' and applying for an emergency custody order for us. 'Jason screamed at her a lot and called her names,' said Melissa – though she never actually witnessed this.

Molly called Melissa the day after killing Dad and told her he had been choking her. 'It was him or me,' Molly said.

Molly said.

The next witness, Helen McCormac, was a mystery. Tracey and David looked at me quizzically when they saw her name on the list of witnesses that morning. I shrugged in response, and Jack was bewildered too. We had never heard her name before, and I didn't recognise her when she appeared on the stand. The defence introduced her as a nurse who was a neighbour of Bobby's in Monroe. That still didn't jog any memories.

She said Molly's relationship with Dad had appeared normal at first but got worse over the years and became 'extreme towards the end'. She claimed that Dad had always watched who Molly talked to. When Molly was in conversation in a group, Dad didn't allow her to stay if a man joined them. I remember Molly being super friendly so I found her testimony ridiculous and not credible. She said he put his hand on the nape of his wife's neck and steered her out of the conversation. I never remember my father being possessive.

She also said Dad had controlled what Molly wore. Most of Molly's friends said this. They testified that Dad was jealous and didn't want other men to look at Molly. I don't know how they could have said that when Molly paraded around in a bikini in public for most of the year. She was a swim coach and spent a good deal of her time at the communal pool. Men saw her in a bikini every day. In good weather, she wore tiny cut-off denim shorts and tiny tank tops. She had a great figure and liked to show it off. But my father didn't care what she or anyone else wore. He had no interest in clothes, and the only time I remember clothes being an issue was when Dad had refused to throw out his old T-shirts, especially an old black Nike top that she hated.

Helen said that, one day, Molly's phone kept ringing. Molly 'fumbled' with it and turned on the speaker. She said she heard Dad screaming at Molly, calling her 'a bitch' and saying she would 'pay for it'. I don't know who or what she heard on Molly's phone, but I find it hard to believe it was Dad.

One after another of Molly's friends spoke about how 'mean' and miserly Dad was. They said he had complained when she left on the lights and fans, and I think all the women mentioned the 'raspberry' incident.

Wasting energy always irritated my dad; Molly's lack of interest in security worried him. It was a regular occurrence for him to return from work to find the doors unlocked, the windows open, everything on and no one home. On a couple of instances, he recorded videos on his phone and sent them to Molly. One day, he opened the fridge and found nothing but a pack of raspberries inside. 'Raspberries!' he exclaimed. His exasperation on the video was clear.

Molly must have showed this video to all her women friends. In court, her friends made a point of saying that Dad had complained about Molly buying the smallest things, like raspberries. But he hadn't been complaining about buying raspberries, he'd been upset that there was no food in the fridge again. He had to do the grocery shopping after work. Just like he usually cooked his own dinner when he got home from work because Molly said he got home too late to eat with us.

But it really incensed me to hear them depict my father as 'miserly'. He was overly generous, and everything he earned was Molly's. However, he didn't like waste. He had spent thousands paying for Molly to go to New York on a trip. He showered Molly with expensive gifts – anything she wanted she got. But he preferred to spend his money on experiences with his family rather than material things. I knew they had rows about money before he died, but I now realise Molly spent money like she had endless wealth. She didn't have an income, but investigations showed she spent $90,000 in the eight months before Dad died.

Jennifer Turner was another witness for Molly. She was married to Dad's close friend, Tony Turner, who lived across the road from us in Meadowlands. He was from England, and Dad and Tony hit it off soon after we moved into the estate.

Jennifer thought it was cute to grab my nose and say, 'Boop!' I disliked being touched on the nose and the way she treated me like a baby. The 'booping' ended about a year before Dad died because Tony and Jennifer divorced and she moved out. But Molly and her were always close.

At the hearing, Jennifer also testified that she had complimented Molly's appearance during a social event. She said that Molly said Dad had called her 'a whore'. Once again, it was 'Molly said'.

In the days after she killed Dad, Molly drove past a condo near Charlotte. We saw an enormous block that looked like houses stacked upon each other with blue roofs and doors. She said her friend Jennifer had moved to one of the condos nearby.

'Would you guys like to live here?' Molly asked.

I remember my stomach fluttering with fear.

'Can't we go home, Mom?' I asked. I wanted to return to Meadowlands to find Dad.

'No, we're selling that now. It's too big for us. But this place has three bedrooms, one for each of us.'

What about Dad? I thought.

When we got home, she showed us photos of the interior online. But Jack and I didn't respond and she got irritated with us. Molly had moved on from Dad and expected us to forget him too. Anytime I think of Jennifer, I remember that condo and the fear and homesickness I felt that day.

CHAPTER 18

THE HOLIDAY

Your Honour
Molly took off her wedding ring almost immediately and told me to stop crying and 'get over it' in the days after she killed him.

Winston-Salem, North Carolina
November 2023

I had so much to say to the judge in my Victim Impact Statement, but I knew there wasn't enough court time to tell it all. I wanted to convey Molly's reaction to ending Dad's life and how I'd never seen her happier than in the days immediately after she'd killed him.

'Guys, we're going to the beach!' she announced the week of Dad's death. 'We're going on vacation! Isn't that fun?'

Her wedding ring had disappeared and she was making plans for her future. After taking us to see the condo in Charlotte, she packed our beachwear and we went on holiday.

As Molly drove, the sun-drenched highway stretched out

ahead of us. She had her sunglasses on, the windows down and her hair whipped carefree around her. Sometimes, she held her hand out the window, fingers spread wide to catch the rushing air. It seemed like her world was full of endless promise.

We were heading for Tom and Sharon's new holiday home on Folly Beach. They had moved from their previous beach house, and we were going to see their new one for the first time. Tom and Sharon were leading the way in the car ahead – my dad's car, a Honda Pilot, which they had started driving immediately after his death.

It was like Dad had never existed, and it was eating me away. I didn't want to go to the beach. I wanted her to tell me everything would be all right. I wanted her to say we'd return home and go to school in September. I wanted to go back to normal. I told her I wanted Dad.

'He's dead. Get over it, Sarah,' she said.

I sat in silence, trying not to cry. She said this to me several times in the days after Dad died. She took Jack and me out for ice cream a day or two after he died and said the same thing.

The Martens' beach house was a large three-storey building with multiple balconies and bedrooms. They sent us to the children's room with two sets of bunk beds, all made up with matching navy bedsheets.

I remember unpacking our stuff, and Jack putting his inhaler on his nightstand as usual. He had inherited our birth mom's asthma and Dad had fretted about his condition. He had continually reminded Jack to bring his inhaler wherever he went. Jack always left it beside his bed, so everyone knew where to find it in an emergency.

Molly gave me a bucket and spade, instructed Jack to carry the boogie boards and we set off for the beach. The dogs – Rory, Homer and Guthrie – darted ahead, their tails wagging like flags as we descended the sandy steps. Tom, Sharon and Molly walked ahead, chatting about shops and restaurants in the area. We could have been an ordinary family heading for the beach, except Mom and Grandpa had killed my father less than a week earlier.

Sharon set herself up with a chair and a book. Tom wandered off with a dog. I pottered about, collecting seashells for my bucket.

Molly was carefree, running into the sea, splashing in the waves. 'Come on, guys,' she said. 'Let's go surfing.'

The Atlantic Ocean was rough, and the waves were high, crashing over my head. Molly had to help me past the foaming breakers and into the calmer, open sea. Jack and I were well out of our depth.

She taught us how to body surf, taking one of us in at a time and leaving the other to tread water until she returned. 'I'll be back for you shortly, Sarah,' she called as she set off with Jack, leaving me alone in the rolling swells.

I faced the horizon to monitor the oncoming waves and avoid them cresting over me. After treading water for a while, my limbs became tired. *They're taking ages*, I thought.

Turning to see what was happening, my heart sank. I'd drifted further up the coast from everyone, so I could barely make them out. Molly was lying on the beach. Jack played nearby, and Sharon's head was still stuck in a book.

Panic gripped me as I realised that they weren't coming back. With no other choice, I started swimming back to shore. But, as I approached the breakers, the ocean's power intensified and churned me in the water. Every wave that crashed over me sent me tumbling under the surface.

Each time I resurfaced, gasping for air, another wave rolled me. It was like being trapped in the spin cycle of a washing machine. I thought I was going to die. I remember waving frantically and screaming, 'Mommy, Mommy!' until the waves rolled me again.

Fortunately, a wave caught me and flung me closer to the beach. Even so, the waves crashed over me as I tried to wade to shore. The sand under my feet shifted treacherously, threatening to drag me back out to sea. Exhausted and choking with seawater, I couldn't free myself from the water.

Then I saw Jack running towards me, splashing through the water. He grabbed me by the arm and dragged me out of the waves. I collapsed on my hands and knees in shallow water on the beach, coughing and sobbing.

I was still crying when we made it back to Molly and Sharon. Sharon didn't look up from her book, and Molly ignored me.

'Mommy, did you not see me?' I cried. 'You said you'd come back for me.'

'I told you to follow us,' she said. 'It's your fault if you won't listen to me.'

'You told me to wait,' I wailed.

'Sarah, I told you to come in, but you stayed. You could have drowned, you know.'

I was shaken because I'd heard her tell me to wait.

When we returned to the house, Molly brought us what I thought were wet peanuts. Now I realise they were boiled peanuts, a Southern delicacy, cooked unshelled in salty brine. I ate some only to keep Molly happy.

'Here, Jack, try one,' she said.

I jumped in straightaway. 'Jack's allergic! You know he can't eat nuts.'

Dad had taken great care to keep Jack from nuts because they made him wheeze, and his eyes swelled up until he looked through puffy slits.

But Molly was in one of her moods. 'I'm his mom, and I told him he can,' she said.

'I don't want any,' Jack said.

But Molly grabbed him and squeezed his cheeks until his mouth formed an 'O', forcing a whole peanut and shell inside.

The living accommodation was open plan, but Tom was oblivious, watering a plant, and Sharon was cooking dinner. Both ignored the commotion going on between Molly, Jack and me.

I was hysterical with fear because Jack's symptoms started straightaway. His eyes began reddening.

'Jack, just go take your inhaler and stop being so dramatic,' Molly said.

I dashed to our bedroom to discover his inhaler was no longer on the nightstand. I suspected straightaway that Molly had taken it. Fuming with her, I ran back to the living room.

'Where is it?' I yelled. 'What did you do with Jack's inhaler?'

I had often seen her hide Dad's car keys and sometimes his phone because watching him search for them seemed to amuse her. She had me engage in the secrecy.

'Why are you asking me?' she replied, indignantly. 'Jack packed his own stuff. He's a big boy now and can pack himself.'

'It was on the nightstand. Where's his inhaler?'

'Stop standing around blaming me – help your brother and go look for it,' she said.

Jack's breathing had become laboured and Molly was a picture of concern. I ran straight to her bedroom and rummaged frantically around in her stuff. I found the inhaler in one of her drawers and rushed back to Jack with it.

'Jack, you shouldn't be so careless,' Molly scolded.

I didn't know if she was referring to Jack 'eating' the nut or 'misplacing' his inhaler.

My trust and security in Molly crumbled that weekend like my sandcastles on the beach. I can only thank God that I didn't know the truth about how Dad had died. I was already scared enough.

CHAPTER 19

RESOLVE

Your Honour

The trauma continues, every day in different ways: the sight of an ambulance brings me terror. I have panic attacks when I see them, I have to look away so I can try to breathe normally. I was with my friend and my mom at a concert of my favourite band, when an ambulance passed, and I broke down.

Courtroom 6, Davidson County Courthouse
Day 6: Monday, 6 November 2023

A wailing alarm erupted deep in the courtroom building, interrupting the proceedings. Immediately, my heart rate jumped, and I knew a bad courtroom day was about to get worse. As the emergency lights pulsed around the room, a familiar vice was already causing my chest to tighten. Each flash of the strobe light infused me with more terror.

The courtroom marshal assured us it was not the fire alarm

– something was happening in the jail facility attached to the courthouse. Tracey wrapped her arms around me and pulled me tighter. 'You're all right, Sarah – close your eyes,' she urged.

She repeated that mantra in my ear, but I didn't feel all right. The room was closing in on me and I struggled to breathe.

I was already transported back to the night when red-and-blue lights painted the trees in shifting colours. Back when my father disappeared forever from my life. A wave of fear and dread was overpowering me, and I felt like I could die.

My legs somehow moved of their own accord as Tracey steered me from my seat and took me by the hand towards the exit. The flashing lights pursued us outside, reflecting off the polished floor tiles in the hall, so Tracey pulled me through the restroom door. I ran into a toilet cubicle and shrunk into the corner where I couldn't see the flashing lights. Supported by the cool metal wall, I tried to catch my breath. My brow felt cold and sweaty, and I brought my arms to my chest as if to hug myself.

'Breathe, Sarah. You're going to be fine,' Tracey said.

She had seen these panic attacks before and knew what to do. I counted my breaths, trying to slow my rapid heartbeat. *In for four, hold for four, out for four.* The panic ebbed from my system, but nausea, shaking and a tidal wave of exhaustion replaced it.

I had been like this since I was eight. A single whoop of a police siren or the flashing light of an ambulance or fire engine was enough to prompt this involuntary reaction. I had improved compared to when I was younger. But today, in Courtroom 6, the events of that August night when the Martens killed my father felt uncomfortably present.

I shut my eyes and breathed deeply. It was Monday, 6 November, day six of the hearing, and it had been a tough day.

You can't defame the dead, meaning a deceased person cannot be defamed since defamation typically involves false statements that harm a living person's reputation. So, Tom's and Molly's defence teams went to town with their character assassination of my dad and his relationship with my birth mom.

Molly's big defence was that she feared being the second Corbett wife to die at Dad's hands. So Molly's attorney, Douglas Kingsbery, hired a succession of well-paid medical experts to rewrite history. Their job was to cast my birth mother as a murder victim. That day, Kingsbery put two forensic pathologists on the stand in Davidson County Superior Court who painted my father as a dangerous sex fiend who strangled women.

Reducing the killers' sentences took precedence over everything for the defence as they spent another day focusing on my birth mom's death. Any emotional distress Jack, myself and other family members felt was irrelevant. It seemed like there was no moral compass in the room and we were just collateral damage.

Dr Bill Smock, a defence witness, described himself as a forensic pathologist who had trained the FBI, police, judges and medical personnel. He claimed to be a forensic expert in multiple fields, including strangulation. He said the post-mortem showed 'that the deceased's face was pale with blushing around the nose and mouth'. Blushing, he said, was one of the 'hallmarks' of somebody whose airways were being blocked.

'It's consistent with strangulation,' he said.

'What is wrong with you?' I exclaimed.

I couldn't help myself. But a loud buzz of murmuring swept through the courtroom, and everyone shifted in their seats. I had to stop myself from leaping to my feet. I looked askance at Tracey and Jack, who also objected. Judge Hall banged his desk with the gavel and ordered everyone to be silent.

I remember staring at Dr Smock, a man with a comb-over and a big moustache. How could he speak like that about a husband and wife he had never met? How could he talk about a woman he had never examined? So many people in my family have asthma. We all know what an asthma attack looks like. Having researched the details of my mother's last moments, I now know that ultimately death from an asthma attack is often as a result of respiratory failure or cardiac arrest due to the body's inability to receive and utilise an adequate amount of oxygen.

How could he and the other defence experts contradict my father, my mom and my mom's sister, who had all recognised an asthma attack? How could they contradict the ambulance paramedics, the hospital doctors and the pathologist – all of whom had met my mom or had examined her body? All he had was a two-page post-mortem report from 2006 – no photos and no other evidence – and yet he was adamant that my father had strangled my mother.

Unfazed by the commotion he caused, Dr Smock continued. 'Certainly, but not with certainty but with probability, Mags Corbett died of an asphyxiated death. The most common cause we are left with is strangulation.'

He said my birth mom's death was a homicide.

To me, he plucked this hideous theory from the sky. And he did it casually, leaning back and swinging in his chair, legs crossed, chatting away with Douglas Kingsbery like two old mates having a coffee.

My birth mom had had a virus that week and had cold sores around her mouth – could that have caused some of this 'blushing' around the mouth? We couldn't ask, and we had no one to ask on our behalf.

I don't know why I felt so shocked about his testimony. Tom and Molly had been saying for years that my dad had strangled my birth mom.

But it struck deeper when so-called experts weighed in and spoke so definitively about what had happened with so little evidence. *Yes, this happened – your dad strangled your birth mother.* And they seemed so casual about creating this horror fiction while Jack and I sat there, struggling not to scream.

Dr Smock then told the courtroom about 'delayed death' that follows manual strangulation. He said many victims exhibited no external signs of injury despite complaining of neck pain, difficulty swallowing or breathing.

His theory was that my birth mom could have been strangled and then died hours later because of swelling in the throat. It sounded ridiculous, almost laughable. I checked the judge's face, searching for a sign of the disbelief and scepticism I felt. Nothing.

In cross-examination, the state put it to Dr Smock that the police photos of Molly on the night of Dad's killing showed little evidence that anyone had tried to choke her.

But Dr Smock said that Molly had claimed that her husband held her in a headlock, which does not always result in obvious bruising.

He said Molly complained of 'difficulties in swallowing' and 'of a sore throat', and they were signs of choking from a headlock. He even thought she had been strangled two or three times that night. The defence resurrected the 'fingernail dig' photo, and he said such marks were common in strangulation cases. Her complaints of feeling nauseous were also common in these cases. I sat there and thought: *Is anyone going to point out the obvious?* Wouldn't you expect even the worst person in the world to feel nauseous after doing what she had done to her husband?

Assistant DA Alan Martin asked if Molly could have felt nauseous because her husband had 'just had his head bashed in'. Dr Smock agreed that she could.

Alan Martin also asked if Dr Smock's evidence came solely from Molly. He used the opportunity to highlight Molly's propensity for lies, asking whether Dr Smock was aware of Molly's 'complicated history with the truth'.

Smock replied, 'I assume they are telling me the truth until I get a finding by a lab or another finding which tells me they are not telling the truth.'

The Assistant DA also asked if Dr Smock knew that Molly 'from time to time told people she was the biological mother of the Corbett children'.

'No, sir,' he replied.

However, in reply to Molly's legal team, Dr Smock insisted that his opinion, as outlined in his report, remained unchanged.

Another defence expert, Dr Thomas Sporn, a pathologist at Duke University and a former assistant chief medical examiner in North Carolina, also rubbished the Irish post-mortem on my mother.

He believed the doctors 'relied' too heavily on her medical

history and family testimony at the time. Asked if he agreed with the post-mortem findings, he replied, 'I don't.'

He said an asthma attack would have been evident in the post-mortem.

'The lungs would be over-extended,' he said. 'There was no investigation of the upper airways or the throat and neck. The pathologist [in Ireland] did not conduct a more in-depth approach. It appears they relied on the information supplied by the deceased's husband, Jason Corbett.'

Dr Sporn also insisted that it was 'likely' that my birth mom had died an 'asphyxial death', meaning my dad had smothered, strangled or suffocated her. But when questioned by Judge Hall, he was suddenly less assured. When he was asked if a conclusion of 'an asphyxial death' was 'speculation', he agreed that it was.

Under cross-examination from Alan Martin, Dr Sporn also admitted that his conclusion of an asphyxial death was not based on any medical findings in the autopsy. He said he could not certify homicide as 'a medical certainty'. Asked why this wasn't in his report, he answered, 'I cannot say as to what I was thinking when I was writing that report.'

Alan Martin remarked that Dr Sporn only introduced the scenario of homicide because the defence hired him to 'pontificate' on strangulation.

The prosecution introduced another expert, Dr William Bozeman, a professor of medicine who provided training to police SWAT teams and bomb squads. He agreed that the autopsy into my birth mom's death was 'incomplete'. However, he did not believe she had been strangled.

When asked why, he replied, 'It is the word "probable". I do agree it could be plausible as a cause of death, but I can't get to the word "probably". It is plausible but not *probably* the cause of death. [Her death] is best described as undetermined.'

We listened to hours of witness testimony and cross-examination, and still no one mentioned that my birth mom's sister had been in the house with her at the time of her asthma attack. And no one mentioned that my dad had driven to meet the ambulance halfway – if you wanted to kill someone, would you do that?

The prosecutors argued that my birth mom could have died from many reasons rather than asphyxiation. Alan Martin told the court that she had gone to the doctor not long before her death complaining of chest pains and pain down her left arm – a classic sign of heart problems. He said the toxicology report showed that she had taken the asthma medication, Albuterol, and this could have increased her heart rate. The medication may have inadvertently made her heart problems worse. But the pathologist didn't examine her heart sufficiently, so the prosecutor said we would never know.

Alan Martin insisted that Molly wasn't truthful in her claims associated with Dad's killing. He said that, according to interviews with many witnesses, Molly told lies. He believed she was also stretching the truth when it came to the night Dad was killed.

Douglas Kingsbery then reminded the judge of (fictitious) testimony that my father got angry when Molly woke him while tending to me during the night. He said the altercation that led to my dad's killing on 2 August began because I had woken him up. He suggested the same could have happened when I was weeks old, resulting in Dad killing my birth mother.

Kingsbery didn't even say my name – just gestured across the courtroom at me. I felt like he was suggesting that I was the common denominator. The thought went through me like an electric jolt. Was he suggesting it was my fault my parents were dead?

'Ignore him,' Jack muttered, grabbing my hand, and Tracey put a protective arm around me.

But I felt like screaming as outlandish perversions of the truth piled up. Every day, I had to sit mute, watching Molly's attorney weave a tapestry of falsehoods and work as a tag team with Tom's defence attorneys. They distorted a lifetime of love and sacrifice and presented my father as a person I didn't recognise.

They described a man who was fun-loving, easy-going and gentle as being dark, controlling and jealous. To them, he was also a drunken, violent wife-abuser and killer. Molly and her father slaughtered my father, and they were still inflicting blows – this time on his good name. I was furious. They put my father's reputation and character on trial, not his killers.

Their twisted narrative flowed on, largely unchallenged by the prosecution as part of this plea bargain. I felt a profound sense of helplessness and frustration. How dare these men tarnish my father's memory and drag my birth mother's name through this courtroom? I resented them talking about my birth mother. She had died seventeen years earlier and had nothing to do with this hearing. Yet, they continued hammering through the foundations of my existence, trying to destroy my entire family history. All I could do was think of the love I had witnessed in old videos of our little family and use those memories to steady myself against the onslaught.

The court spent hours discussing the fiction of my dad killing my birth mom. They hardly spent ten minutes talking about the real killers in the room.

I thought about all of this behind a cubicle door as I waited for my breathing to finally steady. When it did, I felt bolstered with a new-found resolve. I told Tracey I wouldn't listen to them lie about my family anymore. I'd been gagged since I was eight years old and they were still trying to silence me. The Martens had used a metal baseball bat and garden paver to silence my father. Since then, they had used lies as weapons to continue striking him with impunity.

I had to listen as my father's memory was desecrated. I watched strangers discuss and debate the evidence on TV, radio and social media. All this time, I was forced to carry this story inside me, knowing a lot of the truth of what happened, and yet the justice system refused to hear it.

Before I went back into that courtroom, I told Tracey that I wasn't going to remain silent any longer. I was going to write and deliver my Victim Impact Statement, but what I couldn't say in that, I would write in a book. Writing has always been an essential form of therapy for me, and this time my words could also be an opportunity to right some of the wrongs inflicted by the Martens and vindicate my father's good name.

CHAPTER 20

WRITING TO RECOVERY

Your Honour

The grief ruins even the special days. My experience shadows my life – every moment of it is changed.

Winston-Salem, North Carolina
November 2023

The difficulties I had starting my statement had long disappeared. Instead, the words flowed as a stream of consciousness when I sat at my laptop most evenings. I was still writing and rewriting my statement during the sentencing hearing. Every day in court reminded me of more I wanted to say.

Assistant DA Alan Martin had clarified the situation with our Victim Impact Statements. Anyone in the family could write one, and there was no limit to how long we could take to give our statements, but he asked us to focus on our loss rather than Tom or Molly. 'In other words,' I said, 'no Molly-bashing.'

Writing had always been therapeutic for me. I wrote for a few minutes most nights, and as words spilled out, I felt a weight lifting from my shoulders.

I always got relief from taking the jumbled mess of emotions and ideas swirling in my head and making them find order and meaning on the page. Expressing myself on paper has been a therapy since I could write, which was later for me than most children.

Tracey and David had discovered that I couldn't read or write very well when they brought me back to Ireland. Most children have basic literacy skills by age six, but I had little, despite turning nine shortly after I arrived back.

School had not been a priority during my years in America. My attendance was dismal, and the support I received at home was misguided, to say the least. Molly did my homework every morning after Dad went to work. I wasn't good at homework, and she wanted children who were straight-A students. It didn't matter that I wasn't a good pupil, so long as it appeared that I was. Appearances were important. However, it meant the school failed to spot that I had dyslexia – a factor underlying my homework problems. Homework was another secret that we kept from my father. 'Don't tell your dad,' she said.

Wallburg Elementary School was only five minutes away from our home. However, I rarely finished an entire day. Molly often arrived to collect me from school armed with a valid excuse, like a medical appointment. However, we always ended up shopping or at the cinema, somewhere fun. I also feigned illness, so the school would call Molly and ask her to collect me. Molly claimed I had so many illnesses that nobody ever questioned me. She told me I was a coeliac and was allergic to gluten and dairy, so I lived in terror of eating the wrong food.

When I returned to Ireland, Adam gave me bread one day.

'Is this gluten-free?' I asked, always careful.

'Yep,' he lied. He already knew from Tracey and Dave after my doctors' visits that I had never been coeliac or had any food allergies. I did not have a reaction to the bread.

School attendance was not negotiable when I returned to Ireland. I received extra tutoring at my new school and, to help further, Tracey began a word-a-day exercise to build my vocabulary and improve my spelling. With additional resources from the school and Tracey's after-school help, I soon caught up with my peers. I thrived in the comfort and security of a stable homelife.

As soon as I learned to write, putting words on paper became an important way to express emotions I couldn't easily verbalise. I had memories and feelings that I couldn't face saying out loud, and Tracey saw I was struggling at times.

'Why not write what you want to say on a note and leave it on my pillow?' she suggested. 'I'll read it and then we can talk about it.'

I remember hovering over Tracey's pillow many times, note in hand, wondering if I should pull the pin on the grenade rolling in my head. Our note system became a crucial way of communicating thoughts that I couldn't talk about.

Writing provided space for reflection and enabled me to better articulate my thoughts. Putting thoughts on paper also let me disclose information at my own pace. Unlike face-to-face conversations, I didn't feel anxious about seeing immediate reactions like shock, disgust or rejection. Writing notes was always about my insecurities because Tracey only responded with understanding and reassurance.

When I became literate, I found I could express everything better by putting pen to paper. I felt a greater sense of safety and control. My notes became our go-to system for more difficult revelations.

By the time I was twelve, I wrote all the time to clear my mind. A blank page offered a confidante that never judged, interrupted or offered simplistic solutions.

Sitting on a sun-warmed wall one day as I waited for a friend to emerge from her house, I started scribbling some notes. As I wrote, the voices of small bear characters appeared on paper.

'BOOGAWOOGA-WOOGA!' was always Dad's signal for fun. He usually sounded it as Jack and I came down the stairs in the morning. He waited at the bottom of the stairs, and as soon as he saw us, he danced and sang out, 'BOOGAWOOGA-WOOGA!' It's a mystery where his dance and lyric came from, but it always made us laugh.

That day on my friend's wall, I started creating a story inspired by Dad. I wrote about a little bear whose world changed after an evil vulture slayed her beloved dad, Boogawooga. Words appeared freely on the page and a cast of cuddly characters came to life. The rest of the story told how Noodle and her bear brother Paws journeyed to find happiness with a new blended family. The symbolism may not have been subtle, but the story helped me to process what I was feeling and experiencing. Writing was a soothing backdrop to my day, helping me feel a little less alone in my head.

I had also noticed that death was a taboo subject, especially around children. While Tracey and David spoke openly about it, I sensed unease when I mentioned Dad to others. Some parents went to great lengths to hide death from their children – like searching for replicas of deceased pets. I'd heard of grieving parents who waited until their children went to bed to cry. They somehow believed that they should shield their children from their grief. They thought they should construct a fortress around their children and wall out their loss. People deal with loss and grief in different ways, but we all die and shouldn't it be part of living to accept this?

When I lost my dad, I might not have been able to express my feelings clearly, but I felt pain. People think children are too young to understand, but what they don't realise is that they can't protect a child from loss. The child will feel it anyway.

From my own experience, concealing death and grief caused the worst pain because it only made me feel more alone.

After Dad died, we stayed in Bobby Martens' house in Monroe, near Charlotte. Life with Molly and the Martens continued as if Dad had never existed. No one mentioned him anymore.

I remember slipping out of bed at dawn one morning while Molly was sleeping. Deep-orange and soft-pink streaks stretched across the sky, and everything was still and quiet. It was a few days since Dad had disappeared. The outside world seemed normal, but my inner self was distressed. I had a knot of anxiety in my stomach as I climbed into the Martens' treehouse in their garden.

Knees drawn to my chest, I sat in the furthest corner from the treehouse window, hiding myself from view. For the first time, I felt that the world had stopped moving since Dad had disappeared. I sobbed, not quite knowing why I was crying. My fears were intensifying because I couldn't find Dad anywhere, and he still hadn't come back for Jack and me.

The hours passed, and the others began emerging from the house, their laughter and chatter disturbing me and making my stomach twist with fear. My dad had vanished. How could everything be normal? I couldn't understand how they were living like nothing had happened.

Jack hardly spoke a word during those days. When he was around, he only interacted with the dogs and, often, he was missing from Bobby's house. I learned later that he had found a cornfield close to the house and sat in its dense wall of green for hours at a time. No one looked for him. It was a terrifying and lonely time in both our lives.

Failing to acknowledge a child's loss leads to more confusion and fear for that child. When the only sound is silence, it's harder for children to process their emotions. It's frightening when a major part of their life scaffolding disappears and the surrounding adults don't seem to notice. I felt like I was the only person in the world suffering pain and loss.

In my story, *Noodle Loses Dad*, I wrote about what I knew – death, loss and blended families. While I was writing it, the tragic death of a young mom made the news. Emma Mhic Mhathúna, a victim of the CervicalCheck misdiagnosis scandal, left five grieving young children.

I began believing that maybe Noodle's story wasn't just mine and started thinking that the book might resonate with other kids like me.

Tracey and David read my story when I finished it, and their positive response gave me the confidence to tell them about my idea. 'I'd like to make this story into a book to help other children.'

Tracey never saw that coming. 'A book? Like you want it printed and sold in bookstores?'

'Uh-huh,' I said, pleading. 'You wrote a book and I think I'd like to write one too.'

Seeing Tracey write a book a year earlier had inspired me to think I could do the same. She wrote a bestselling book, *My Brother Jason*, detailing the story of my father's killing. She didn't allow me to read it, but I'd watched her and journalist Ralph Riegel working on the manuscript together.

However, I could see that Tracey wasn't convinced about my idea. She said I could do it when I was older but needed to concentrate on school for now.

'But I've already written it,' I argued. 'It wouldn't take much time.'

I had no idea of the amount of work needed, but I wheedled, reasoned and argued.

'I suppose we could look into it,' Tracey finally conceded.

My book, *Noodle Loses Dad*, was released in November 2019, when I was thirteen years old. Its publication catapulted me into a world of excitement. I promoted it everywhere possible, even appearing on *Fox 8 News* in North Carolina.

That same week, like families all over Ireland, we settled on the couch for the annual ritual of *The Late Late Toy Show*. When host Ryan Tubridy held up a book mid-show, my jaw dropped. I glanced at Tracey in confusion, but she also gazed in disbelief at what was unfolding. Ryan was showing everyone my book.

He explained he had met me on his radio show that week and

added, 'She's written a book about what happens when sadness comes to your family; maybe your parent doesn't make it and life becomes tricky.'

'Oh, my God!' was all Tracey could muster as we both burst into tears. We were overwhelmed by what had just happened.

The notebook given to me by the prosecution during the sentencing hearing became a valuable therapy tool too. Every day, I used it to scribble question after question. After the hearing or the following morning, I posed my questions to the Assistant District Attorneys.

However, I also began using that notebook in the courtroom to express my feelings. They were often negative ones, like powerlessness, frustration and sadness. My pen pressed harder into the pages at times, and I underlined words like 'ANGRY!' and 'FURIOUS!'. Writing in that notebook was often the only alternative I had to cracking up or screaming. I tore out these pages filled with sadness and anger and binned them afterwards.

I realise that writing is another gift from Tracey, who has encouraged and supported me ever since I went to live with her and David.

Today, when I'm dealing with thoughts that are difficult to manage, writing is still the one thing I can do to make myself feel lighter. When I start to write, the anxiety that sometimes clouds my mind dissipates and is replaced by greater clarity.

Writing is another way to bring calm into my world and ground me. And I need every bit of help I can get because sadness tinges even the best days now. Every celebration has a void – the space where Dad should be. And while that sadness and emptiness remains, I will continue to write.

CHAPTER 21

THE SCHEME

Your Honour

I loved her even after all the abuse she put me through. I had no idea what adoption was, only that she wanted to do it so badly. And worst of all, I trusted her ... I thought Molly loved me, but I was just her entertainment, someone who would do anything she said and be like a doll she could dress up.

Courtroom 6, Davidson County Courthouse
Day 7: Tuesday, 7 November 2023
According to a psychologist who examined her for hours, Molly was obsessed with taking Jack and me from Dad. On day seven of the sentencing hearing, we learned that Molly had such an unhealthy preoccupation with us that she never had a genuine interest in building a life with Dad.

Dr David Adams had met Molly on 12 July 2022 and conducted a four-hour interview before compiling a psychological report for the state prosecutors.

His report was both frightening and upsetting. Dad had offered Molly a lifestyle that enabled her to be the stay-at-home mom she had wanted to be. However, his evidence was that my father was ultimately disposable because her obsession was about Jack and me.

The psychologist believed Molly's plan all along – from soon after she had arrived in Ireland to work as our nanny – was to take us.

'A primary focus of her existence from before she married Jason Corbett was to adopt these children, then divorce him and take these children,' said the Massachusetts-based forensic psychologist.

His words were extraordinary, but not surprising. I'm sure he was as shocked as we were when Molly baldly stated that she'd consulted a divorce lawyer even *before* she married Dad.

'I wanted to get legal options about divorce and getting the kids and consulted a lawyer,' she had told him.

This divorce lawyer gave her much the same advice that she got from our neighbour Melissa Sams in early 2015.

'He told me to start to document my activities with the kids and also [document] the physical violence. He told me my chances for adoption were minimal. He told me to get a restraining order. Also, the lawyer said the kids would have a say when they got older – twelve or so. That was my goal.'

He discovered that she had investigated how to achieve her goal of getting us before she laced up her designer gown on her wedding day, 4 June 2011. At worst, Molly reckoned she might have to wait until we were older. Twelve, perhaps.

We were appalled. Hearing Dr Adams' report made me scared

for the child I had been. Her own words in his report revealed far more truth than we'd heard in all the courtrooms over the years.

For me, her revelation that she met with a divorce lawyer before marrying Dad was horrific. It said a lot about her real feelings, or lack of them, as she married him. I felt so sorry for my father, realising he was just another pawn in Molly's games.

Only weeks after we moved to America, Dad and Molly got married in a place ominously called Bleak House, a magnificent white mansion overlooking the Tennessee River. As a four-year-old flower girl, I was concerned with the swish of my ballerina dress and the shine of my new shoes. Floating through the day on a cloud of white tulle and joy, I didn't notice the undercurrents of tension and an atmosphere thick with doubts.

Molly began planning her showcase wedding as soon as she and Dad announced their engagement in Limerick on Valentine's Day in 2010. The wedding became her main focus. Dad continued working and we went to creche and school while she travelled to the US months before us to ensure a fairytale wedding experience. She organised the day with military precision, sparing no expense.

Bleak House manor had been a Confederate headquarters during the American Civil War. However, wedding planners had replaced drill sergeants, taking advantage of its lush tropical garden and elegant white pavilion.

Dad's family and friends flew over from Ireland, and their familiar accents were a comforting reminder of the life we'd left behind. Violins played and the heady scents of summer blooms filled the gardens as guests arrived. Staff welcomed everyone with canapes and champagne. They served dinner on the terrace under a magical canopy of lanterns and fairy lights. The place was an enchanting setting for an outdoor wedding, despite its unlikely name.

All I cared about was that Bleak House offered the perfect backdrop for my white 'princess' dress with its pink cummerbund and silk rose. Daddy assured me the venue was *my* castle.

Molly's parents lived a few miles away from Bleak House. They had a home on Comblain Road, an upmarket neighbourhood in East Knoxville. Tom and Sharon were well-heeled, well-educated professionals regarded as pillars of Tennessee society.

The Martens' family and friends comprised most of the hundred guests at the wedding. All that week, Tom posed as the lavish father of the bride, funding his daughter's big day. We didn't know until years later that Dad had sent two cheques amounting to €50,000 from his AIB account to Tom Martens to pay for the day.

I also didn't learn until later that Dad's family and friends from Ireland attended a tension-filled, pre-wedding barbecue at Tom and Sharon's house. Molly never even appeared at the party. Instead, Tracey found her curled up crying in a basement bedroom for no reason she could discern.

I was probably the happiest person at Dad and Molly's wedding. I loved seeing everyone dressed in their finery and all the people we'd known in Ireland around us again. More than anything, I loved spinning around on the dance floor with my dad. He hoisted me in his arms and swirled me around the floor for our dance. I remember uncharacteristic shyness overcame me when his best man, Brendan O'Callaghan, handed me the microphone during the speeches. I can still feel Dad leaning into me and whispering, 'It's okay. You can do it.' It was all the encouragement I needed to give my 'speech'. Jack also was involved in the ceremony that day as the ring-bearer.

I don't know how Dad felt that day. Only weeks earlier, he had confided in Paul that he had learned Molly suffered from mental-health issues. Those issues became evident on the wedding day. One bridesmaid quit early after Molly had exchanged words with her. Molly also screamed at David in front of all the guests, accusing nine-year-old Adam of offending her. Adam had an allergy to eggs and everything on the menu contained them. Molly had been aware of that allergy for years. Someone kindly went to a drive-through to get something for him to eat. But Molly erupted when she saw him with food that wasn't on her menu. She flounced to the manor in tears with Sharon in hot pursuit.

None of this interfered with my day. My focus was lovely frocks, towering wedding cakes (Molly couldn't decide, so she bought two), fairy lights and the people I loved. I was a princess, and the world sparkled, full of happy-ever-after promise. The day was magical to me. As with all fairytales, however, shadows lurked beneath the surface.

Molly also claimed in her interview with Dr Adams that she and Dad had started their relationship six months after she arrived in Ireland. Tracey has emails Molly sent to Dad with images of wedding dresses and pleas not to reconsider their relationship three months after she moved to Ireland.

Molly's interview with Dr Adams also included an admission that she had been 'dealing with depression' before travelling to Ireland.

A former fiancé of Molly's said that she had been taking sixteen prescribed meds daily and another ten 'as needed' months before she left the US. Molly had met Keith Maginn through a dating website. The Ohio man, who worked for a non-profit organisation, said they fell in love 'pretty fast' and even became engaged. However, they struggled as her mental health deteriorated and her meds use became chaotic.

'She later suffered a miscarriage,' he said in a newspaper interview. 'When I found out she was pregnant, I was horrified as she was on a tremendous amount of medication at the time … and I was worried how that could have affected things.'

He added: 'It's hard looking back now to know if anything she told me was true. So much of it … I found out a lot of it was lies.'

At the time, Molly and Keith had lived in an apartment on Berlin Drive in Knoxville, an investment property owned by Tom and Sharon. Tom had charged the couple rent and refused to reduce it when Keith said he could not meet the monthly payment, with Molly unable to work.

He described Tom and Sharon as 'exasperated' by Molly's condition. After five months of illness, the Martens admitted Molly to a psychiatric unit at Emory University Hospital in Atlanta, Georgia, miles from their Tennessee hometown.

Keith lived in a cheap motel nearby to support and see Molly during visiting hours. However, we know now that, within weeks of that psychiatric treatment, she flew to Ireland.

'She told me about going to Ireland to become a nanny for a widower and said she would only be there for a short period as we were engaged at the time,' he said. 'I didn't hear anything for several days and then got an email thanking me for keeping her alive and loving her. She said I was her angel, but she didn't know if she was ever coming back to the US.'

'I just wanted to get away,' Molly told Dr Adams.

When twenty-four-year-old Molly replied to my dad's advert for a nanny in February 2008, it must have seemed like the answer to his prayers. Her CV made her stand head and shoulders above any other candidate. She was the dream nanny – a qualified Montessori teacher who had been vetted as a foster parent. She was also a graduate of the highly regarded Clemson University in South Carolina and was an avid swimmer who had been vying for the US Olympic swimming team. Dad knew nothing about her medical history until shortly before the wedding, three years later.

The attraction between Dad and Molly was immediate apparently and, within months, they were in a relationship. People who loved Dad were happy to see his old sparkle return. They say he found his smile again for a while.

The psychologist's evidence tallied. Molly had told him her relationship with Dad was 'wonderful at first, romantic, appreciative ... I felt worthwhile'.

However, most of Dad's family and friends had reservations about the speed of the romance. In hindsight, it bore all the signs of a transitional relationship. I have a lot of compassion and understanding for Dad at this time. He was still visiting my birth mom's grave daily, clearly still grief-stricken, and when he was at his most lost and lonely, he thought he had found a sweet and caring woman devoted to his motherless children. Molly seemed like an angel in disguise.

However, the cracks in their relationship soon appeared. She complained to the psychologist that she was unhappy when Dad didn't buy a car or an internet subscription for her. This was untrue. Everyone remembers that Dad bought her a car, and she used his bank card to buy whatever else she wanted.

Even after their marriage, Molly admitted that she'd continued to look for custody of us. She sought advice from two more divorce lawyers, including her friend Melissa Sams. Molly's true nature came into focus in Dr Adams' report.

We saw other signs of her unhealthy preoccupation with Jack and me, including efforts to mould us into a reflection of herself. Perhaps she felt that if she could recreate us in her likeness, she could make everyone else believe we were her children. She had an obsession with being seen as our mother.

One summer's day, she led Jack and me into the bathroom and used permanent dye to colour our hair a pale sandy colour like hers. Dad was taken aback when he came home to discover what she had done.

'What did you do to the kids' hair?' he asked.

But Molly had it all worked out. 'It's a fad with the kids using lemon juice and sunlight to lighten their natural hair colour,' she said. 'Jack begged me to let him do it because everyone in his class did it, and then Sarah wanted it done too.'

Dad accepted her explanation that it was just a harmless kids' craze. Jack was unfortunate, though. His hair dye reacted with the pool chlorine and ended up a terrible shade of ginger.

She also liked to dress me to look like a miniature version of herself. I became a pocket-sized extension of Molly and a dress-up doll rolled into one. We had matching cowgirl outfits with shirts, denim skirts, boots and Stetsons. We dressed as 1920s flappers for Halloween with matching curly blonde bobs. However, it didn't need to be a special occasion for us to dress the same. We had dozens of matching outfits for any day of the week. Stores like Old Navy and Gap sold Mommy-and-me-style matching ranges, and Molly must have been their best customer. Our matching outfits helped feed her apparent craving for attention.

Dr Adams' assessment that 'getting the kids' was her 'goal' helped sweep away Molly's web of deceit. For the first time, we were offered a clear and chilling perspective on her character and motivation. Molly's claims about Dad's jealousy and controlling behaviour rang hollow against the backdrop of her long-term scheming and manipulation of Jack and I. I've since learned that before she met my dad, Molly claimed on a blogging site that she had a boyfriend who had a daughter aged eight. She was seeking advice on what phone to buy so she could communicate with the young girl without her mother knowing. Discovering this really shook me as I realised how far back her behaviour went.

However, not many outside the courtroom got to hear about Dr Adams' interview, report and findings. His words and Molly's were lost in all the media coverage about the 'botched' Irish post-mortem and the strangulation allegations.

The worst part for me was the realisation that, from the outset, Molly's relationship with Dad was not based on genuine affection. I felt an aching sorrow for Dad afterwards. He had welcomed Molly into his life and his heart. Everyone in his family had. And all along, she had been playing a game. A long, patient game, where, for some reason, Jack and I were the desired prize.

CHAPTER 22

A BADGE AND A BAT

Your Honour

What Molly and Tom Martens took from me, I can never get back. No member of the Martens family has ever shown me any remorse. I only got betrayed. Molly and Tom Martens have used me – and words I was forced to say as an eight-year-old child – to escape the just consequences of beating my dad to death.

Courtroom 6, Davidson County Courthouse
Day 7: Tuesday, 7 November 2023
Much of day seven was about Tom, the quintessential stern-faced and 'unemotional' FBI agent. His defence team wheeled out a psychologist and several character witnesses to portray him as a by-the-book professional and devoted family man.

During his thirty years at the FBI, Tom had what his defence counsel, Jay Vannoy, called 'a stellar career'. He began life as a lawyer before being recruited by the FBI to run their offices in Knoxville and Cincinnati for thirteen years. His job also involved running violent-crime task forces, where he gained an expert knowledge of crime scenes. He trained Drug Enforcement Agency and FBI agents on how to interview suspects.

His extensive background in law enforcement and the law meant he knew how to provide a compelling narrative for his and Molly's defence. Tom was a formidable opponent for the prosecution, able to use his intimate knowledge of crime-scene protocols, investigative techniques and judicial proceedings to his advantage.

Upon retirement from the FBI, Tom went to work in counterintelligence for the US Department of Energy. He worked in Oak Ridge, one of the two original sites for the Manhattan Project – the Second World War research programme that produced the first nuclear weapons.

Tom had a Q-level security clearance, the highest in the US government. It allowed him to access top-secret documents and, according to one of his former FBI colleagues, he could access a couple of levels higher than 'top secret' if he needed to. His job was to defend US nuclear energy secrets from spies – mostly Chinese, Russian and Iranian.

The defence counsel hired a psychiatrist to evaluate Tom. Forensic psychiatrist Dr George Corvin's job was to find mitigating circumstances that might justify a lighter sentence for Tom. In January 2023, he interviewed Tom for two and a half hours and carried out an assessment of Tom's 'behaviour and control' on the night of Dad's death. His commissioned report also offered character evidence, highlighting his positive attributes.

Dr Corvin told the court that he believed Tom Martens was a 'Type A personality' who was 'meticulously polite' and didn't show any emotion when interviewed.

I looked up 'Type A' – Dr Corvin didn't say that this personality type is also associated with competitive, impatient and aggressive behaviours, and is easily angered or hostile in stressful situations.

'He arrived very early for his appointment,' said Dr Corvin. 'He was meticulously polite with the staff. I found the interview with him was very easy. He lived a life in which order is important and organisation is important. He was deliberate and analytical – a classic Type A personality. He would be inclined to use logic over emotion, and he follows the rules rigidly. He had a Q security clearance with the Department of Energy. He was a pro-social man driven to find solutions and help other people.'

Dr Corvin added, 'I don't want to say that he is devoid of emotion, but he likes to deal with situations that are just the facts. He was not very emotive.'

That much had been clear from the 911 call Tom had made on the night he killed Dad. Detectives reviewing his 911 call even remarked that he 'sounded like he was ordering a pizza'.

I wished Tom had been asked how long he waited before making that 911 call. Maybe the medics could have given their expert opinions. But we never heard the testimony from Davidson County sheriff's deputies who found dried blood in the bedroom. Or from the paramedics Amanda Hackworth and Barry Alphin who reported that Dad's body was cold to the touch.

However, despite his extensive FBI training, Tom's recall of events in Dad's bedroom was patchy. He claimed he didn't notice the bloody brick paver in the room and never saw Molly using it.

Dr Corvin explained gaps in Tom's memory as being normal in a 'sudden, severe, scary and life-threatening situation'.

The forensic psychiatrist said he believed Tom went into the room to diffuse a row, but it escalated. No one asked why, if Tom intended to diffuse the row, he had carried a baseball bat upstairs with him or why he shut the bedroom door behind him when he entered the room. If my dad had been able to leave that room, I believe he never would have returned to the house and Molly could not allow that to happen.

Dr Corvin said when Tom witnessed his daughter being choked, a fight-or-flight response kicked in. This is the body's 'emergency overdrive' when it perceives imminent danger.

The psychiatrist ultimately found Tom to be 'meticulously responsible'.

The Martens' plea agreement even conceded the amount of force employed in their self-defence was excessive. A pathologist testified that Dad's head had been struck at least a dozen times. He said any one of those individual blows could have rendered my father unconscious, ensuring that he was no longer a threat. But Tom and Molly continued their savage attack. Was that 'meticulously responsible' behaviour? But no one asked that question either.

After Dr Corvin stepped down, the courtroom was treated to a convention of the Tom Martens fan club. An assortment of family and friends took the stand to talk about his sterling character, incredible work ethic and wholesome family values. I struggled to reconcile this virtuous figure with the man I knew as a killer, who had never shown a morsel of remorse for taking my father's life.

Sharon's brother Mike Earnest stepped up first. Mike was in the US Navy and was also a federal agent, working with a

Washington-based organisation that oversaw the reconstruction of Afghanistan. He had positioned himself as the family spokesperson and chief defender of Tom and Molly.

Mike said his sister Sharon had found 'the perfect match' when she married Tom in 1973. He spoke about their four children. Their eldest, Bobby, was a federal agent with the Bureau of Alcohol, Tobacco, Firearms and Explosives (ATF). Their second child and only daughter was Molly. Their other two sons were Stewart, an engineer, and Connor, who worked in sports marketing.

'They met at Emory University, and I remember Sharon bringing Tom home to meet our parents,' said Mike Earnest. 'I would say we have been quite close in the fifty-three years since. In the seventies, Tom was in the FBI on his second assignment in Washington, DC, and I was in the navy in Delaware, so over those two and a half years, we spent a lot of time together.'

Mike said he and Tom often played golf together and his brother-in-law was a stickler for the rules. 'There's a lot of rules in golf. You play with Tom, you play by the rules. He would say, "Why play the game if you're not going to play by the rules?"'

After establishing Tom's rules-driven integrity, he then painted a portrait of an exemplary husband and 'an exceptionally dedicated father'.

He said this devoted father read bedtime stories to his children and introduced them to *The Hobbit* and *Lord of the Rings* author J.R.R. Tolkien. I thought about all the stories I missed from my dad and all the stories his grandchildren will never hear. Mike said Tom also coached the children's swim, soccer and T-ball teams. I wanted to tell the courtroom that my dad used to coach us too.

Mike told the court that Tom was also an incredible chef. He quipped that he had even learned to use a phone to google how to make a vindaloo. He spoke about how Tom followed recipes like he followed rules, and never improvised. I thought about how I'd never get to have a Friday night barbecue watching dad flip burgers. I swore that he was going to get down on one knee and ask Tom to marry him at one stage. It all got a bit weird. He must have talked about how much he loved him for twenty minutes.

Tom's son Stewart also appeared as a character witness, describing his father as 'my role model who leads by example'. He told the judge that Tom was a marvellous grandad, rolling up his sleeves and changing nappies for Stewart's two children.

Former FBI agent Todd Sandstedt, who had worked with Tom, told the court to 'open up the dictionary, look up the word 'gentleman', they'll have a picture of Tom Martens beside it'.

Or look up the words 'felon' and 'killer' and they'll have a photo of Tom Martens too, I thought.

This sentencing hearing was supposed to be about a man and his daughter beating my dad to death. Instead, we had to sit through a courtroom rom-com. We had stories about how this killer had fallen in love and how great he was in the kitchen. And we had another FBI agent saying how strict Tom was and taught him so well. I couldn't understand why they were allowed character witnesses, and my dad wasn't.

I said this to Assistant DA Alan Martin. 'Why are there character witnesses for Tom and Molly? Where are the ones for my dad? He's not here. If Tom and Molly want to take the stand and testify for themselves, they can. My dad can't. I'm happy to do it for Dad.'

Two weeks' worth of hardworking taxpayers' money was spent

on a sentencing hearing that focused largely on how great Tom and Molly were. The defence tried to paint them as solid, respectable citizens. It made my blood boil how they kept repeating that neither Tom nor Molly had committed a crime before that night.

My dad had no criminal record either. He never committed a crime in his life. He was a good citizen who paid his taxes, held down a good, responsible job, and loved and supported his family. If anyone should have character witnesses, especially after the defence team's character assassination, it was my father. But he was denied that. My dad would have had a stream of colleagues and friends from all over the world who respected and cared for him. They would have spoken about how he raised €36,000 for the Asthma Society after my mum died. They would have told how he invested everything in his family. Family, love and loyalty were extremely important to him.

I got more and more vocal with the prosecution as the days went on because I realised with a growing sense of panic that this hearing would soon end, and so would my final opportunity to be in a courtroom, trying to defend my dad.

CHAPTER 23

ENDGAME

Your Honour

Sitting inside this courtroom has been a traumatic experience. I was hoping there would be a retrial, so my truth and my brother's truth could both be heard. Instead, all we have is this, a Victim Impact Statement.

Courtroom 6, Davidson County Courthouse
Day 7: Tuesday, 7 November 2023
When I first entered the sentencing hearing, I'd planned to study for a criminal-justice degree after finishing school. By day seven of the courtroom process, I started to doubt that decision. Maybe, naively, I thought that the law was a profession that could help people, but what I witnessed in Davidson County Courthouse made me see that the law is more focused on winning than seeking truth or justice. The District Attorney's office of Lexington appears to be constrained by an underfunded budget and overworked staff.

In our case, the District Attorney made unilateral decisions not to proceed with a retrial. It's debatable whether a retrial would have required significantly more time than the farcical proceedings of the sentencing hearing that ultimately wasted the time of the court and its employees.

I got more insight into the 'guns for hire' courtroom culture with the defence's next witness, seeing first hand how it sidelines empathy and human decency. Many witnesses made me feel that the system doesn't care about the victims and their families.

Dr Scott Hampton, an expert in domestic violence for the defence, also took the stand on that seventh day. He'd reviewed multiple sources of information provided to him by the Martens' defence team. He spoke as an expert on domestic violence, but never spoke to the only independent witnesses in the house – Jack and me. Nor did he seek any documentation on our recanted claims after we'd been taken out of the Martens' custody.

Rather than the phrase 'domestic violence', Dr Hampton said he preferred to use the term 'intimate partner violence'.

He listened to the 'pancake' tape and deduced from the only tape presented in Molly's defence that she was a victim of abuse.

'There was constant berating of Molly,' he claimed. 'She was trying to resolve the situation. She was protecting the children, setting boundaries. Molly is trying to appease Jason. She is trying to protect, guide and set boundaries. She tries to make pancakes to resolve the situation.'

He said Dad had a 'sense of dominance and entitlements' that had begun before they met. 'He didn't meet her on a dating app,' he said. 'He was looking to employ her. He has already established himself. You have no rights.'

No one mentioned that Dad had sold the home he'd built, left a job he'd loved and uprooted his children from family and friends to move to America – all to please someone who had 'no rights'.

Dr Hampton also claimed Dad had trapped Molly in the marriage. 'If you don't get to adopt the kids, you can't leave,' he said. 'That's how he kept her trapped.'

Assistant DA Alan Martin said Molly had placed recording devices around her home to manufacture evidence of abuse that never existed. She only had one tape to present to Dr Hampton in which Dad raised his voice. 'All the others were destroyed,' he said.

He also raised the psychological assessment carried out by Dr Adams, which found that Molly's primary aim was to do anything she could to get us from Dad. 'Adoption was her desire,' Alan Martin said. 'And she would stop at nothing to achieve it.'

He told the court Molly had 'an extraordinary ability to dissemble, deceive and manipulate others through lies'.

Dr Hampton said he didn't like the word 'lie' because there were good lies too. He said good lies were when someone didn't tell the truth, but they did it for what they believed were 'good reasons'.

'Everyone can agree Molly was all about the kids. She applied for the job and she was all about the kids,' he said.

However, Alan Martin continued to reveal Molly's deceit as he cross-examined Dr Hampton. He asked the psychologist to explain what 'good reason' Molly had for lying that she was a foster parent or was on the swim team of a prestigious university. 'Why would she lie about something like that when, in fact, she didn't even complete a semester at that college?' he asked.

Dr Hampton described Molly's lies as 'future-pacing', which he explained as, 'This is what I want my life to be and I'm going to talk about it until it happens.'

But Alan Martin hit back, presenting another of Molly's lies as 'emotional manipulation'.

'Say when I was in college, I had a roommate. I had a photograph framed in my dorm room, and I had the picture in it that came within when I bought it. And when asked about it, I told my roommate. "That's my sister, she died of leukaemia." And I never had a sister, and certainly not one who died of leukaemia. This is emotional manipulation.'

But Dr Hampton refused to describe it as manipulation. 'Some people create non-factual events because they want their life to be better,' he said.

'So, I'm going to fake a sister who died? That's bordering on delusional. It's very manipulative. She had an extraordinary way to manipulate other people's emotional states.'

Alan Martin also referred to Molly telling women at a Bible study group about giving birth to me.

According to Dr Hampton, this was still not a lie – it was 'wish fulfilment'. I felt like we were in some kind of horror version of a Disney movie. Wish fulfilment?

'They were things she wished for. It's not unusual for people to exaggerate things. Lying on the stand is different.'

When Molly lied about being an editor of a magazine in Ireland, it meant she *wished* she was the editor of a magazine. It seemed delusional. Dr Hampton offered endless justifications and excuses for Molly's many acts of lying.

Alan Martin didn't accept the 'wish fulfilment' or 'future-pacing' excuses either. He said Molly had invented a conversation with my birth mom, claiming Mags had asked Molly 'to take care of Jason and Jack and Sarah' if anything happened to her. He clarified that my mother *never* met Molly. When he said those words, it was one of the few times I ever thought my mother was lucky.

Alan Martin said this claim was another example of Molly's 'insidious lies'. 'We know all these things are false,' he said.

Dr Hampton claimed it made no sense for Molly to stage a violent confrontation because, if Dad were to survive it, he could divorce her and take us to Ireland, and, if he died, Molly would lose us anyway because she had no custody rights. He said Molly was prepared to stay in the marriage for another few years until we were twelve when we could determine who we lived with after a divorce. 'She was highly motivated to gut it out the next few years.'

For similar reasons, Dr Hampton insisted that Molly had to defend herself from Dad but was 'highly motivated' to save him from dying the night she and her father had killed him.

'She had to use the right amount of force that's necessary to stay alive,' he said. 'She had to ensure that Jason wasn't dead. That was a high priority because if Jason is killed, she hasn't adopted the kids, so she won't have access to the kids. How to decide how much force to use and keep that balance of keeping Jason alive is very challenging.'

No one mentioned at this stage that there was evidence that Dad was planning to take us back to Ireland without her. What if Molly had realised she couldn't 'gut it out' for the next few years?

Alan Martin took advantage of Dr Hampton's statement about Molly needing to use 'the right amount of force' to confront him again. He showed Dr Hampton photographs of Tom and Molly at the scene – both clearly unharmed. Then, he showed him photographs of Dad 'with his head bashed in'. I looked down immediately, not wanting to see.

'Does that look like a reasonable amount of force to you?' he asked.

Dr Hampton hardly missed a beat. 'I believe it's a measure of how terrified Tom and Molly were,' he said. My mind whirled as I wondered, *Was I your last thought, Daddy?* I've read that some scientists believe that the brain might remain active for a short time after death, possibly for seven minutes or more. They aren't sure what happens during this time, whether it's a dreamlike experience or whether the person relives memories from their life. If you did get to relive memories, Dad, I hope they took you far away from your pain and what you experienced that night.

As Dr Hampton's reply led to horrified gasps around the courtroom, I sat there wishing that my dad's final memory was filled with peace and love and that he knew that he was the brightest thing in my life.

Judge Hall reacted immediately, warning that no public displays of emotion were allowed. He told everyone in the public gallery that we could leave if we couldn't handle the testimony.

But I felt appalled that Dr Hampton saw photographs of a man bludgeoned to death and tried to justify that brutal savagery. According to him, the evidence did not show excessive force. *The reason they kept striking my father on the head – even as he lay unconscious – was because they were so terrified.* All I could think of was the terror, confusion and agony Dad must have felt as his wife and father-in-law rained blow after blow on him.

However, like all 'hired guns' in a courtroom, Dr Hampton

had a job to do. He prioritised being a witness for felons over any empathetic consideration for the victim's children and family. The entire process was dehumanising. To make matters worse, as he left the stand, he flashed a winning smile at Tom and Molly and the defence team. Job done.

Most days in the courtroom, crime-scene and autopsy photographs were a constant hazard for Jack and me. My family had seen those photographs, and they have never been able to forget the viciousness they contained. But I have never seen them and never want to. I have, unfortunately, heard and read the accounts of veteran police and investigators, who have all said they had never experienced violent scenes like it.

Three of the four bedroom walls were blood-spattered. Some walls had prints of my father's bloody head striking them. Indentations from the force of the killers' weapons had pockmarked the plasterwork. Pools of blood stained the carpet, and blood spatters appeared on the blinds and skirting board. There was more blood spatter on the underside of the quilt, the lamps, everywhere. A bloody hand mark smeared the bedroom door handle.

I had the misfortune of seeing one crime-scene photograph in the media. It was a close-up of one side of my dad's bedroom door. It showed a bloody handprint sliding downwards – which was, I believe, evidence of my dad's doomed attempt to escape that room. That photograph and that handprint still haunt me.

Throughout the hearing, I had to work hard to avoid the crime-scene images. The defence displayed them on laptops, which they often swung in the courtroom with abandon. Prints were casually strewn on desks. On countless occasions, I was forced to look down and study my knees until my neck ached, but I was determined not to be traumatised further. I never want to witness my father's death scene.

Alan Martin made a brief but chilling closing statement on the second last day of the hearing. He said Molly knew 'the endgame was coming'.

He said the marriage was loveless and a lie. And that Molly had provoked an argument the night Dad died hoping to get a domestic violence order that would have given her custody of Jack and me because she feared Dad was about to take us to Ireland.

He was careful to say that the prosecution was not suggesting 'premeditation' in the killing (he couldn't because it was part of the plea deal) but he said that Molly had tried to engineer an incident on the night of 2 August. He also added that she needed her husband alive.

She took advantage of having her father, a former FBI agent, in the house that night to unleash an explosive event that turned out to be lethal. On 2 August, he said, 'the clock was ticking' on 'Molly's years-long plan to get these kids'.

'Molly had a plan, and that plan came into fruition well before she married Jason Corbett. She was talking to a divorce attorney [before the marriage] about how to get the kids. She entered a marriage in full and open contemplation of divorcing someone to take somebody else's children. She lived a lie … she was motivated by the refusal to let go of what she wanted, but she could not have [Jack and me]. All she had to do was quit living the lie. Molly was all about the kids,' he said. 'And they are not her kids.'

He repeated his mantra that Molly was skilled at scheming and deceiving, and had a 'complicated relationship with the truth'. He said Molly's account of what happened the night Dad had died was as unreliable as all the other lies she had told.

He urged the judge to consider the carnage at the scene. He said the problem about the night of 2 August was 'that Jason's statement died with him'. However, he added, 'Jason's statement [his blood] was on the carpet; it was on the wall and it was on the ceiling. He was silenced.'

He went on, 'Is Jason a monster as he has been portrayed to be? Is it fair? No, it is not. Was this a happy home? No. That does not justify what happened.'

Alan Martin said Tom had accepted responsibility for his actions in the death of his son-in-law, but Molly had not. He said Molly blamed Dad for everything that happened before he was killed, and everything afterwards on her own father.

He also expressed relief that we did not have to endure seeing the weapons used being presented to a jury again. 'There will be no demos of a bat and brick pounding on the table,' he said, reflecting on the original trial when he'd struck his desk with the bat in his closing arguments.

Alan Martin's voice trembled as he turned and spoke about Jack and me. 'It is nothing but a miracle that these two children do not have the sights and sounds of that night scarred into their brains. Nothing but a miracle.'

He pointed at us, and the judge followed the direction of his finger. For nearly the first time in the entire sentencing hearing, Judge Hall looked directly at Jack and me. Until then, he seemed to actively avoid looking at us.

Jack and I and most of the family left the courtroom when Tom and Molly's attorneys got up to make their final arguments. We'd heard it all before.

I learned that Molly's attorney Douglas Kingsbery said that Dad was the aggressor on 2 August 2015. After killing Dad, he said Molly got into a foetal position outside the home because she was in such distress. The entire incident could have ended if Dad had released his chokehold on Molly as her father had demanded. He argued Molly was the victim of a long-running campaign of domestic abuse in their marriage and that Dad was an abusive husband who used physical and emotional violence to control her.

Once again, Kingsbery displayed his exceptional talent for concocting narratives to suit his client. 'Jason woke up and he was angry ... Molly was assaulted for getting up at night to tend to an eight-year-old,' he said. 'This was a trigger for Jason. Even the children knew not to wake him up at night.'

We made the right decision to leave the courtroom. I never want to hear that nonsense again.

Before he finished, Kingsbery also flung Tom under the bus, adding it was him – not Molly – who had killed Dad after striking him repeatedly in the head with a baseball bat. It was little wonder that the pair barely seemed to look at each other by the end of the hearing.

Tom's counsel Jay Vannoy claimed that Tom had tried to defuse and calm the scene he had encountered in the bedroom. He said Tom had lived a blameless life and had been trapped in a tragic event, not of his making.

Not of his making? Who wielded that bat? I wondered when I heard what he'd said afterwards.

'Everything about this case is extraordinary,' he said. 'There is nothing normal about this case. It is unusual. It is extraordinary.'

One of his other lawyers, Jones Byrd, said Tom had already served over three and a half years in prison for an unfair conviction. He said it would be a 'manifest injustice' if he had to go back to jail after the errors in the 2017 trial. He added that as Tom had pleaded guilty to voluntary manslaughter, he would lose his ability to hold high-level security clearances, which were part of his job and his identity.

The judge was reminded again of Tom's terrible trauma when Sharon had been diagnosed with ovarian cancer in January 2016. Tom missed the second round of her chemotherapy because he was in jail.

Tom and Molly also addressed the judge at the end of a long day. We came back into the courtroom in time for Molly's statement. She never apologised, of course. She only used the opportunity to justify her actions. 'I protected my father from certain death,' she said.

Tom said he was a lawman and took responsibility for his actions. However, he was only protecting his daughter.

'I have great respect for the law. I used the law to protect our nation's security. I realise my actions were excessive and were in violation of the law. I accept responsibility and I am sorry. I repeatedly begged Jason to let her go. But when he started to drag her down the hallway, my instincts to save my only daughter took over. I had no choice. Maybe a better man could have produced a better result, but I did the best I could.'

The seventh day of the hearing was long and traumatic. We heard Dr Adams' shocking revelation that Molly had consulted a divorce lawyer *before* she'd married Dad. We were forced to listen to character witnesses for 'meticulously responsible'

Tom. Dr Scott Hampton claimed the violence wreaked on my father was 'a measure of [how] terrified' Tom and Molly were of him.

Then we had Alan Martin's chilling closing statement about Molly realising 'the endgame was coming'.

The day felt like hell. During a break in proceedings, we had left the courthouse for some fresh air. I felt shaken and upset by what we'd heard. The sun was beating down, and I felt overheated and overwrought. So many people were milling around and cameras were pointing at us. The people who had killed my dad walked right past me.

I felt I couldn't do it anymore. I didn't want to be in America anymore. I just wanted to go home. Dad's American friends and neighbours came to the court sometimes, and others met us for lunch. We went to restaurants where we'd gone with Dad. North Carolina seemed to have a vast gaping hole in it where Dad once was. I wanted my dad. I barely made it down the road from the courthouse before I dissolved into tears.

Tracey said David would take me back to the house in Winston-Salem for the rest of the day. But I had made it this far and was determined to see this case through to the end.

We sat in the car and turned on the air-con, and I cooled down and stopped crying. I was determined not to be seen crying in public or to be viewed as a broken little girl. Because I'm not. I'm a strong person, but I was just worn out at that stage. Later, media videos and photos appeared of me tearfully hugging Tracey, and I cried again, seeing a moment of raw emotion and grief turned into a public spectacle.

CHAPTER 24

REHEARSALS

Your Honour
It was only when I went to live with Tracey and David in Ireland that I knew the true meaning of family. I now know what a loving mother is. I've always known a loving father, and Dave is that now too.

Courtroom 6, Davidson County Courthouse
Day 7: Tuesday, 7 November 2023
After the hearing, we went to the District Attorney's office and waited for everyone to leave the courthouse. Judge Hall had just confirmed that the case would end the following day, so the prosecution team wanted us to read through our Victim Impact Statements before we delivered them.

I asked that Jack and I should also be able to show photos of Dad to Judge Hall. Real photos – not crime-scene photographs and autopsy photographs where Dad was a crime statistic and a case number.

I wanted Judge Hall to see photos of Dad as a father, husband, son, brother and friend. Photos that showed him smiling, happy and whole. I wanted him to see Dad as a real person. The prosecution attorneys shrugged. There was nothing prohibiting this in the plea deal, but they warned that the defence might still object.

When the courthouse was quiet, Assistant DAs Kaitlyn Jones and Marissa Parker led us via the jury rooms back into Courtroom 6 for our rehearsal.

I was already wound up and apprehensive about delivering my statement. My heart had plunged earlier in the week when I'd read a news report revealing Jack and I would personally deliver our Victim Impact Statements.

I hadn't wanted anyone to know that in advance. I didn't need the added pressure of the world knowing that I would speak on my dad's behalf in court for the first time. The media interest was spiralling anyway, and this report only amplified the stress and piled on more expectations and coverage.

Eight statements were to be delivered in the courtroom on the final day of the hearing. Tracey, Jack and I would read our statements ourselves, the District Attorney's team would read the others' statements to the court. In his, Wayne described how the Martens had lied to him about how his twin had died on 2 August 2015. A joint statement from other family members, including David, Dean and Adam, spoke about how Jack and I had been retraumatised by the Martens' efforts to reduce their jail time. Marilyn's statement would describe how an image of 'Jason's battered body haunts me every day'. A statement from my granda was also read.

The prosecution would read most of the submissions. Assistant DA Marissa Parker would read the statement on behalf of my birth mom's family, the Fitzpatricks. This would be the first time the judge would have heard that my birth mom's sister Catherine was in the house when the asthma attack started, something the defence had not mentioned in the courtroom despite days of 'evidence' about my birth mom's suffocation and strangulation. Tracey, Jack and I would stand and read our own statements.

Jack, Tracey, David, Adam and Dean sat at the back of the court for the read-through as Kaitlyn and Marissa brought me to the front to read my statement.

I had read less than half of it when my tears blinded me and my hands trembled. My emotion, stress and dyslexia snowballed, and the page turned into a jumble of blurred letters. I went into meltdown. It was impossible to read any more, so I stopped and despaired. *There's no one in the courtroom besides my family, and I'm like this!* I felt ten times worse. I knew I had to face this again in front of a packed courtroom in the morning.

Anxiety and fear had got the better of me. I breathed deeply, trying to regain control. In my heart, I realised I cared too much, but it was little consolation. I was overanalysing and overthinking everything, and piling more pressure on myself.

Tracey came up and hugged me. 'Don't worry about it, love,' she said. 'You can practise it a few more times later.'

I knew everyone wondered if I could do it. I wondered myself. I felt discouraged rather than motivated after the read-through, but I still didn't want to give up. Everyone knew how important making this statement was to me. It was my first and final opportunity to speak on behalf of my dad, but I had tried several read-throughs, and they all ended the same way – failure and tears. I couldn't get to the finish line.

Jack went up, and we all went quiet as he unfolded his pages and began to speak. His voice quivered to begin with, but he gained strength with each word. We had heard excerpts from each other's statements, but I'd never heard much of Jack's before that evening.

'Every single day I wake up with the weight of guilt, loneliness and depression, knowing I will never get to see my dad again …'

His words painted a vivid picture of a struggle to survive in a world that seemed cruel and unpredictable. One by one, we were all overcome with emotion. Everyone wept, listening to the raw pain he expressed. Jack never discussed his emotions or feelings, so hearing him expose his soul in his statement nearly broke me.

'When I was a young teenager, I used to think sometimes it would be easier if I wasn't here anymore and at least that way I could be with my dad and my mam and apologise and feel safe.'

I knew Jack had gone through very dark times after Dad died. But it was awful to hear my brother admit he had thought about killing himself. He'd never said that aloud before. It was tough for Dean and Adam to hear too.

Jack and I had both struggled after Dad died, but I'd always feared that my brother had found it harder. I have my ways of coping – therapy, talking and writing help me. I know how to make myself feel better. But for a long time, I suspected Jack hadn't engaged in enough ways to express or release his pain. He has rediscovered his love for music and I don't worry about him as much anymore. But hearing how he felt at his worst moments was heartbreaking.

Then we heard Tracey's powerful statement. She highlighted how the Martens had not only stolen my dad's life but tried to steal his good name. 'To serve their own ends, they tried to destroy the good name of the man whose life they had just taken.'

She also spoke about the heartache of losing her and David's foster daughter, Isobel. She'd been twelve years old when they'd brought Jack and me from America. I shared Isobel's room in the beginning.

They'd been investigating the process and possibility of adopting her when Dad was killed. But she'd been taken back into the foster system after we arrived because Tracey and David didn't have the physical space in the house for her to remain with them. Nor could they take on three children with multiple needs. Isobel was another innocent victim of what happened on 2 August 2015. Another life irrevocably changed by what Tom and Molly Martens had done.

'I remain devastated by the loss and I miss mothering her,' said Tracey. 'There has been so much of our lives impacted by Jason's killing.'

Everyone felt emotionally wrung after the read-throughs, but we comforted each other with a family hug before leaving the courtroom. We had dinner back in the house that evening. Everyone tried to act like the following day wasn't the big day, the culmination of all our efforts, but there was a tension in the house that hadn't been there before.

Nobody said it, but everybody felt it. With so much one-way evidence in Courtroom 6, we all feared that Tom and Molly Martens might walk free the next day.

But everyone did normal things that night. Dean and Paul called their wives. Marilyn called her kids. Tracey called her dad, John.

The sentencing hearing was tough on Granda. My dad was the youngest of his eight children. He was even the youngest of the twins, so he was his baby. He'd read the headlines in the newspapers back home and watched news reports about Dad killing my birth mom. The hearing had been challenging for him. He's very stoic, the strong and silent type, but behind it all, he's a complete softie.

He was also still grieving my nana, Rita Corbett, who had died in 2020 during Covid-19. He hadn't been allowed to be there to comfort her during her last days, and I knew that had had a lasting effect. He missed her a lot. We all did. Then the Martens were released from prison less than a year after she passed. I'm only glad that Nana never lived to see that.

Before we left Ireland, Granda had hugged Jack and told him, 'Don't look down. Look them in the eyes.' So, that's what Jack made sure he did.

Later that night, Tracey tried to prepare me for delivering my statement. She said I had to distance myself from my words or risk breaking down again. 'Just read what's on the page. Try taking the emotion out of it. Think as if you are reading a book.'

Even if I couldn't make it to the end, Tracey assured me she would finish it for me. This took some of the pressure off me. It was some comfort to know that if I made an absolute shambles of my statement, Tracey would step in and read it for me. And I knew no one important to me would judge me for it.

I went into Tracey and David's room that night because they had a dresser on which I could rest my laptop. I added a few more lines and began rehearsing like an actor learning her script.

I concentrated on the beginning and the end, reading both silently and aloud, getting familiar with the lines.

I thought that learning the words would reduce the likelihood of being caught off-guard by my emotions. And if I broke the statement into sections, I could concentrate on getting through one section at a time.

I tried to breathe and pace myself. I had to remember to pause if I felt myself becoming emotional. The Assistant DAs said nobody could tell me to hurry. I could pause for an hour if I wanted. I would need to use every strategy I could to get myself to the end.

'This Victim Impact Statement is about your dad and you. It's not about being critical of Molly,' the prosecutors had warned. But it had to be about Molly too, because her actions had significantly impacted my life. I should have been thousands of miles away with my school friends at Munger Community College studying for the Leaving Cert. Yet eight years after she had killed my father, I was back in North Carolina for a sentencing hearing. Instead of writing an English essay, I was in front of my laptop writing how her actions had impacted my life.

I'd had a meeting with Liam O'Mahoney, the school principal, before leaving for America. I got his trademark fist bump and his assurance that everyone in the school had my back. The staff were always supportive and discreet. They never said anything in front of other students, which I appreciated. When I'd returned from my first court proceeding about Dad the year before, several students had said they'd heard I was in America.

'Lucky you,' they'd said, adding they hoped I'd had a good holiday.

'I did, thanks!'

I was glad many people never watched the news. I liked returning to routine and not dwelling on my other life.

My teachers were amazing, always doing their best to ensure that I didn't fall behind. They uploaded lessons to the Google Classroom platform for me. I tried to do an hour here and there to keep up, but my mind wasn't always in the right place for schoolwork.

I continued to re-read my statement. Tracey assured me it was okay to show emotion but to focus on why I was delivering this statement, not its content. But even as I rehearsed again that night, I cried. A lot.

The statement contained lots of excerpts from pieces I'd written between the ages of ten and fourteen – each paragraph was a piece of my life. Every version of myself had a voice, which was important as I'd had no voice during those years.

The Victim Impact Statement was the only opportunity afforded to me to talk in an official capacity about Dad. I thought about what Jack had said during the evening run-through. He said that Molly was 'a monster' who abused him in every way imaginable. *If Jack has the strength to do this*, I thought, *so do I*.

I would talk about my experiences with Molly too. People had to know. The more I thought about it, the more determined I became. I would stand at the front of that courtroom and read my statement from beginning to end.

CHAPTER 25

BAD HABITS

Your Honour

I was used by her. All I have ever been is a piece on her chessboard. She taught me how to shoplift, how to vomit, how to be the most convincing liar.

Winston-Salem, North Carolina
November 2023

I couldn't tell the judge that Molly had physically scarred me, but she had marked me in other ways. Her impact on me went far deeper than Tracey and David realised for a long time.

I remember a shrill alarm sounding when Molly and I went to leave the department store one day. A uniformed security guard stopped us by stepping into our path. 'Ma'am, you'll need to move aside and open your bags for me, please,' he said.

Other shoppers flowed around us, stealing curious glances at the well-dressed woman clutching store bags and a small girl's hand. I was six or seven years old.

Molly had a big shopping habit, so we spent countless hours wandering in Hanes Mall in Winston-Salem. However, she also had another habit of taking items without paying for them. Her technique was to buy things and slip an extra item or two into the shopping bags or conceal garments in the changing rooms.

'What do you think, Sarah?' she'd said, modelling a top and turning before the mirror.

Then she'd balled up her old top and stuffed it in her handbag, and we exited the store with her new top under her jacket. She sometimes made me an unwitting accomplice – carrying a bag containing her plunder.

The guard asked us to stand aside as he rummaged in Molly's plastic store bags containing her purchases. I can see her now, rolling her eyes, her face a picture of indignation.

Finding nothing suspicious in the bags, the guard focused on me. 'What about the hat?' he asked, eyeing the bucket hat Molly had perched on my head.

She'd said I looked so cute that I should wear it home. Molly glanced at me and gasped, 'Oh my Lord! You can't do that, Sarah!'

Confusion washed over me as I looked from one adult to the other.

'I'm so sorry,' Molly said, plucking the hat off my head and returning it to the security guard. 'My daughter must have picked it up.'

She gave the security guard a tinkling laugh as if to say, *Kids will be kids*, and we left the store. She was brazen. She thought she could get away with anything and, as a result, she often did.

Since Molly also paid for things at the register, I had some vague notion that adding extra items to your shopping bag was acceptable. I was a kid. I rarely questioned anything Molly did. I thought taking items was a normal part of the shopping process.

The hat incident remains clear in my mind because the guard confiscated my new headwear, and I felt hurt that Molly had scolded me after telling me to wear it home.

Not long after I returned to Ireland, I was in Brown Thomas and running my fingers through a jewellery rack. A pretty tennis bracelet caught my eye. Tracey was browsing through a clothes rail, and I tugged at one of her shopping bags, intending to drop the bracelet in.

Tracey yanked her bag away from me. 'What are you trying to do, Sarah?' she said, eyes flaring.

I held out the bracelet, confused by her reaction. 'I was just putting this in your bag,' I said hesitantly.

I saw Tracey's lips form a rigid line, but I was bewildered.

I didn't know that what I was doing was wrong. I'd never even heard of the word 'shoplifting'. Popping a few little things into a bag was normal shopping behaviour for me. *Isn't this what we do?*

'We'll talk about this later, but put that back,' she said, her voice measured.

Tracey wore an impassive mask that day, but, years later, she admitted she was deeply concerned about my behaviour. She explained why I could never do that again. It must have been very difficult for her. She never expected to have such a large family or anticipated how much support we needed. Every week brought a new revelation from either Jack or me. New learned behaviours we'd been exposed to that demanded a lot of love, understanding and care.

Shoplifting was not the only issue she had to deal with because Molly had led me down the path of other risky behaviours too.

One day, when I was very young, I'd heard strange noises coming from Molly's bedroom ensuite. I remember freezing in the open doorway, unsure if I should have witnessed what I did. Molly was kneeling, crouched over the toilet, holding her hair back with one hand and retching with two fingers from her other hand in her mouth.

She got to her feet, wiping her mouth with the back of her hand when she saw me.

'Are you okay, Mom?' I asked, concerned.

'Yes, I'm good,' she said. 'It's nothing. I'm just keeping myself slim for swimming.'

Molly's troubled relationship with eating had already affected Jack and me. She used food as a tool to manipulate – using starvation as punishment and feeding as a reward. She also criticised people's body shapes, demeaning Dad for his weight. Fearing similar disgust, I was growing wary of food. If staying thin meant vomiting into a toilet, I was happy to do it. And if Molly was doing it, how wrong could it be?

I was about six when I started, and it took a while to learn. I'd put my fingers in my mouth and wonder why it wasn't happening. I had underestimated how far my fingers needed to reach for the process to be effective. But I learned by watching and practising.

I became preoccupied with food and weight long before I heard of eating disorders like bulimia, but I was lucky because the behaviour never became ingrained. Purging never became a daily thing for me. Tracey discovered the issue, and another bad habit was curbed thanks to some early intervention.

CHAPTER 26

A HOLLOW VICTORY

Your Honour
My dad had a life to live. He had a really important job to do –
being my dad – and he loved it. He loved me.

Courtroom 6, Davidson County Courthouse
Day 8, Wednesday, 8 November 2023
Jack stood before the court, tall and straight, and began delivering his statement in his natural, quiet-spoken manner.

Tracey, David, Adam, Dean and I sat close behind, holding hands, caring for each other and willing Jack on. We had discussed who should go first and last. I wanted to speak after Jack had spoken. I thought I might feel braver after watching Jack speak. Jack is so private that I knew reading his statement felt like a massive violation for him.

He never wanted to be in front of a courtroom addressing the judge. He tore every carefully guarded word from deep inside him. I knew it must have filled him with dread to lay bare his innermost feelings and private thoughts in such a public forum. But, like me, he felt a desperate need to be heard. He wanted to set the record straight, tell the truth about Dad and explain his own part in this twisted narrative that had played out in the courtroom.

The bravest and most impactful sentence for me was Jack's opening lines. 'The first thing I want to state clearly is: I was a liar. From the age of four to ten years of age – I was taught how to lie and manipulate people by Molly Martens. During this time, I was abused by Molly Martens in every way you can imagine, and then some.'

Almost immediately, Molly began whimpering. During Tracey's statement, she had looked away, never once sobbing. Tracey had spoken of her bigger blended family and how she loved Jack and me more than words could express. She'd pleaded for Jack and me to have the time to heal.

But Jack was only half a minute into his speech when Molly began making heaving sounds. She was close to the defence's microphone so no one in the courtroom could avoid hearing her. Her sobbing echoed around the room, and there was a danger she might drown out Jack's voice. But Jack wasn't thrown. He was there to tell the judge in a court of law that he lied in his original interviews. He was there for redemption. We had anticipated Molly's behaviour, so he just raised his voice and spoke louder.

'I have felt lost for so long, not really knowing where I will end up. I have lost so much of myself. I lost my love for sport. I lost my trust in people, and I have lost myself day by day, year by year, since the day he was taken from me. I constantly second-guess myself, not sure if people really care about me. I can't trust anyone because I can't even trust myself because of how Molly taught me to lie for so many years. I have to work to see the best in people.'

Molly had angled her chair away from us, but her sobs got louder every time he mentioned her name. Tom gazed straight ahead and didn't even attempt to comfort his daughter sitting feet away from him. The dynamic seemed odd between them throughout the hearing, with very little interaction.

Jack kept going despite the disturbance in the courtroom.

'The bright boy and happy kid everyone used to see was buried deep inside of me, and I don't know if he will ever come out again. The tragedy and trauma I have had to deal with growing up destroyed me. I am drowning every day in pain.'

Jack's head remained high, only dipping to read his statement or to gather himself, especially while talking about Dad.

'I didn't just lose a parent. I lost my biggest supporter, my teacher, my protector, my hero but, most of all, I lost my best friend,' he said. 'My dad was the most caring, funny and gentle man you could ever meet. He could light up a room with his smile. He brightened my world and, since then, my life has been dark. I'll never hear his voice, feel his warmth or hear that perfect laugh ever again.'

Molly grew even louder as Jack reached into his soul and expressed his thoughts about her. But he continued to speak with quiet assurance as he revealed the real abuser in 160 Panther Creek Court.

'Your Honour, don't be fooled by this mask of civility of Molly Martens. There is a monster lurking underneath the exterior. She systematically broke me down and drip-fed me untruths. I want to be clear: I had never witnessed my dad hit Molly Martens – ever. I am not under duress now. I want you to look at me standing here today and know the truth. It is a travesty of justice that Molly Martens wasn't charged with first-degree murder, as was considered by the DA.'

The courtroom struggled to hear Jack over Molly's groans. Jack had to stop, pausing to gather himself at times. But he drew in one deep breath after another and fought on.

'Molly Martens needs to be locked away for as long as possible, so she cannot do this to another family, another child. It is my biggest fear and gives me nightmares. She will do it again if she finds the opportunity.'

The Martens' family exchanged glances, with some members crying when Jack highlighted another important issue that hadn't been raised during the sentencing hearing.

'My father's mobile phone, laptop and hard drives vanished after his death, and they were never located afterwards,' he said. He also revealed where he'd last seen them.

It required every bit of resolve not to break down during his heartfelt disclosures. Listening to his words was devastating, and it was even more difficult to realise his experiences differed from mine. Neither of us knew what the other went through because Molly kept us apart. Regardless of how tearful I felt, I gulped the emotion down because I knew if I started crying, I would never stop.

Around this point, Judge Hall issued a single warning that he would not allow the courtroom proceedings to be disrupted.

I hugged Jack after he had finished speaking. I knew it had

been so hard for him that I wanted to say, 'Right, we're done. Let's get out of here.'

But it was my turn, and with my heart beating hard, I stepped forward. I felt petrified, but I also felt a surge of determination burning inside me. My biggest fear at that moment was not being able to finish – I hadn't yet got to the end of my statement in read-throughs.

But my brother had done it, and seeing how he delivered his statement with such bravery and grace gave me the courage I needed. I felt the surrounding support. Jack stood at my shoulder. When I glanced left or right over my shoulder, I saw everyone I loved. Tracey, David, Marilyn, Adam, Dean and Jack were in the front-row seats behind me. They were almost within prodding distance of me, urging me to succeed. I wanted my voice and truth to be heard, so I began with Dad.

Your Honour
You know my dad as 'the deceased', but he had a name. It was Jason.
He had blue eyes. He worked really hard. He was a good golfer.
He was my baseball coach.
He was my soccer coach.
He was my biggest supporter.
He tucked me into bed at night.
He made me laugh.
He made me feel loved and secure.
But most importantly, he was just my dad.
Jason Corbett was my dad.
All I ever wanted was to have a father–daughter dance.
I will never get that.

He is never going to be there for me when I get my heart broken or when I graduate.
He didn't even get to see me graduate primary school.
He will never know I wrote a book in his honour.
I will never get to tell him how much I admire him.
Or how I wish I had his courage.
He will never walk me down the aisle.
He will never meet my children, his grandkids.
That future was taken from us.
Instead, my life is filled with anniversaries of death.

While I spoke, the judge looked through the photos we'd given him of Dad. We had printed them up and handed them to the prosecution that morning. Assistant DA Alan Martin announced that Jason Corbett's children requested that Judge Hall see photographs of their father while they delivered their Victim Impact Statements to the court.

The defence was surprised, but it would have appeared churlish to object. So, they didn't.

Your Honour
I wish that you could have met my dad.
He had this big, warm personality. He was so good to others and always tried to make other people's lives better.

I was glad that Judge Hall heard about the man who had read my bedtime stories and taught us to play soccer and baseball. I wanted the judge to see our resemblance to him and realise that he'd been a real person and we were a proper family.

A TIME FOR TRUTH

My dad. The person who gave me my name, my chubby fingers, the colour of my eyes, my loud laugh, my singing voice and even the shape of my head.

I'm reminded of Dad's hands whenever I examine my fingers. As a child, I often wrapped my hand around one of his big fingers. And he got his fingers from his mother, Rita Corbett because my nana's fingers were the same. I also inherited the 'chubby' Corbett fingers and the same shaped head and eye colour as both.

My name is Sarah. My dad explained to me that my name means 'princess'. He would call me 'his little princess'. He would wrap me in his hugs, read to me ...

The tears flowed and I broke down several times. But I wiped those tears from my face, took a deep breath and continued. I knew this was my only chance. If I messed up, Tracey would step in for me, and no one in my family would have cared – but I would have been devastated because I had been waiting since I was eight or nine years old to speak on my dad's behalf in court.

I would never speak before the judge or the Martens family again. I wanted my words documented for posterity, part of the legal record. And I wanted Tom and Molly to hear me and know I remembered. I remembered everything.

Not once did I say I didn't love Molly Martens, but after weaponising my love for her and [because of the] abuse I endured, I can stand here today and say I do not love Molly, and she is not my mother.

Molly's sobbing and moaning reached fever pitch. At one stage, when I started speaking about how she'd taught me how to shoplift, I paused on purpose. I let her emit an anguished lament to the court. Then, I raised the volume of my voice about five levels.

I don't care if I sound like I'm shouting, I thought. *You will not drown me out. Everyone will hear this whether you like it or not.*

I told the judge how, on returning to Ireland, Molly had contacted the child beside me in school. He reeled back and glowered at her. Molly collapsed onto the table in front of her, face down, arms hanging, wracked by violent weeping. I had to pause again before continuing.

She took everything I loved away from me, everything. She took my dad, the person I am supposed to go to when I need advice. He was supposed to teach me how to drive. He was supposed to be there for my Holy Communion and my Confirmation. He was supposed to be there for my first day of secondary school.

I said that Dad and I would never sing 'The House That Built Me' or 'The Streets of New York' at the top of our lungs in the car again. And that I'd never say goodnight to him again.

My dad used to tuck me in every night ... 'as snug as a bug' ...

I remembered how Dad approached the 'tucking-in' aspect of his job with dedication. He 'chopped' the blankets around me, binding me like a mummy under the bedclothes. I sometimes squealed as he squeezed me, but he said he had to make sure I was 'snug like a bug in a little tiny rug'. It was the cosiest feeling.

He'd leave my bedroom door cracked, so I didn't get scared at night, and he was always there to take care of me when I had a nightmare. My dad was my hero. He always will be. When I woke in the mornings, he would greet me and my brother with the saying 'Boogawooga' in his booming voice and laugh his loud laugh. It made me laugh, and I felt safe and loved. I will never feel that security again in this world.

Friday nights were our official 'Dad' nights. I looked forward to Fridays all week. On those evenings, Dad lit up the barbecue, kneaded his favourite blend of meats and seasonings and made up his delicious burgers.

I still picture him behind our big grill, tongs in hand, standing in the wafting smoke and the heat of North Carolina's long summer evenings. I insisted on 'helping', so he'd scoop me up, gave me the tongs and let me flip the burgers. The night wasn't complete until I heard the juices hiss and watched the flames jump as I flipped the meat patties.

When our back garden seemed filled to bursting with the smell of charcoal and seared meat, we'd all sit together with a big bowl of salad and Dad's quarter-pounders. Some of my best memories of North Carolina were Friday nights with Dad and his homemade burgers.

Then I told the judge other memories so he'd learn more about my dad.

Just weeks before he died we were at the local Sheetz, a petrol station and convenience store. Jack and I were in the car, and Dad was outside 'pumping gas'. Dad started talking to a woman at the next pump. Her hair was bound back into a tight ponytail, and she looked tired and distressed. She had three crying kids in the back of her station wagon.

I couldn't hear the exchange between them. But I saw Dad and the woman walk into the store, and when they emerged, they were carrying shopping bags. She pumped gas into her car, and Dad put the bags in her vehicle. I saw her thank him as he got back into our car.

Jack asked, 'Who's that lady?'

Dad said he didn't know, but he bought some groceries and gas for her.

'Why?' I asked.

'She doesn't have money and I do, so I could help her. It's good to help others because we never know what's happening in people's lives. Someone else may do the same for you one day.'

It was just a random act of kindness, and that was our dad: pure kindness.

Judge
You didn't have the pleasure of meeting my dad, Jason Corbett. I think of my dad all the time, and when I think of him, I remember his kindness. Two weeks before he died, we pulled up in a Sheetz ...

Before I finished, I also pleaded for a sentence to reflect the seriousness of Tom and Molly Martens' crimes.

Next year, I am due to begin my BA in criminal justice. It will take four to six years. I want to change the world for the better. I want to do good in the world. I ask you to let us adjust and get out from under this. Please, my dad's life is worth more than a few years in prison. He didn't want to die ...

I've seen my father's bloody handprint on the door of his bedroom. There was nothing voluntary about his death. I know in my heart he tried to leave that bedroom. He didn't choose to leave us; he was taken from us. HE was the victim.

I believe in the justice system; I am innocent of any crime, but I have lived under this crime for more than half of my life. I am pleading with you to give me my freedom by giving the maximum possible sentence to Molly and Thomas Martens.

I'd reached the end of my statement, my throat sore and eyes red with grief. I felt raw and exhausted, but I made it to the final line.

I am proud to be the daughter of such a kind and gentle man. I am proud to be Jason Corbett's daughter.

Jack and I poured out our hearts and exposed our souls in our Victim Impact Statements. We both pleaded with the judge to make his sentence reflect the crime the Martens had committed against our dad and us. We hoped the statements would make a difference in sentencing Dad's killers.

'Thank you, young lady,' the judge said as I assumed my seat on the bench with the rest of my family.

Then he said words that were like a hammer blow to me. He hardly paused for thought before adding that nothing we had said in our Victim Impact Statements had swayed him in his judgment.

'I've indicated that what I heard would not change my judgment in any way. It has not,' he said.

He said his decision was predetermined and unaffected by anything we'd said in the courtroom. I was stunned. I also thought his remark was inappropriate. I'd always assumed that Victim Impact Statements were vital to the judicial process. They were to guide the judge to make a more informed decision regarding the sentence length. Not in our case, apparently.

'Every criminal case of any kind that comes before the court should be a search for the truth,' he said. 'I do not know the truth.'

I do not know the truth.

I despaired when the judge said that. How could so many people with such formidable intellect and vast academic achievements be so blind to the truth? All Judge Hall had to do was compare the photos of my father with those of Tom and Molly Martens on Sunday morning, 2 August 2015. My father lay naked in a pool of blood with his head caved in. Meanwhile, Tom and Molly's nightwear was undamaged; Tom's spectacles were unscratched, and Molly's fine wrist bracelet was intact. The only obvious marks on the two killers were spatters of my father's blood.

Their 'evidence' of self-defence comprised a litany of witnesses stating, 'Molly said,' and a single recording of my father raising his voice. They had found a miniscule mark on Molly's neck after she had been digging at and kneading it for hours. The 'evidence' that my father had killed my birth mother was farcical, considering her sister had witnessed the traumatic events of that night.

The judge continued. 'I have listened intently. I have clung to every detail of everything presented, and I have used every bit of experience of my life to make this a fair and impartial proceeding. Then, when called upon, to enter judgment in a fair and impartial way. It is a case with a number of holes [that] only the three people in that room could ever fill. I say at best because I don't know what the emotional and mental state of Mr Martens and [Molly] were at the time.'

In his statement, the judge emphasised that Jack and I were 'blameless'.

'The directness of ... Jack and Sarah are as compelling to me as the statements I heard. Based upon my experience, I found those to be believable,' he said. 'What is important for the family of the victim, particularly these two young adults, and irrespective of what I find, they were and are blameless in this matter. Completely. Not mostly. Completely.

'At the time eight and eleven, and they stand before me nineteen and seventeen, they were and are blameless. And any statements they made and any statements they make now, the court system has done the best. I have done my best with them. They are blameless and must always be treated as blameless in this absolute tragedy. And it is, you've heard me say, a homicide.'

He continued by talking about the shortcomings of the law.

'The law is imperfect. If the law were perfect, Jason Corbett would be back with us. The court cannot restore that. The court cannot adequately punish or the court cannot adequately rehabilitate. The court cannot adequately deter others. It's an imperfect process.'

He also referred to my plans to study criminal justice.

'I am glad that the young lady, Sarah, is going to be a part of it moving forward. She may make it more perfect. But it is imperfect.'

He questioned Tom and his wife Sharon's actions on the night.

'The one thing that I am struck with is – and it will be reflected in sentencing, but in an appropriate way. The one thing I am struck with from the time that Mr Martens heard this noise upstairs, the banging, the words, sufficient to grab a baseball bat. What does an experienced law-enforcement officer do when he realises that deadly force may need to be deployed? Call backup. There was no call to 911. There was the wife I've not heard from. That's another big hole in this matter.

'I don't fill it with my own supposition. I don't fill it in a way that would further jeopardise these defendants. [Sharon's] words, at least as documented, are that she heard it, she heard some banging, but she thought that Tom would take care of it. It makes no sense.

'Mr [Alan] Martin's term that this is not a silent crime rings true to me. And from the very moment I started receiving evidence, the notion that one gentleman, a very experienced pillar of the community, absolute servant of the people, and charged with protection of life and liberty, would choose a baseball bat without [saying], 'Honey, wake up. Call the police. I'm going to take care of this. Honey, call the police', or that woman on her own who heard this thing would not call the police, not call 911 contemporaneously, in addition to responding with a baseball bat, is something I will never understand.

'Had I heard [Sharon's] testimony, I don't think I would understand it … There are things that simply do not make sense.'

He did comment on the contrast between the unscathed appearance of Tom and Molly and Dad's body after the killing.

'The other great dichotomy we have [is] a gentleman with a career you cannot emulate. A young lady who has clearly – I've heard some things today that could change the analysis – but from everything I have seen and heard, was raising two wonderful children.

'There is an enormous disparity between Jason Corbett's body and the bodies of Mr Martens and Ms [Martens]. I understand that oftentimes, when one is choked or strangled, it is not apparent. There was redness on the neck. There was something that could very well be a nail dig.

'… these folks came away with really not a mark on their body, and Mr Corbett, without going into any detail, is – his condition was diametrically opposite to that, and that's very hard to reconcile.

'The delicate bracelet on Ms Corbett's right arm is intact. The pyjamas that were not stretched. The gentleman's shirt was not stretched. They're blood-spattered but not stretched.

'I wasn't there. I will never know. I don't know the absolute truth.'

He rejected the prosecution's argument that our presence in the house on the night of Dad's killing was an aggravating factor in the killing.

Then, Molly stood for sentencing.

'She shall be imprisoned for a minimum of fifty-one and a maximum of seventy-four months. This is an active sentence. It will resume essentially immediately. She will receive credit, which the law requires, for all time spent in custody towards service of that sentence.'

Sentencing in months was confusing, especially as we had to subtract time served already. We turned to each other, trying to work out the maths.

Molly was sentenced to four years and three months up to a maximum of six years, two months. But she and her father had already served forty-four months – three years and seven months – in prison between August 2017 and March 2021.

We knew Molly would be incarcerated, but not for long. Tears stung my eyes. *At least they'll go back to prison*, I thought.

The attorneys said afterwards that each would serve only another seven months behind bars. Good behaviour earned during the time already served ensured they wouldn't serve the entire six years.

We could never have been happy with the results. We had no possible 'win' situation in this plea-deal scenario because we could never walk out with a first-degree murder charge. Even their original second-degree murder charge and sentence of twenty to twenty-five years could never make up for the permanent loss we'd suffered.

The judge learned that Molly had battled bouts of depression and had been diagnosed with bipolar disorder. After witnessing Molly's hysteria in court, Judge Hall requested a full psychiatric assessment of her by the North Carolina Department of Corrections.

'Now, I am concerned. I am concerned because of the pain that she has expressed during this proceeding. But she is in my care now, and I order that she be immediately assessed for suicide precautions. I order that she receive the benefit of all mental healthcare, psychiatric if necessary. I'm going to order a psychiatric examination by a medical doctor, not a psychologist, and that she be afforded any treatment that may be indicated.'

Molly howled even louder, prompting Judge Hall to ask her to pull herself together. 'Please comport yourself, please,' he urged.

He also said he was 'concerned for other reasons about the family of the victim'.

Alan Martin, one of the Assistant DAs, replied by requesting 'the imposition of the longest possible no-contact communication order with any of the children or any of the family members of Mr Corbett or Ms Fitzpatrick'.

'So ordered,' said the judge. 'I understand she will be subject to post-release supervision and that is an order of this court.'

Molly held out her hands to be cuffed by the sheriff.

Judge Hall then asked Tom to stand.

'When I say pillar of the community, sir, I mean it, and I do have respect for you.' He said his 'service in the FBI and in defence' was a mitigating factor in his sentencing. He gave Tom the same sentence as his daughter.

'I wish you the very best, sir,' he said. 'He is in your custody, sheriff.'

Molly continued to sob, but Tom's expression was inscrutable. If he felt anything, he concealed it well. He took off his coat and handed it and his wallet to his son, Stewart. He told a tearful Sharon, 'Everything is going to be okay.'

He also experienced the harsh click of cold metal being secured around his wrists. Each time it happened, it must have seemed like an ironic reversal of fortunes for a man who had performed that ritual countless times with suspects or felons throughout his career.

I watched as the sheriffs led Tom and Molly away to Davidson County Jail. I assumed they would soon be moved into the North Carolina state prison system to serve the remainder of their sentences.

I can't say I felt satisfaction at seeing them being marched out of the courtroom in handcuffs. It was more of a relief. After all the skewed and one-sided evidence I'd witnessed during the hearing, I'd feared the Martens would walk free based on time served. Everyone had feared that.

So, seeing them clapped in handcuffs gave me some closure, maybe even some small sense of gratification. After a ten-day sentencing hearing, I was glad that Tom and Molly knew that Jack and I were sitting there and watching their final humiliation.

CHAPTER 27

AFTER THE STORM

Enroute to Washington Dulles International Airport
Wednesday, 8 November 2023

The car hummed steadily along the highway, and I sank deeper into the back seat. Through half-closed eyes, I watched an endless blur of trees and fields. Fragments of soft conversation from the front seats occasionally filtered through the haze in my head, but I couldn't muster the energy to engage.

Everyone bundled into our cars immediately after the sentencing hearing and we began our long journey home. We'd already packed up and left the house in Winston-Salem and our vehicles outside Davidson County Courthouse were laden with our suitcases and belongings. We were wasting no time heading back to Washington's Dulles International Airport. I travelled with Tracey, David and Jack. Meanwhile, Adam and Dean had their own rental car, and Marilyn, Sharon, Wayne and Paul were in another. We all wanted to go home.

We had one final shock before leaving the courthouse. It

happened within seconds of Molly and Tom being taken away. Everyone was getting ready to go when someone yelled Tracey's name in the courtroom.

I saw one of Molly's friends, her face twisted in fury, rushing towards Tracey. A Davidson County police officer and a bailiff rushed to intervene but, in an instant, Paul and David stepped in front of the woman.

'Back off,' Paul said to the woman, palms raised.

The officer and bailiff grabbed Molly's friend and, with little ceremony, they escorted her from the building. The commotion was over in seconds, but it took us a few minutes for us to gather ourselves again. The day had been stressful enough without that.

We had already said our farewells to people who had known Dad. Some colleagues and neighbours had turned up for that final day. 'We'll see you the next time you visit,' they said. And I wondered with a sinking feeling if I'd ever see them again. We had never *visited* since Dad died. We had only gone there for court cases; now the cases were over, so were our reasons to go to North Carolina.

As awful as all the courtroom hearings, pre-trial hearings and trials had been, they were a constant reminder that my father wasn't gone. But, with the end of the hearing, I felt like I was losing Dad all over again. Or I was losing an important connection with him. Up until the end of the hearing, Dad had remained at the forefront of our minds. We still had unfinished business for him.

But the life I'd shared with Dad in North Carolina was over that day. A new chasm of grief opened, and that stark realisation that Dad was gone and never coming back struck again. The last connection that had tethered us to North Carolina had been severed, and I felt disillusioned with the world. Any imagined or hoped-for triumph had evaporated, and the judge's words, so long awaited, felt empty. It was all over. I felt sadness, a sense of anticlimax and an overwhelming loneliness that I hadn't expected.

No one spoke after we left the court. There was nothing to be said. Tracey readied a statement from the family that was to be released the following morning.

'While this is not a moment of celebration for us, we can still find a path to move forward in our lives. While we may not be satisfied with the sentencing, we would like to acknowledge the dedication and hard work exhibited by the Davidson County Sheriff's Department and the District Attorney's office throughout the past eight years. We are deeply grateful for the support we have received from the people of North Carolina and Ireland. We thank the media for their interest and reporting. We kindly ask for privacy as our family processes this experience ...'

I wondered if I'd ever be able to process it. The adrenaline that had sustained me during the hearing was gone. I was quiet in the car because all I felt was bone-deep exhaustion and deflation. The things they had said about Dad, the seven-month sentence, all swirled together in a nauseating mix. I could see the same weariness and sadness in the faces of the others.

Even though I had seen Tom and Molly Martens being returned to jail, I felt no sense of jubilation. At most, I could exhale a little. However, the result was underwhelming and disappointing.

An additional seven months for a man's life? It seemed like a mockery of an exchange. People got longer sentences for stealing a car in America all the time. I couldn't shake the feeling that I was still waiting for justice that would never come. I drifted in and out of sleep listening to the monotonous drone of tyres on asphalt, and losing track of time and place.

The landscape darkened, the streetlights multiplied and soon the traffic thickened. It was dark when our small convoy pulled into a motel in Richmond, halfway between Davidson County and the airport. We gathered in the restaurant for a kind of 'debriefing' over dinner and to discuss the day's events.

Everyone felt fortunate to be part of such a close and supportive group. We talked about how proud we were of each other. People said Mom and Dad would have been proud of Jack and me. I knew they were doing their collective best to lift my spirits. We talked about how we'd made the pilgrimage together and that, even though we might not have achieved the desired outcome, we had represented Dad with integrity, loyalty and love. And we continued to talk into the night about everything and nothing. Despite the traumatic day we'd just had, we laughed.

The weight of the previous ten days still pressed on all our shoulders, but the weight felt lighter somehow when we were all together. I knew that the following day would bring more challenges. Many moments would arise where the events of recent weeks would churn in my mind. But that night, in a restaurant on the outskirts of a strange city in Virginia, I relaxed and let the healing power of family and friends ease that troubled day.

CHAPTER 28

DISBELIEF

Shelbourne Hotel, Dublin
Monday, 4 December 2023

Tracey woke me, moving around our plush Dublin hotel room a few weeks after we'd returned to Ireland. She was already packing and getting ready to leave. I stretched and rubbed my eyes, looking in surprise at the time on my phone. We were only staying one night in Dublin. Why were we in such a hurry to leave and return to Kilkee?

Tracey had urged everyone to move on and immerse themselves in normal life again as soon as the sentencing hearing had ended. However, it still felt like there was no escape from the Martens. My stomach sank when I went into a local shop one day and saw Molly's face looming from the front page of a newspaper with a headline bearing Jack's branding of her as a 'monster'.

Weeks later, Tracey and I were invited to a Christmas show in Dublin's National Concert Hall held by wellness coach Georgie Crawford. We liked to follow Georgie's journey in her *Good*

Glow podcasts. Tracey thought the show would be a girls' night out and a pre-Christmas treat for us. Then David made it extra special by booking a room for Tracey and me in the Shelbourne Hotel. I'd never stayed in such a luxurious hotel in my life, and I knew Tracey was looking forward to our one-night getaway as much as I was.

I expected to have a relaxing morning and maybe luxuriate in the marble bathtub, but Tracey was in a hurry. She wasn't even having breakfast before heading home. She seemed tense, so I didn't question anything and got ready to go too. Tracey insisted everything was fine, but she would never usually leave in a rush, so I knew something had happened.

As she drove along the quays by the Liffey, I asked again. 'Really, is everything okay?'

Tracey was silent for a moment, and then she said it. 'It seems the Martens are getting out of prison tomorrow.'

I was horror-struck. 'What? That can't be right!' I said, pulling out my phone and starting to search.

The courts had only imprisoned the Martens on 8 November – meaning they were getting out less than a month after the sentencing hearing. I felt my heart start to pound and my skin become clammy. My hands shook as I tried to type.

The uplifting show and our beautiful hotel room faded in an instant. Nausea set in. No wonder Tracey couldn't stomach breakfast.

An Irish newspaper's front-page story reported the pair were about to be released. The journalist had tried to contact Tracey the previous night, but we were at the show and missed the calls.

I realised I was getting a glimpse of what Tracey had faced down the years. She'd received many of these jolts that sent shockwaves through her and ruined her day or week. She'd always kept this news to herself until she could give us the privacy and space to process the latest twist in the case. Tracey and I sat in the car in virtual silence, hoping there had been a mistake this time.

However, when we got home and checked, the records office in Raleigh confirmed Tom and Molly were about to be released. The North Carolina Department of Adult Correction also released a formal statement with more information. Tom would be released the following day and Molly the day after. The prison service said both felons would have twelve months of supervision by a parole officer after they left prison.

We started emailing and calling the North Carolina Department of Adult Correction and the District Attorney's office, trying to get more information. How could they be getting out within a month of the hearing? But it was still early in the morning in North Carolina and nobody answered.

Even after the working day began in North Carolina, no one called us back. I felt more distraught and frustrated as the day went on.

My therapist had asked me to keep a diary and to document my feelings and events. I have only one note on my phone for that day: 'This can't be happening!' I wanted to fly to America and confront whoever had made this decision.

When we managed to speak to someone in the District Attorney's office, they insisted it had nothing to do with them. Tracey got through to the correctional facility and gave Molly's inmate number, but they said Molly wasn't there. So where was she? Tracey called the Davidson County Jail, and they confirmed Molly was there. So was her father.

That explained why no one had seen them being moved from jail. We knew some media waited days to get footage of people being taken to prison. Felony cases typically spend little to no time in county jail after sentencing, they're sent within hours to correctional facilities. However, weeks later, Tom and Molly were still in Davidson County Jail, enjoying more relaxed conditions and greater freedom of movement and visitation than in a state prison.

All day and into the night, we faced walls of bureaucracy or received conflicting information about the Martens' fates. My head was pounding with a stress headache as the day continued.

I called and left messages. Jack called. All the family were making calls. Nobody from the justice system in North Carolina got in touch with us to explain or offer any support. However, in Ireland at least, the news of the Martens' imminent release stoked outrage on radio and social media all day.

Tracey only got a confirmed update around 10.00 p.m. that night.

'They're not getting out,' she said finally.

The prison service said that the online information referring to the Martens had been taken down and was being updated.

Then, they released a second statement. 'After further review, the initial projected release dates calculated in response to re-sentencing for Molly Corbett and Thomas Martens were found to be incorrect.

'The current projected release dates for both are 27 June 2024.

[Tom and Molly] Martens will be transferred to state prison facilities to complete the remainder of their sentences.'

The pressure bubble popped, but I didn't feel elation, only drained and tired. We all felt the same.

The prison service in North Carolina said that the confusion over the imminent release was due to 'human error'. We were incredulous that the authorities could have made such an error in their calculations. We wondered how they could make the exact same error with two inmates.

After discovering the 'error', Molly and Tom were moved to the North Carolina state prison system to serve the remainder of their sentences.

Molly was admitted to the North Carolina Correctional Institution for Women in Raleigh, a multilevel security prison. Tom was sent to a medium-security prison, Piedmont Correctional Institution in Salisbury, with shared cells and tight supervision.

'These offenders may be transferred to other prisons after the completion of the admission and evaluation process,' the prison service said.

North Carolina's prison service normally kept inmates with a serious Class D felony conviction in medium- or maximum-security facilities. However, Tom was soon switched to a minimum-security facility even though they are normally reserved for prisoners with non-violent offences. In Caldwell Correctional Center in Lenoir, Tom was accommodated in a single cell and a more relaxed environment.

District Attorney Garry Frank said his office had had no input into the decision to release the Martens early. He said under North Carolina law, an administrative unit called the Combined Records

Section managed the prison population. This unit set the release date for prisoners based on data from several sources. According to the Combined Records website, these sources include federal enforcement agencies. I thought this was interesting, considering the Martens' considerable federal connections.

The fact that no one had moved Tom and Molly from the county jail made it seem even more suspicious. It was as if someone had thought that moving them into the larger prison population was not worthwhile.

Whoever caused this debacle, it created another nightmare day for us. If the Irish media and Justice for Jason supporters hadn't reacted forcibly to highlight this injustice, I believe the Martens would have been out in plenty of time for Christmas that year.

CHAPTER 29

WHEN CRIME PAYS

After my birth mother died, Dad had packed a large suitcase with her cherished possessions, mementos of Mom and Dad's time together. He also kept another case with her wedding dress and shoes. He'd left the case with Tracey when we moved to America.

We sometimes take out Dad's old suitcase and rummage through it, usually on an anniversary or other family occasions. The case now contains his passport and a handful of documents, and sentimental mementoes. Recently, I must have rummaged deeper than usual because my hand brushed against something cool and smooth. I pulled out a bottle of Dad's aftershave, a scent Mom had given him as a gift after they first met.

Mom and Dad were first introduced by their mutual friend, Lynn Shanahan. She knew my father from the time they were in National School together. In February 1997, Lynn brought her friend, Mags Fitzpatrick, to Dad and Wayne's twenty-first birthday party in the Sallyport, a Limerick club. As soon as he met Mags, Dad was smitten.

The first gift Mom bought Dad after they started dating was the Dior fragrance, Fahrenheit. Because Mom had bought it, the scent was special, and Dad continued wearing it until the day he died.

Tracey picked up the bottle, shook it and sprayed it into the air. The scent hit me like a blow. I had forgotten that scent, but it came back to me in a rush. The warm and rugged aroma instantly transported me back to another world. With the fragrance came memories of being hugged in Dad's powerful arms and his big smile.

I felt a bittersweet ache – happiness for the memories that his scent brought back and grief for what I'd lost. I started sobbing, releasing a torrent of emotions. The familiar smell brought me closer to Dad than I had felt in years and was like a comforting reminder of him in the room. I sprayed some on my arms to carry around for the day.

Jack arrived home later, and the leather and woody notes immediately hit his nose. He stopped dead and stared at me, confused at this sudden echo of our past. 'Where did you get that?' he said. He recognised the unmistakable scent that had always clung to Dad's clothes the minute he walked in.

I feel so blessed that Dad had curated this collection of his and my birth mom's love in that old suitcase because we have so few mementoes to remember him by.

Dad had appointed David as the executor of his estate in his will, so his fiduciary duty was to protect the estate for Jack and me. The month after Dad died, the estate got an order prohibiting Molly from removing property from the house that was owned either solely by Dad or jointly with her.

Two months after Dad died, Tracey and David returned to North Carolina for the start of a civil hearing. They had asked Jack and me to list the things we'd like from our Panther Creek Court house, saying they would try to find them and bring them home for us.

I asked for some teddy bears and my birth mom's rings. Dad always said he was keeping them for me. She was wearing her wedding ring when she was laid to rest, but she had an engagement ring and two eternity rings that Dad had bought for her on Jack's birth and mine.

However, Tracey and David couldn't find the rings, and Molly said she didn't have them or know of their whereabouts. Tracey returned to Ireland with Dad's wooden sign reading 'Jason Corbett's Pub' with its Irish flag and shamrock emblems. She also brought his golf clubs and a golf trophy he'd won. These are the only things of sentimental value we now have belonging to Dad.

Dad's neighbours in Meadowlands contacted Tracey a fortnight after prosecutors charged Molly with murder in January 2016. They told her several moving trucks were outside our Panther Creek Court house. We soon discovered Molly had removed almost all the household contents except for Dad's clothes and some furniture he'd bought with my mom.

David moved to enforce the consent order taken out the previous September. He sought a restraining order preventing Molly from taking anything else from our home or selling the items she had taken.

During the ensuing hearing, Molly admitted that agents acting for her had removed the items from the house as she was planning to bring them to her native Tennessee. She argued that everything she took had been gifted to her or bought by her or her parents. She said the purchases were made using a credit card solely in her name.

However, the court found that Dad's earnings had paid all her card bills. The court ruled against, forbidding her to take or sell the items, citing potential harm to Jack and me as the estate beneficiaries.

Molly was given thirty days to return the property taken from our house. She could keep her clothes, bathroom toiletries, two lamps, a trunk, paintings, a coat rack and a mirror. The court ordered her to pay $4,900 to the estate for Dad's car, which her parents had been driving. Dad's furnishings and other belongings were eventually placed in secure storage.

The fight for the house contents was one of several civil-court hearings with Molly. At some stage in the proceedings, Molly finally surrendered my mom's rings in court without providing any explanation. I have them now, and they are precious to me; I hope one day to pass them to my own daughter.

After the Martens went to prison, Tracey and David called the storage unit to retrieve Dad's belongings. They planned to bring Jack and me to the unit to choose items of the most sentimental value to bring home.

I remember the worried discussions Tracey and David had about us visiting the unit but they decided that we needed closure for the specific feelings of trauma we felt about our sudden upheaval, as we had been given little notice or opportunity to process things at the time. The prospect of revisiting and sorting through our belongings held the promise of a cathartic or healing experience for Jack and me. The night before we visited the storage unit, we eagerly talked about the anticipation of reconnecting with our past possessions and were filled with a sort of hopeful feeling. However, when David phoned the storage company to arrange our visit, we received devastating news. The storage business told David that a relative of the Martens had sold off all the belongings, including Dad's pool table, furniture and bar. The unit holder sold off the remaining items to pay for the storage. There was nothing left.

The realisation that everything had disappeared struck us deeply. To us, it further proved that Molly had never cared about Jack's or my feelings. Tracey and David were already immersed in other court cases involving the estate and upcoming appeals, and no one had the energy to go on another tangent and pursue this one. What was the point? Everything belonging to Dad was already gone.

Molly did her best to depict Dad as tight and miserly throughout the sentencing hearing, but the truth is she'd enjoyed his hard-earned income and spent it with abandon.

Investigations showed that she spent $90,000 in just eight months before Dad died, and she filled almost three rooms of our house on Panther Creek Court with her clothes. She also spent lavishly on clothes for me. Someone counted over eighty dresses hanging in my room.

She'd made sure she wouldn't be short of cash after Dad died and had cleared out their joint account of $30,000 within days of killing him.

The head of the investigation into Dad's killing, Detective Lieutenant Wanda Thompson, looked into Dad's life-insurance policies. He had taken them out through his employer, MPS. The

Unum Life Insurance company confirmed the total value of the policies was more than $600,000.

Dad had told Tracey and David that he had set up his life insurance to give his children 25 per cent each and the other half to Molly. However, Detective Thompson's investigations revealed that 'Jason Corbett had recently changed his beneficiary status to Molly Corbett'.

Detective Thompson enquired how this was done and wrote in her report: 'Ms [Unum Insurance employee name] could not advise me how recently that transaction took place. She advised that due to privacy laws, she did not believe she could share any further information about Jason Corbett's life-insurance status.'

All we've learned since is that the policy was changed online in 2014.

After Dad's death, Molly stood to benefit from a life-insurance policy and a house with a combined worth of one million dollars.

'Jason Corbett's alleged comfortable financial status provides an additional possible motive for his untimely death,' Detective Thompson wrote in the documents filed while seeking a search warrant for access to Molly and Dad's bank statements, email and phone records.

However, Mike Earnest, speaking on behalf of the family, later insisted, 'Neither Molly, Sharon nor Tom were aware of this life-insurance policy through his employment, until after his death.'

In July 2017, David, as executor of Dad's estate, sued Tom, Molly and Sharon for Dad's wrongful death.

The civil lawsuit claimed that Tom and Molly had wilfully and maliciously assaulted our dad, causing his death, and that Sharon had aided and abetted the incident. It also stated that Jack and I had lost income, services and protection because of Dad's death.

While Molly and Tom were in prison, their lawyers settled the wrongful death lawsuit filed by Dad's estate. This resulted in a payout to a trust fund for Jack and me – although there was no admission of negligence or wrongdoing by the Martens.

As part of that 2019 settlement, the Martens paid $180,000 and an insurance company, State Farm, paid an additional $20,000. After paying attorney fees and litigation costs, $149,000 was deposited into our trust fund from the Martens.

However, another $601,000 was deposited into the trust fund from Dad's life-insurance policy. The insurance company refused to pay Molly for the insurance as she was deemed 'a slayer' and legally prohibited from benefiting from the death of the person she had killed. David ensured that she renounced any claim to the funds so that they could be used 'for the benefit of the children'.

After that, David resigned as our trustee, leaving Grant Thornton Accountants in Ireland as our independent trustee.

A lot of that money has gone. It was used to pay legal bills, travel and living expenses incurred while flying over and back to America over the past five years.

Tracey and David financed everything before that. The Limerick community also raised almost €60,000 to assist with the costs, which were huge. The legal fees for the guardianship battle alone amounted to €250,000 in two weeks. Tracey and David had to liquidate everything they owned to meet the bills. But Jack and I wanted to take over, using the trust fund and Dad's money to represent his and our interests when we could.

Our house in Panther Creek Court was also put up for sale. It took some time, but Mays Gibson Real Estate in North Carolina sold it for $345,900 in 2018. The house sold for $50,000 less than Dad had paid for it in 2011, most likely because of the property's tragic and brutal history.

Under US law, half the sale amount went to Molly despite her being in prison for Dad's second-degree murder at the time. Dad had paid for the entire property, spending $400,000 on our American home from the proceeds of the house he and Mom had built in Ballyneety.

Molly never held paid employment after she married Dad. She contributed less than $10,000 to their income during their entire marriage but had owed $12,000 on her credit card the month Dad died. Dad wrote cheques for $50,000 for her dream wedding and another for $75,000 to furnish our house. Yet, after making no financial contribution to the home or contents, Molly profited from killing my father by receiving $173,000 for 'her' half of the house. She was effectively provided funds for her legal bills with money she received from killing Dad.

Maybe we could have fought her in the courts over the house proceeds, but it was a case of picking our battles. Tracey and David would have had to open us to another legal front, and they were already engaged in a war to keep the Martens in prison. Molly was 'all about the children' after all, so Tracey requested that she return the proceeds from the house and lodge them to our trust. Of course, that never happened.

Yet, throughout the sentencing hearing, Molly's lawyers tried to paint our generous and loving Dad as the one who was grasping and mercenary in Panther Creek Court.

CHAPTER 30

RELEASE

Blackrock Health Galway Clinic
Wednesday, 5 June 2024

Propped up by pillows, I lay in a hospital room, my mind torn between the Leaving Cert paper on my over-bed table and the Martens leaving prison. I felt suspended between two worlds again.

I answered questions on the English Paper with my writing hand tethered to an IV drip. The clock ticked relentlessly, but I was distracted. My focus flitted between the exam and the real world outside.

North Carolina's prison service first scheduled the Martens' release date as 27 June 2024. However, the Department of Adult Correction made further recalculations on their sentences and decided their new release date was 6 June, the same week that I was due to start the Leaving Cert. It was far from ideal, but I was powerless to do anything. I had to push the Martens into the furthest recesses of my mind.

My health problems began the week before the exams started. We had our Sixth Year graduation party in the Strand Hotel at the end of May. My throat felt terrible the following day, but I blamed it on too much talking and singing, and expected the soreness to resolve in a day or two.

Two days before the start of the Leaving Cert exams, I woke up with my throat so swollen, I was struggling to breathe. I felt as if I'd swallowed a tennis ball. Tracey brought me to ShannonDoc in Kilrush, the emergency doctor service near our home in Kilkee. After prescribing antibiotics, he instructed Tracey to bring me straight to A&E if things didn't improve.

The next day, I felt worse, and Tracey thought I needed to go to the hospital. As my exams were starting the next morning, she didn't want me to spend hours waiting in University Hospital Limerick A&E. After consulting with my doctor, she decided to take me to Blackrock Health Galway Clinic, an hour and a half's drive north of Kilkee.

The decision was the right one because an ear, nose and throat specialist saw me within minutes. He diagnosed a peritonsillar abscess, a complication of tonsillitis, which blocks the airways and makes it difficult to breathe. However, he shocked me by insisting that I had to be admitted for treatment. I was never sick and hadn't been in hospital in years.

The doctor asked if I was experiencing any stress because I seemed to be run down. Tracey and I looked at each other. If my throat had allowed me, I would have laughed.

I had tried not to let the Martens' impending release affect me. But it was hard to face the fact that my father's killers would soon be free again and, this time, forever. The news reports about the Martens' release date combined with the exams and feeling unwell meant the entire week felt like a complete overload.

The doctor prescribed rest, IV fluids and antibiotics. However, there wasn't much rest with English Paper 1 the following morning. Tracey contacted the school, and they were amazing, facilitating the exam in hospital at the last minute.

The weight of isolation and being in a hospital bed hit me the next morning. I missed the reassuring presence of friends and the nervous energy that filled the room before an exam. I had to settle for the company of my own private invigilator – my school had dispatched a special needs assistant to supervise the three-hour exam. The nursing staff also stuck a 'Do Not Disturb' notice on the door.

The nurses had tried but failed to find a vein in my left hand. So, my writing hand dragged the IV line across the page accompanied by the sound of the insistent beep from attached medical equipment.

Afterwards, I lay staring at the ceiling, wondering how my school friends had done and thinking about the Martens getting out the following day. I had hoped to sit my Leaving Cert like any normal teenager, but it didn't happen that way.

The Martens' release was scheduled for around 2.00 p.m. Irish time on Thursday, 6 June – as my second English paper started. I stayed away from my phone until after the exam when I googled news on their release. Photos of Molly leaving the North Carolina Correctional Institution for Women in Raleigh popped up. She had emerged twenty minutes before I had opened my exam paper – around 8.40 a.m. in North Carolina.

She beamed for the cameras, her hair tied up as she wore a

jaunty blue-and-white striped sundress. With her sunny outfit and cheery disposition, the images suggested she was leaving a summer garden party rather than a facility housing death-row murderers.

She climbed into the back of a car branded 'North Carolina Department of Adult Correction' with two probation officers and waved and smiled at the media from the car as she passed. *Do all prisoners get chauffeur-driven home by the prison?* I wondered.

It was disturbing seeing her smiling and waving. Everything about Molly suggested that the gravity of her crime and the pain she had inflicted on others meant nothing to her. Rather than even a show of remorse, we saw the true face of Molly – self-centred, callous and insensitive.

Molly's attorney, Douglas Kingsbery, followed in the same vein, issuing a self-serving statement on behalf of his client. Molly was 'thankful to be alive because there are many women who are in abusive relationships who aren't so fortunate'.

Molly was keen to portray herself as a brave survivor of domestic abuse and it hurt me deeply to see her create this false narrative and exploit the pain of real victims of abuse.

We also couldn't understand why the prison service released Molly at the same time as Tom. He had been a model prisoner. However, Molly had violated prison rules several times, which should have disqualified her from early release.

Her infractions included unauthorised leave from a specified area. She had also breached prison rules by possessing 'non-threat contraband' and disobeying an order from a prison officer. However, those and other infractions failed to affect her 'good behaviour' record.

Tom left his cushy minimum-security prison in Lenoir just under two hours after Molly was released. The prison was a three-hour drive from where Molly had been incarcerated. He strode out a picture of self-assurance and left with one of his sons, who was waiting outside the gates.

I know nothing of what happened to them since, nor do I care. All I know is, as felons, father and daughter may not live with each other and cannot socialise unless approved by parole boards.

Fox TV had asked for a statement, which I sent from the hospital.

'Molly Martens manipulated my love, trust and feelings from a very young age for her own gain. The Martens chose self-interest over considering the harm caused to innocent individuals, especially children.

'Despite serving their sentence, the repercussions of their actions will have a lasting impact. The truth, known by all involved, will eventually come to light for the world to see.'

And I believe the truth about what happened that night will emerge.

I left the hospital the following morning with lots of medication to take during my maths exam that afternoon. When I returned to school, however, I didn't seem to feel the same nervous energy or excitement as everyone else. It was strange, but my perspective had shifted over the previous months without my even realising it. My friends seemed more invested in the impending exams and analysing the questions than I was. The Leaving Cert had once loomed like a mountain to climb. After the experiences of the sentencing hearing, however, the exams had become a molehill. Many of life's other challenges, including the Martens' release, had made these exams seem almost inconsequential. The little things didn't seem to matter as much.

In one way, I envied my classmates caught up in their normal concerns. But my new-found outlook had its advantages as I sat each exam with a sense of detachment and calm. I didn't fret over a few points in the Leaving Cert.

The day I finished the exams, I walked ten minutes from the school to the Castlemungret Cemetery to see Mom and Dad. A mix of rural fields and urban sprawl surround the modern cemetery stone walls. Its neighbours consist of bungalows, open pasture, GAA sports pitches and a busy road.

Turning left inside the gate, I walked to near the back of the cemetery. I could find Mom and Dad's polished marble gravestone blindfolded. The brown headstone bears a small wedding photo in the top left-hand corner of the stone. Mom and Dad are in each other's arms, looking at the camera with Mom's red wedding bouquet resting on Dad's shoulder. It makes it easier to talk to them when they're smiling out at me.

Dad picked the headstone out for Mom, and the dedication reads: 'Cherished memories of a wonderful wife and mommy, Margaret (Mags) Corbett (Nee Fitzpatrick).'

Dad's name is now inscribed below hers. Their ages will remain thirty-one and thirty-nine forever as Jack and I get older.

The stone has two inscriptions: 'Suffer little children to come unto me. Erected by her loving husband Jason, son Jack and daughter Sarah.'

On the base is a second inscription that my dad used to read to us every time we visited Mom.

There's got to be a reason, and we have to understand,
God made us and at any time, he'll reach down for our hand.
There might not be a warning.
We won't know where or when.
The only thing I'm certain of is we will meet again.

Often, there are fresh flowers at the bottom of the stone, so the words are not always visible. But Jack heard Dad read it so often, he can recite the inscription off by heart.

The cemetery is a peaceful place despite the nearby traffic. I love being around the stillness of their resting place. It sounds morose, but it's the only constant in my life. The cemetery has always been there for me. I remember my father bringing us there to see Mom, and now I'm there for both of them. Other people I love, including Nana and my cousin, are always there too. I stayed for about an hour with Mom and Dad, relating everything happening in our lives.

A middle-aged woman approached, asking if I was the Corbetts' daughter. She said nothing more, just stood for a minute, maybe saying a silent prayer. Then she said, 'You're a very brave girl', hugged me, and walked away. Sometimes, lovely things happen out of nowhere.

Despite the unwelcome distractions, I got good points in the Leaving Cert and a place on the course I had applied for. Yet, it was still a piece of paper for me, and unimportant in the great scheme of things. I had already decided to postpone plans to attend third-level education to pursue another unexpected passion.

Exams may be important, but I've learned more valuable life lessons outside the classroom walls. After my experiences, I've gained a deep appreciation for the unpredictability and fragility of life. And when it comes to shaping my life and future, for me, exam results pale compared to the power of resilience, love and family bonds.

CHAPTER 31

AFTERMATH

Kilkee, County Clare
2024

I've had two persistent nightmares since I was a child; both feature Molly.

In the first, I'm skiing down a snow-covered mountain, even though I've never skied in my entire life. To my left is a line of snowbound conifers stretching down the slopes. A fence lies beyond the trees. I glance left and my heart misses a beat because Molly is behind the fence, watching. I continue skiing but, when I look again, she's still there, staring. I feel terror. The cold air rushes against my face, but no matter how long or fast I ski down this dream snowscape, Molly is still behind the fence, watching. When the Martens were released from jail, the fence disappeared, and she advanced on me through the trees. I woke many times soaked, my heart pounding with distress and fear.

In the other dream, I'm on holiday with a husband and two kids – young versions of Jack and myself. We're in Busch Gardens, the amusement park in Tampa, Florida. I've been there in real life with Tracey and David and the rest of the family.

In the dream, I see an older lady talking to my kids. As soon as the old woman sees me, she's furious. She grabs me by the shoulders and screams into my face. It's only then that I realise the figure is an older Molly. I can't understand what she's screaming about. She is incoherent with rage, but I know she's planning to take the children, and I have to save them. My husband and all the other park-goers have vanished. It's just me struggling with Molly and desperately trying to hold on to my kids. She has a vice-like grip on one of my arms and with her other hand is grabbing at my daughter. She feels glued to me, making it impossible to pry her away from me.

For years, those nightmares haunted me. I'd wake, my heart hammering in my chest, adrenaline coursing through my veins and every nerve on alert. I often fled from my bed to Adam's room. His calming presence always comforted me.

The nightmares still recur but no longer wield the same power over me. When they happen these days, I can roll over and go back to sleep. But they were a sign of ongoing stress and anxiety, especially when I was younger.

It's taken a while to readjust since the sentencing case and the Martens' release. Judge Hall stated that no matter how severe the sentence, it would never bring Dad back. But the weight of injustice still sits heavily with me, and I don't think I'll ever come to terms with the Martens' sentences. They took my dad's life and, in return, they lost four years of their own. The sentence 'voluntary manslaughter' still rings hollow and derisory.

Tracey raised something that also stuck in my mind. Imagine

for a moment if the circumstances on 2 August were reversed, and my father had beaten Molly with a baseball bat and a brick so severely that he smashed her skull.

Would the police have sent Dad home after questioning? Would they have given him custody of his wife's two children after he'd slaughtered her? Would a judge have sentenced him to four years for savagely killing her like that?

My experience with the judicial process shook me, particularly witnessing how it deprives victims of a voice. The contrast in sentencing within the same court was also disheartening. I saw people receive harsher sentences than the Martens for far lesser crimes because they couldn't afford any high-powered lawyers. The scales seem to tip in favour of the wealthy. I had to question the integrity of a process I had once wanted to be part of.

Because Dad wasn't just a victim of Molly and Tom Martens. He was a victim of the legal system too – one that stereotypes women as victims and men as perpetrators of abuse. The court didn't recognise that coercive control and domestic abuse can affect anyone, regardless of gender, and the perception still exists that there are no male victims. Jack spoke about this at our balloon release for Dad before the sentencing hearing. Molly had painted herself as a victim, but Dad, Jack and I were the victims of what happened in our house in Panther Creek Court.

Molly presented the court with a carefully crafted image of the perfect woman in a desperate situation. She did this masterfully because she is a chameleon who has been role-playing all her life. When she'd come to Ireland, she had been a shy but accomplished nanny. She'd posed as the devoted suburban wife in America. Then, she became the abused wife of a tyrant on other occasions. However, her most cherished image of herself was of the exemplary mother who had dedicated herself to the lives of her children. She juggled multiple narratives, each tailored to a different audience, and most of them lies.

As the prosecution had said, lies were Molly's way to manipulate and control people. When I was a child, she told me that my dad had cheated on her, raped her, choked her and murdered my birth mom. She told me Tracey was a bad person. I heard so many lies that I doubted what I saw with my own eyes.

She manipulated a small cohort of women into believing she was a victim of domestic abuse. I wonder if Shannon Grubb still believes the story Molly told her when she asked her to bring shoes to the park for me.

The webs of deception grew more complex as Molly went along. Why would she tell people who *knew* she wasn't my birth mother about being in labour with me? Either she was a fantasist who believed her own lies or she told so many lies she couldn't keep track of them.

I don't understand the root of her obsession with Jack and me. I think Molly loved *the idea* of having me as a daughter. She liked the public image of having two little (dyed) blonde children hanging off her every word and adoring her.

But Jack and I were real children who had lost their mom and came with all the challenges of that. We were messy and needy, required nurturing and unconditional love like all children.

But we were never individuals or real people to her. I believe she never wanted real children with all their complexities and demands. She wanted small reflections of herself, so she micromanaged my clothes, hair, our activities, food and every aspect of our lives. To all appearances, we were doing great at school and succeeding in her favourite sport. She saw this as her achievement. *Everyone, look, I'm such a great mom.* We were her trophies to be displayed in public.

Our emotional landscape was a complete minefield with Molly. We never got to experience unconditional motherly love. We faced rage or withering disappointment when we failed to 'win' or meet her expectations. She lavished us with love and affection one minute and gave us the silent or hairdryer treatment for some perceived slight the next. She turned off her love as effectively as a tap when we failed to please her. She couldn't control many aspects of her life, but it was easy to control two small children.

Adjusting to life in a loving, stable family with a caring mother figure took some time. Jack and I were confused when we started living with Tracey. We had to learn that when she corrected us or was upset by our behaviour, it didn't mean she didn't love us anymore.

I had loved and feared Molly at the same time. I was desperate for her approval and affection and fearful of her rejection. I rarely thought about what I wanted. I was too focused on pleasing Molly. Living under that sort of control can be as damaging as any physical abuse. However, there is no bruising with coercive control, so it is harder to recognise or prove.

I anticipated what Molly wanted me to do and say. She didn't need to do a lot of coaching for the interviews with social workers after Dad's death. After years of training, I knew how to please her.

My father spent much time and effort trying to please her, too. We were all on edge, trying to keep her in good humour. But we knew one innocent remark or a misplaced object could trigger a scalding tirade of screams and accusations. Behind closed doors, she effectively controlled the three of us. She was talented at intimidation, isolation and manipulation.

We had to be alert because Molly's personalities shifted like sand in a desert storm. Sometimes, we had happy Molly, who was upbeat and full of wonder, joy and affection. My dad fell in love with that side of her. On those days, she was giddy and charming, and her enthusiasm for life was contagious. Happy Molly rarely lasted, however.

Sometimes, we had desperately sad Molly. All vibrancy disappeared and she'd become a ghost of her former self. That's when Molly drew the curtains and lay in the dark or sat for hours in a bath until it was stone cold. Dark and sad Molly presented occasionally, and the house became eerily quiet.

On other days, we had competitive supermom Molly. When she was in this mode, she'd burst through doors, barking orders and setting impossible deadlines. Her eyes burned with fiery determination. *You must work. You must study. You must train. You must win.* That Molly was relentless and exhausting. That was swim-coach Molly.

Furious Molly was a frequent face around our house. She flung accusations like daggers, and her anger was indiscriminate. She was erratic and terrifying then, and Jack felt the brunt of her violence if Dad wasn't home. Furious Molly was the hardest to live with.

Many witnessed the frightening side of her behaviour because she couldn't maintain her public face for long. The mask slipped often. That's why I now believe she'd wanted to move to America.

She didn't want outside influences, like Dad's family and friends, to question her behaviour and challenge her authority.

On one occasion, when Paul Dillon and his girlfriend were visiting, they were backseat passengers in a car with Dad and Molly. Molly was driving on the busy highway between Charlotte and Winston-Salem. Dad said something innocuous, but Molly slammed on the brakes, tyres screeching, and stopped the car in the middle of several lanes of speeding traffic.

Horns blared around us as other vehicles swerved, desperately trying to avoid crashing into us. Paul and his girlfriend were petrified and begging her to move but Molly was too busy screaming at Dad to care. The incident was part of Paul's statement to investigators, illustrating the kind of concerning behaviour he'd witnessed.

I think Dad made a lot of allowances for her behaviour, knowing she had mental-health problems. He tried hard, often spending hours trying to calm her over some perceived insult. He bought her flowers, wined and dined her, and attempted to make her happy. But she gaslighted Dad, making him feel foolish and negligent by giving him the wrong times for our events. She antagonised him by being wasteful, leaving appliances and lights on and going out. Instead of supporting him, she hid his car keys and phone. I saw it all and stayed silent.

Molly wanted her own children, of course. I learned later, from public reports, that she had suffered miscarriages and Dad had paid $25,000 towards fertility treatments. At Molly's request, he had samples held in a sperm bank at a clinic in North Carolina.

But taking someone else's children was fine too. The psychologist Dr David Adams' professional opinion was that her primary focus was to adopt us, divorce Dad and take us. Her dream was to look like the perfect mom – and she needed Dad's ready-made family to achieve that look.

Molly's psychologist said she was 'all about the kids'. However, she wasn't 'all about the kids' in a healthy way. Brian Shipwash, the judge who had removed Jack and me from Molly during the guardianship case, was more accurate in his description of her. According to an interview with him after the sentencing, he believed Molly felt a 'deranged entitlement to the kids'.

Dad grew to realise this. He grew wary of her controlling behaviour and obsessiveness concerning us. He was under continual pressure from Molly and her parents to let her adopt us. It must have been stressful fighting their demands.

Investigators into Dad's death reported that a senior employee at his company in North Carolina said my father had refused to use Molly's citizenship to help arrange an American visa. 'He did not want [her] to have any legal grounds to maintain custody' if they later divorced, according to the report summary.

Wayne had come on holiday to North Carolina just before Dad was killed. We all went to Washington during his visit, where we stayed with Sharon's brother Michael Earnest and his wife Mona. Sharon came with us too. We went to all the usual tourist sights, the White House, the Lincoln Memorial and the Washington Monument. Wayne remembers how Sharon brought up the subject of Molly adopting us in front of everyone.

'Jason, if you'd sign those papers, we can look at sorting colleges out for Jack,' she said. Tom and Sharon were always prodding him to let Molly adopt us. Dad didn't need assistance to pay for our college, and he was never going to allow the adoption to happen. This was in the weeks near the end of his life when I believe he had given up trying to save the marriage. The atmosphere in the house was terrible.

Molly's frustration grew. When she'd married Dad, she had got the house and lifestyle she wanted. The obstacle to her ultimate happiness was her husband. Dad stood in the way of her 'deranged entitlement' to the children.

Dad knew if he was to end the marriage, he must get us to Ireland first and then address his problems in America. As he told Paul, he would need to be on a plane before the Martens even knew he had left.

Investigators believe the trigger to the events on 2 August was Molly learning about Dad's plans.

'The Ireland trip was allegedly for the purpose of moving him and his minor children back to his native homeland permanently,' said Detective Lieutenant Wanda Thompson in court documents for the 2017 trial.

She added, 'Additional information received from business partners of Jason Corbett indicated that in preparation for that trip, [he had] allegedly discussed transferring some of his financial assets … to his home bank in Ireland.'

In the days before his death, he also hinted at these plans when Jack and I were in the car with him. 'How do you feel about moving back to Ireland?' he asked. I remember he moved the rearview mirror to watch our reaction.

My immediate response was, 'With Molly?'

It was an odd question for a child to ask, but I felt something serious was happening. This was around the time that Molly had jumped into my bed and accused Dad of killing my birth mom.

Dad replied, 'I don't know yet.'

All the signs were that Dad was on the point of leaving. Jack had seen the suitcases in his bedroom the night he died. We'd also seen him on his laptop on the Aer Lingus site looking at flights a few days earlier.

The prosecution said Molly brought her parents to our house to be a witness to whatever plan she had for that night. Investigators think she hoped to engineer a situation where she could expose his 'domestic abuse', disrupt his plans to leave and gain custody of us.

What actually happened that night has affected my entire life, and the negative impact is exacerbated because I feel guilt over it. Dad would have left Molly sooner if I had told him what was happening. Knowing that continues to hurt me.

By the end of the sentencing hearing, I was turned off the idea of studying criminal justice. I've realised since that I don't need to be a solicitor or barrister to help others. I feel that sharing my story is an act of being a change-maker. For that reason, I want to keep telling my story because it's not only my story. Behind closed doors, other people are living lives like we did in fear, anxiety, confusion and doubt, being manipulated and monitored. It's not always easy to recognise coercive control, especially when you're in the thick of it. This form of abuse is often subtle but insidious.

In the future, I'd also like to advocate for all victims of domestic abuse, regardless of gender. Spousal abuse of men remains hidden and under-acknowledged. I've had heated debates with people who dismiss the notion of men as victims of domestic violence or abuse – but they are. We need to change societal assumptions that women are the only victims. Everybody should be protected, and everyone's rights and safety matter.

The Martens used a metal baseball bat and garden brick to silence my father. After that, they used lies as weapons to continue striking him. However, they were helped by a judicial system blind to the possibility that a father and children could be victims of a wife and mother.

Throughout the hearing, Molly's attorneys portrayed her as a nurturing mother and a frightened wife. Her friends' testimonies highlighted the fear and peril they believed Molly lived in. She and Tom claimed they had fought for their lives to survive an attack by a brutal domestic abuser.

In the courtroom, Molly had presented herself as a fragile and tragic figure, dabbing her eyes and struggling to maintain her composure. Justice should be blind to physical appearance, but everything about her appearance was designed to elicit sympathy. She was skilled in presenting herself as an innocent victim of domestic abuse.

In the sentencing hearing, Judge Hall chose not to listen to our Victim Impact Statements as adults. He told the court they didn't influence his decision in the sentencing. Instead, he chose to listen to the statements we'd given social workers as children. Those statements also helped overturn the Martens' murder sentence. Even though we recanted them, the appeals courts didn't care and insisted the original trial had erred by excluding them.

No one cared that we were eight and ten years old. Or that we said what we were instructed to say after being subjected to coercive control for years.

No decision-maker has spoken to us once in all the years since those interviews took place. Not a single lawyer, social worker or judge took the time to listen to us. We only got to say this in our Victim Impact Statements. They never considered why two children would or could lie.

There was little surprise that the Martens only had to serve months in prison. Dad couldn't defend himself, and Jack and I weren't listened to. The killers slipped through the cracks of a justice system that failed to see beyond its own prejudices.

The nightmares I have about Molly no longer concern me. The nightmare for me is knowing that she and Tom successfully weaponised my words to get away with killing my dad.

I try to accept that what happened wasn't my fault. But that's difficult because I still feel complicit in many of Molly's schemes against my father. I helped her hurt him when he was alive, and then I hurt his memory and aided his killers with the statements I made to social workers in the days after he died.

Some days will be darker than others. I think about what happened and feel a mixture of rage and despair rise inside me. It's a struggle sometimes, but I try to fight those emotions. I realise it's pointless to harbour negative feelings because I only hurt myself.

Instead, I try to recognise pain and acknowledge it without letting it consume me. I know that, as a family, we did all we could to get justice for Dad. And I know my father would never want me to be defined by what had happened to him.

Yet, even years later, I find myself standing before Dad's headstone and saying, 'I'm so sorry. I didn't realise what I was doing.'

CHAPTER 32

A NEW WORLD

Kilkee, County Clare
July 2024

Checks completed, the dive master gave me a thumbs-up. I'd never seen the weather so bad in Kilkee Bay. The rain was horizontal, and the rib pitched and rolled with each white-capped angry wave. I perched on the edge and, using one hand to secure my mask and regulator, signalled that I was ready to enter for my first ocean dive.

Taking a deep breath, I tucked my chin to my chest and back-rolled into the choppy waves. The cold shock of the Atlantic Ocean hit me despite the barrier of my thick neoprene wetsuit. On resurfacing, the swell lifted me and then dropped me as fast, waves crashing over my head. Remembering my training, I formed a circle with my thumb and index finger, giving the okay sign to the dive master. I bobbed like a cork in a spin cycle, waiting for everyone else to flip back into the water.

A thrill of anticipation ran through my veins as my dive

'buddy' descended the anchor line, and, adjusting my buoyancy, I followed. At first, turbulent water and a flurry of bubbles surrounded me, and then something amazing happened: the sounds and motion of the everyday world disappeared. The waves above became a muted rumbling, and a remarkable calmness enveloped me. The gentle hiss of the regulator accompanied every breath I took, followed by a popping stream of air bubbles as I exhaled. I sank further into the glorious sound of silence.

The rough conditions had stirred up sand and sediment, so visibility was poor. As we continued to descend into the murky depths, the water's clarity didn't improve. I didn't care. From the moment I submerged, I felt the soothing embrace of the ocean and a profound sense of peace. It was just me in another world, floating into an alien landscape. The other divers were close but distant, blurred shapes. They were separate and distinct from me. I felt the bliss of being alone.

After Tracey and David had brought me back to Ireland as a child, I'd tried competitive swimming at school but it brought back too much trauma. I didn't enjoy it. However, in my later teens, I returned to the water recreationally and grew to love it again.

A few years ago, Tracey started managing a non-profit called Kilkee Waterworld. It aims to teach people in coastal west Clare to swim and engage with the ocean. Jack and I joined a lifeguard course there and it was one of the best decisions of my life. I made friends I'm still close to. Training as a lifeguard led me to complete the assistant teacher course, and then I trained to be a full swimming teacher.

I began working as a part-time instructor in Waterworld, teaching all ages from children to adults who came from schools and clubs in the region. I particularly enjoyed teaching small kids.

Helping a frightened child discover the joy of swimming filled me with a sense of accomplishment. My journey had been different – I had never feared water. Instead, I'd feared my teacher. My experiences with Molly shaped my teaching philosophy: no child would ever feel that kind of anxiety in my class.

When an autistic child joined our class last year, he was terrified of the water. With patience, I coaxed him into the pool, but submerging his face petrified him. 'That's all right,' I said. 'Can you put your chin under the water?'

By the end of that session, the child was diving beneath the surface and loving it. I'm not sure who had the biggest smile, him or me. My goal was to make every student feel exhilarated before the end of their class – eager to return and learn more skills.

Swimming is more than just a pastime; it's a crucial life skill and, without it, we're limiting our enjoyment of what the Irish coastline offers. By fostering a love for water in my students, I wasn't just teaching people to swim. I felt I was opening up a world of possibilities for them to explore and enjoy in the future.

At the beginning of last summer, Tracey launched a snorkelling and diving programme with the local dive centre and scuba club. David and I started snorkelling and exploring Kilkee's famous natural rock pools, the Pollock Holes. Then I joined the scuba-diving course and started training in a pool. I took that first sea dive in the bay in July 2024 and, even though it was mid-summer, the rain was driving, and the ocean tossed and rolled.

The seabed had been ploughed up, and sediment was everywhere. No one could see any fish in the cloudy conditions.

Our only sightings were a couple of hardy hermit crabs scuttling along the muddy bottom of the sea. But moving underwater felt incredible, its buoyancy providing a languid grace. Every movement felt like a graceful ballet or meditative Tai Chi.

I felt I could have stayed underwater forever, but the dive instructor gave us the signal to ascend, bringing us to the surface early because conditions were so bad. Breaking the surface that day was like waking from a surreal but wonderful dream.

I clambered back on the boat, exhilarated by a new-found passion.

I beamed. 'That was completely amazing! Please, can we do it again?'

Scuba diving exhilarated me from the start. With that one dive, I found not just an incredible pastime but a new lifeline – a way to reset my mind and soul.

That first dive also opened up a world of new possibilities that I could never have imagined. Kilkee is also one of the best diving locations in Europe, and it's right on my doorstep. I feel privileged to live here, so close to the ocean. I also love the life and the people in this area. They took me under their wings and helped me grow into a skilled snorkeller and diver.

As I progressed to deeper dives, my passion grew. I trained as a coxswain to get my licence to operate a boat. Within weeks, I had applied to Ireland's only commercial diving training programme at An Bord Iascaigh Mhara (BIM). The competitive course in Castletownbere in County Cork accepts only fifteen or so students.

The day of my debs dance was an exciting one. Hours before this rite of passage and the official end of my schooldays, I received notice BIM had accepted me on the course. I was on the first step towards a career in diving.

With further training, a commercial diving qualification offers opportunities worldwide. I could work in any number of different fields, from ecology and conservation to aquaculture, oil rigs or diving schools. My dream is to travel the world, teaching diving and swimming, and experiencing marine life in all its diversity. I hope to dive in Hawaii and the Great Barrier Reef in Australia someday. I may need to work in aquaculture or oil rigs to fund this dream, but diving is my vision for the immediate future. College may be on the horizon, but I'll focus on this path for now. In five years, I'll be twenty-three, and who knows what will happen? I may be ready for an entirely new adventure.

In a family where everyone has their 'thing', I've finally found mine and each day brings a new adventure. 'Shark-infested' isn't a term associated with the Irish coastline. However, Kilkee and Loop Head became one of the best places in Europe to see basking sharks in early summer 2020. The world's second largest plankton-feeders returned in 2024, and it was a wonder to see these amazing creatures swimming in their circle formations. Marine biologists have since explained the behaviour as 'shark speed dating' along the Atlantic coastline of County Clare.

I've also had an encounter with one of the smaller creatures of the Atlantic – a pipefish – a relative of seahorses with a horse-like head and snake-like body. Normally shy and camouflaged in seagrass, the pipefish approached, weaved through my fingers and wrapped its tail around my arm – a behaviour none of the other divers had witnessed before. It was an unforgettable interaction.

I love to dive. Calm settles in as soon as we head out in a boat, with flocks of seagulls wheeling overhead. Everyone leaves their phones on the shore, which makes the experience even more relaxing. The real world can be noisy, intrusive and hectic, but from the time we leave the pier, no work email or news of an emergency can reach me. When I'm on that boat, time slows down. There's no stress, only anticipation of the magical world underneath.

As soon as I submerge, my only concern is to check in on my cylinder and depth. The whole outside world goes quiet, my mind is at rest, and I'm absorbed by this excursion to another planet. I've never experienced freedom and relaxation like it in my life before.

Underwater, I escape from everything and every concern and worry that I feel in real life. I've lived much of my life in the public eye, and will continue to advocate for others suffering domestic violence, but, when I'm under the water, the fish are indifferent. I'm just another interloper exploring their vast underworld city and they go about their business around me. I just enjoy the privilege of having this brief visitor's pass to their habitat.

I never want to surface and am always eager for the next dive. Wrestling back into a damp wetsuit is hell, yet I'm happy to do it if it means a second dive in a day. Whatever it takes to get back under the water is worth it.

Focusing on the many things that bring me happiness helps me navigate the ebb and flow of the more negative emotions I sometimes feel. The ocean, even in its worst moods, has become my latest sanctuary and therapy. It helps balance me.

Yet, sometimes, it's bittersweet because diving is another life experience that I'll never get to share with Dad. I expected my father's absence to hurt less as I got older. However, I felt a greater sense of loss and sadness in the past year and as time moved on.

Dad's ninth anniversary was probably the hardest one for me, perhaps because it was the first year when he felt truly gone. We had no impending trial, no more court dates and no motivation to stay strong for him.

The past year also marked many significant milestones in my life. I went to my graduation, sat the Leaving Cert, had my debs dance and discovered a new passion and career direction. Since the sentencing hearing, I have had countless experiences that remind me how much my dad is missing and how profoundly I miss him.

I know I'll always defend my father and his legacy, but the way I plan to honour Dad's memory in the future is by embracing this life that he can no longer share. I know that's what he'd want for me.

The scars of what happened run deep, and I don't know if I can ever fully heal after everything. However, I know scars can fade. Through all the difficult times, my family's love, support and unity have been and continue to be my greatest strength. I have my dad's love and foresight to thank for that. He knew Tracey and David would protect Jack and me as fiercely as their own children, and we have had constant love, support and guidance since the day they collected us from the social services office in Thomasville in August 2015.

As a family, we've faced a lot of adversity, but that has only strengthened our bond. Whatever challenges we face in the future, I know we'll always protect each other and find shared joy and laughter even in the worst of times. Because we are the Corbett-Lynches, a blended family united by blood and an enduring love for each other – and my father, Jason Corbett.

ACKNOWLEDGEMENTS

Mom, thank you for being the only person who understood me when nobody else did. Thank you for protecting me and trusting me, for believing me when others tore my words to pieces. Thank you for allowing me to use my own voice when everyone else silenced it. Thank you for teaching me how to hold my head up high when everyone else told me to stay small. Thank you for being the mom I never thought I would be lucky enough to have. Everything I am today you helped me to become.

Dad, thank you for making me laugh when I didn't think I could smile. Thank you for holding me every time I cried. Thank you for our drives and singing 'Sweet Child O' Mine' on our travels, and for listening to all my rants on the way to school.

Dean, thank you for being the big brother I hope one day my daughter will have. Thank you for always giving me the advice I need, not the advice I want. Thank you for taking so much time out of your life to protect me from the world.

Kelly, thank you for being the sister I always wished I had, for being the girl to give me her hand-me-downs and do my nails. Thank you for always making time for me, like that time we played in the snow, and for taking me on day trips with Oscar and Maya. Most importantly, thank you for making me an aunt to Max.

Dear Nana, although you are no longer with us, I want to say thank you for making me feel so special. Thank you for all the times you would comb my hair and make me feel safe. Thank you for the dinner and cups of tea we shared. To my granda, thank you for showing me the beauty of nature.

Kathryn, thank you so much for your patience, kindness and love of writing that resulted in this work. You helped me share a story that needed to be told and I am forever grateful.

Ciara Doorley and the team at Hachette Ireland, thank you for giving me the platform to share my story and to use my voice finally after years of being silenced. Thank you for supporting me in every way through this process. Thank you for listening and giving me the confidence and opportunity to finally be heard. I have been so lucky to have met such a kind and caring team of people.

Nuala, your humour and kindness has lit up every room I have ever entered with you. Thank you for being a confidant, a friend and family. Thank you for speaking out when I couldn't and for never letting anyone forget my dad and mom.

To my Aunty Marilyn, Sharon, Uncle Wayne, Kate, Jenny, Logan and extended family, thank you for making me feel the comfort of being part of a loving family. I treasure it and I love you all.

Jack, thank you for holding my hand when we were in that van and I felt so alone. You gave me comfort. You may be older but remember I will always protect you.

Adam, thank you for being my safe space when I was growing up and for making me feel so safe like nobody in the world could hurt me. Thank you for taking care of me when I would get nightmares in the middle of the night and for never complaining about my random conversations.

To the Fitzpatrick family and community of Pallaskenry, I am and will always be my mother's daughter. You should be very proud, and I want to thank you for defending my mother and father's enduring love.

Ralph, thank you for your kindness and the advice you have shared with me over the years; you gave me such confidence in myself as a writer to start this book.

To the people of North Carolina and America, thank you. For those who came to the courthouse, posted online and kept us in their prayers, thank you for your solidarity and the courage you gave me.

To all of the people who supported the fight for justice for my dad, the friends, colleagues and acquaintances and the people of the Meadowlands, thank you for your kindness, support and friendship. Even though you are miles away, I always appreciate and never forget your kindness.

To the Davidson County Sheriff's Department team, including Brandon Smyth, Wanda Thompson, Michael Hurd and Sheriff David Grice, thank you. To the DA's office, especially Alan Martin, Garry Frank, Ina Stanton, Greg Brown, Marissa Parker, Kaitlyn Jones, Karen Coe and everyone else on the team, I wish you peace and comfort. It is a difficult job that you do. To Clay Dagenhardt, there are no words I can say that will convey how thankful I am that you were there that night. You made me feel secure in a world of chaos I woke up in, and I will forever be grateful for that.

To the people of Limerick and all across Ireland, I want to say a heartfelt thank you for all you have done for me and my family. I am indebted to you for raising awareness of my dad's killing and lighting the way home for me and Jack. It has made a massive difference to my life.

To the Loop Head Peninsula people, especially Kilkee in Clare, thank you for welcoming me into your community with open arms and hearts. You shielded me, accepted me and you all gave me the opportunity to live the life of a teen. You allowed me to be myself. It is where I have healed and found peace. They say it takes a village, and I am lucky to be part of one. Thank you especially to Ocean Life Dive Centre, Kilkee Waterworld, Clare Sports Partnership, Diving Ireland, Board Iascaigh Mhara and the Kilkee Sub Aqua Club for your help, mentoring hours and skills that resulted in my qualifications as a commercial diver and a love of the ocean.

To my parents, Jason and Mags Corbett, thank you for bringing me into a world filled with your love. I miss you and love you. I am proud to be your daughter.